Tune My Heart

Tune My Heart

Bible Narratives Devotional Guide for Families or Individuals

Second Edition

Scott Aniol

G3 Press

Tune My Heart
Bible Narratives Devotional Guide for Families or Individuals
Second Edition

Published by G3 Press
www.G3Min.org

First Edition printing, 2020
Second Edition printing, 2022
Printed in the Unites States of America

ISBN-13 979-8-9855187-9-5

Contents

Introduction

Stories shape us.

When we read a story, we enter a world that the author has created and thus become shaped by that world. Experiencing the world of the story forms our imaginations of reality, our perceptions and affections, and even our worldview and beliefs.

The same is true—perhaps even more so—with the stories of Scripture. Biblical narratives shape our imagination of who God is, what he is like, and what he expects of his people. The difference, of course, between biblical stories and fictional stories is that the narratives of Scripture actually happened, but the power of stories in the Bible is no different—they help to form who we are. When we read biblical narratives, we enter the stories of historic events in God's providential plan ourselves, and they affect us as if we were living those stories ourselves.

This is exactly why God gave us his revelation in various aesthetic literary forms. Scripture is filled with narratives and poetry; even the more didactic portions of the Bible are filled with poetic devices that shape our minds and our hearts. God the Holy Spirit, "carrying along" men of God (2 Pet 1:21), inspired the stories of Scripture—he literally "breathed them out" (2 Tim 3:16)—in order to form us into the people he intended for us to be.

The aesthetic forms of Scripture provide a way of communicating God's truth that would be impossible with systematic statements of fact alone. Since God is a spirit and does not have a body like man, since he is infinite, eternal, and totally other than us, God chose to use particular aesthetic forms to communicate truth about himself that would not have been possible otherwise. These aesthetic forms are essential to the truth itself since God's inspired Word is exactly the best way that truth could be presented. There is a reason the Bible calls God a "king" rather than simply asserting the doctrinal fact of his rulership. There is a reason the Bible calls God a shepherd, fortress, father, husband, and potter rather than simply stating the ideas underlying these metaphors. These images of God paint a picture that goes far beyond mere doctrinal accuracy. They communicate something that could not be expressed in mere prose. They shape our imagination of who God is, both expressing and shaping right affections for God, which are central to Christianity.

All of these realities emphasize the need for all Christians to regularly read the Word of God. Immersing ourselves in the Word—all of it, but especially the stories and poetry—helps to grow us in our knowledge and love of God and to live in a way that brings him glory.

It is important to regularly read all of Scripture, but sometimes it might be helpful to give focused attention to the narratives and poetry of Scripture. This could be helpful for any Christian—spend some dedicated time slowing down and really immersing yourself in the Bible's stories. This could also be helpful especially for young children, who might not be ready to read through the whole Bible in a year, or for times of family worship, where attempting to read through the whole of Scripture in a year might be too much.

Components of This Resource

The goal of this Bible narratives reading guide is to provide such a resource. I have created a 52-week Bible reading plan that focuses only on the narratives of Scripture, along with all of the psalms and proverbs. Further, the plan schedules readings for five days per week, giving readers the weekend to catch up if they fall behind.

Additionally, I have also created a 52-week catechism, compiling focused questions and answers from historic catechisms like the Westminster Shorter Catechism, the Heidelberg Catechism, Benjamin Keach's catechism, and Charles Spurgeon's catechism. Narrowing this tool to 52 questions and answers allows an individual or families to memorize one per week, and then review again in subsequent years, allowing these doctrinal statements to form and shape belief.

In this guide, I have provided notes, summaries, and questions for personal reflection or group discussion. The notes are designed to answer some of the more challenging issues of the texts, give historical context, or provide classic, conservative interpretation and application.

Finally, each week of reading also has a passage of Scripture to memorize and a hymn to sing, both of which usually correspond to the primary themes of the Bible readings, the catechism, or both.

Ways to Use This Resource

This resource could be used in a number of ways. An individual could use this for personal Bible study and meditation. The plan also works perfectly for upper elementary age children (my two oldest children have used this reading plan three years in a row now, ages 8 and 10 when they started it), and the study notes will help answer questions they might have. Parents could use this for family worship as well, reading the passages together and using the questions for discussion. The notes will also help the parents be able to answer questions their children (or they themselves!) might have as they read. Or a whole family could read through the plan together, parents and older children reading the passages individually earlier in the day and using the memory passages, hymns, catechisms, and reflection questions during family worship. My family has done this for a couple of years, and we have benefitted greatly.

I originally intended for the plan to be used beginning in January and running through the calendar year, but you really could start any time during the year, maybe beginning at the start of a school year or any other time. It is designed to begin on Monday, however, so even if you begin in January, wait to start on the first Monday of the month.

My prayer is that this guide can be a useful resource for helping the stories and poetry of Scripture to shape us into mature, God-fearing Christians, to the glory of God.

Visit www.tunemyheart.com
for supplemental resources.

5 Day Bible Narratives Reading Plan

To download a printable reading plan, visit www.tunemyheart.com.

Week 1: Creation and Fall
☐ Gen 1:1-2:3
☐ Gen 2:4-24
☐ Gen 2:25-3:24
☐ Gen 4:1-16; Prov 1
☐ Gen 6:1-8:19

Week 2: Abraham and Isaac
☐ Gen 8:20-9:29; 11:1-9
☐ Gen 11:26-12:20
☐ Gen 13:1-14:16
☐ Gen 14:17-15:21; 16:1-16
☐ Gen 18:1-15; 21:1-7

Week 3: Lot
☐ Gen 18:16-19:29
☐ Gen 20; Ps 1
☐ Gen 21:8-21; Pss 4-5
☐ Pss 6-7
☐ Gen 23; Ps 8

Week 4: A Just God Justifies
☐ Gen 22:1-19; Rom 4
☐ Pss 9-10
☐ Gen 24
☐ Prov 2; Gen 25:19-34
☐ Gen 26

Week 5: Trust in the Lord
☐ Prov 3
☐ Gen 27
☐ Gen 28:1-29:30
☐ Gen 29:31-31:3
☐ Gen 31:4-55

Week 6: God's Good Plan
☐ Gen 32-33
☐ Gen 35, 37
☐ Gen 39-41
☐ Gen 42-43
☐ Gen 44-46

Week 7: God Raises Up a Deliverer
☐ Prov 4-5
☐ Exod 1:1-2:10
☐ Exod 2:11-25; Ps 90
☐ Exod 3:1-4:18
☐ Exod 4:19-31; Ps 77

Week 8: God Saves His People
☐ Exod 5:1-6:13
☐ Exod 7-9
☐ Exod 10-12
☐ Exod 13-15
☐ Exod 16

Week 9: Worshiping God at Sinai
☐ Exod 17-19
☐ Exod 20; Deut 6
☐ Exod 24, 32
☐ Exod 40
☐ Lev 10:1-11; Ps 11

Week 10: Wandering in the Wilderness
☐ Num 11-12
☐ Pss 12-13
☐ Num 13-14
☐ Num 16-17
☐ Num 20-21

Week 11: Preparing to Enter the Promised Land
☐ Num 22:1–23:12
☐ Pss 14–15, 105
☐ Deut 34; Ps 16
☐ Josh 1:1–3:6
☐ Josh 3:7–5:12

Week 12: Invasion of the Promised Land
☐ Josh 5:13–6:27
☐ Josh 7–8
☐ Josh 9–10
☐ Josh 14, 23–24
☐ Job 1, 42; Ps 49

Week 13: Judges
☐ Judg 1–3
☐ Judg 4–5
☐ Judg 6
☐ Judg 7–8
☐ Judg 9

Week 14: Samson
☐ Judg 10–12
☐ Judg 13–14
☐ Ps 17
☐ Judg 15
☐ Judg 16

Week 15: Ruth and Boaz
☐ Pss 19–20
☐ Prov 6–7
☐ Prov 8
☐ Ruth 1–2
☐ Ruth 3–4

Week 16: Samuel and Saul
☐ 1 Sam 1–3
☐ 1 Sam 4; Ps 21
☐ 1 Sam 5:1–7:2
☐ 1 Sam 7:3–8:22
☐ 1 Sam 9–10

Week 17: Saul's Rise and Fall
☐ 1 Sam 11–12
☐ 1 Sam 13; Ps 72
☐ 1 Sam 14
☐ 1 Sam 15; Ps 28
☐ 1 Sam 16

Week 18: David and Saul
☐ 1 Sam 17
☐ 1 Sam 18; Ps 18
☐ 1 Sam 19; Ps 59
☐ 1 Sam 20; Ps 52
☐ 1 Sam 21–22; Pss 34, 56

Week 19: The Pursuit of David
☐ 1 Sam 23–24; Ps 57
☐ 1 Sam 25; Ps 54
☐ 1 Sam 26–27; Ps 37
☐ 1 Sam 28; Ps 83
☐ 1 Sam 29–30

Week 20: David Becomes King
☐ 1 Sam 31; Pss 76, 110
☐ 2 Sam 1–2; Prov 9
☐ 2 Sam 3:1–5:4
☐ 1 Chron 11:1–25
☐ 1 Chron 13, 15:1–16

Week 21: The Davidic Covenant
☐ 2 Sam 7–8
☐ 2 Sam 9–10; Ps 23
☐ 2 Sam 11; Prov 10
☐ 2 Sam 12; Ps 51
☐ 2 Sam 13; Prov 11

Week 22: Absalom's Rebellion
☐ 2 Sam 14; Prov 12
☐ 2 Sam 15; Ps 3
☐ 2 Sam 16–17
☐ 2 Sam 18; Ps 45
☐ 2 Sam 19; Ps 24

Week 23: David's Reign
- ☐ 2 Sam 20; Ps 25
- ☐ 2 Sam 21; Ps 26
- ☐ 1 Chron 21; Ps 27
- ☐ 1 Kings 1; Prov 13
- ☐ 1 Kings 2; Prov 14

Week 24: Solomon's Reign
- ☐ 2 Chron 1; Prov 15
- ☐ 2 Chron 3-5
- ☐ 2 Chron 6-7
- ☐ 1 Kings 10-11
- ☐ 1 Kings 12-13

Week 25: Elijah
- ☐ Prov 16-18
- ☐ 2 Chron 11-12; Prov 19
- ☐ 1 Kings 15-16; Prov 20
- ☐ 1 Kings 17; Ps 29
- ☐ 1 Kings 18

Week 26: King Ahab
- ☐ 1 Kings 19; Ps 30
- ☐ 1 Kings 20
- ☐ 1 Kings 21; Prov 21
- ☐ 2 Chron 18; Prov 22
- ☐ 2 Chron 19-20; Ps 118

Week 27: The Start of Elisha's Ministry
- ☐ Pss 31-32
- ☐ 2 Kings 2; Ps 33
- ☐ Pss 35-36
- ☐ 2 Kings 4; Ps 38
- ☐ 2 Kings 5; Ps 39

Week 28: Elisha's Continuing Ministry
- ☐ 2 Kings 6:1-23; Pss 40-41
- ☐ 2 Kings 6:24-7:20
- ☐ 2 Kings 8
- ☐ Pss 42-44
- ☐ Pss 50, 53, 55

Week 29: Turn to God
- ☐ Ps 58, 78
- ☐ Pss 60-61
- ☐ Pss 62-63
- ☐ 2 Chron 24; Ps 64
- ☐ 2 Kings 13; Ps 65

Week 30: Jonah
- ☐ Jonah 1-2
- ☐ Jonah 3-4
- ☐ Pss 66-68
- ☐ 2 Chron 26; Is 6; Ps 87
- ☐ Pss 69-70

Week 31: The Fall of Israel
- ☐ Pss 71, 73
- ☐ 2 Kings 17; Ps 74
- ☐ 2 Kings 18-19; Ps 75
- ☐ 2 Chron 32
- ☐ 2 Kings 20; Ps 79

Week 32: Jeremiah
- ☐ 2 Kings 21; Ps 80
- ☐ 2 Kings 22; Ps 81
- ☐ 2 Kings 23; Ps 82
- ☐ Jer 1; Ps 84
- ☐ Jer 18-19

Week 33: Babylon Invades Judah
- ☐ Dan 1; Ps 85
- ☐ Dan 2; Ps 86
- ☐ Jer 24, 37
- ☐ Dan 3
- ☐ Jer 38-39

Week 34: Babylonian Captivity
- ☐ Jer 43; Ps 88
- ☐ Jer 52; Ps 89
- ☐ Ezek 37; Ps 137
- ☐ Dan 4; Ps 91
- ☐ Dan 5, 9

Week 35: Return from Exile
- ☐ Dan 6; Ps 92
- ☐ Ezra 1, 3; Ps 93
- ☐ Ezra 6; Pss 94–95
- ☐ Neh 8–9
- ☐ Pss 96–98

Week 36: The Birth of Christ
- ☐ Pss 99–101
- ☐ Luke 1
- ☐ Luke 2:1–39; John 1:1–18
- ☐ Matt 2; Ps 102
- ☐ Luke 2:40–52; Ps 103

Week 37: Jesus's Early Ministry
- ☐ Matt 3:1–4:11; Ps 104
- ☐ John 1:19–2:12
- ☐ John 2:13–3:21; Ps 106
- ☐ John 4:1–42
- ☐ Luke 4:14–44; Is 61

Week 38: Jesus's Ministry in Galilee
- ☐ Mark 1:21–45; Pss 108–109
- ☐ Matt 5–7
- ☐ Mark 2:1–12; Pss 111–112
- ☐ Pss 113–116
- ☐ Luke 7:1–17; Ps 117

Week 39: Jesus Heals and Forgives
- ☐ Luke 7:36–50; Ps 120
- ☐ Mark 4:1–34; Ps 121
- ☐ Luke 8:22–39; Ps 107
- ☐ Pss 122–124
- ☐ Matt 9:18–32; Pss 125–126

Week 40: True Repentance and Faith in Christ
- ☐ John 5
- ☐ Mark 6:1–29; Pss 127–128
- ☐ John 6:1–21; Pss 129–130
- ☐ John 6:22–71
- ☐ Mark 8:27–38; Pss 131–132

Week 41: The Light of the World
- ☐ Mark 9:1–29; Ps 133
- ☐ Matt 17:24–27; Luke 9:37–50
- ☐ Matt 18:7–35; Ps 134
- ☐ John 7:1–8:30
- ☐ John 9

Week 42: Parables of the Kingdom
- ☐ Luke 17:11–18:14
- ☐ Luke 10:25–42
- ☐ Luke 14; Ps 135
- ☐ Luke 15; Ps 136
- ☐ Matt 13:44–52, 25:1–46

Week 43: Holy Week
- ☐ Luke 16:19–31; John 11
- ☐ Matt 20:20–28; Mark 10:46–52; Luke 19:1–10
- ☐ John 12:1–11; Matt 21:1–11; Luke 19:39–40
- ☐ Mark 11:12–12:12
- ☐ Matt 26:14–29; 1 Cor 11:17–34

Week 44: Jesus's Death and Resurrection
- ☐ Matt 26:30–56; Pss 46–48
- ☐ John 18:12–27; Mark 14:53–65; Matt 27:1–10
- ☐ Luke 23:1–25; Is 53
- ☐ Matt 27:27–61; Ps 22
- ☐ Matt 27:62–28:15

Week 45: Jesus Ascends and Sends the Holy Spirit
- ☐ Luke 24:13–45; Pss 138–139
- ☐ John 20:24–21:25; Ps 140
- ☐ Matt 28:16–20; Luke 24:44–53; Acts 1:1–11
- ☐ Acts 1:12–2:47
- ☐ Acts 3:1–4:31; Ps 2

Week 46: The Persecution of the Early Church and Spread of the Gospel

☐ Acts 4:32-5:16
☐ Acts 5:17-6:7
☐ Acts 6:8-8:3
☐ Acts 8:4-40
☐ Acts 9:1-31

Week 47: The Gospel Spreads to the Gentiles

☐ Acts 9:32-43; Ps 141
☐ Acts 10:1-11:18
☐ Acts 11:19-30; Ps 142
☐ Acts 12; Ps 143
☐ Acts 13

Week 48: The Gospel Moves into Europe

☐ Acts 14; Ps 144
☐ Acts 15; Ps 145
☐ Prov 23-24
☐ Acts 16
☐ Acts 17; Prov 25

Week 49: Paul Begins His Final Missionary Journey

☐ Prov 26-27
☐ Prov 28-29
☐ Acts 18; Prov 30
☐ Acts 19
☐ 1 Cor 1-2, 13

Week 50: Life by the Spirit and Word

☐ Ps 119
☐ Eph 5:18-6:20
☐ Phil 3-4
☐ Rom 1, 3
☐ Rom 8, 12

Week 51: Paul on Trial

☐ Acts 20:1-21:16
☐ Acts 21:15-22:29
☐ Acts 22:30-23:35; Prov 31
☐ Acts 24-26
☐ Acts 27; Ps 146

Week 52: Jesus Comes Again

☐ Gal 4:4-7; Tit 3:3-7; 1 Tim 1:15-17
☐ Acts 28; Pss 147-148
☐ Rev 1, 4-5
☐ Rev 21; Ps 149
☐ Rev 22; Ps 150

Tune My Heart Catechism

The Tune My Heart Catechism has deep roots in the traditions of Christians who have gone before. It is based on historic catechisms, including the Heidelberg catechism, the Westminster catechism, Benjamin Keach's catechism, and Charles Spurgeon's catechism. Since it has 52 questions, it is manageable to teach children and then regularly review through the years, allowing families to focus on one question per week and progress through the catechism every year. The catechism covers the most significant doctrinal issues, broad enough so that really any evangelical Christian with any denominational or eschatological position can use it (particular denominations can supplement this with their own specific Questions and Answers). It helps teach core doctrines but also is personal, devotional, and addresses the heart.

To download a printable catechism, visit www.tunemyheart.com.

Younger children can memorize the italicized portions.

1. **Who made you?**
   God made me.
   (Gen 1:26, 27; 2:7; Eccl 12:1; Acts 17:24–29)
   What else did God make?
   God made all things.
   (Gen 1, esp. verses 1, 31; Acts 14:15; Rom 11:36; Col 1:16)
   Memory: Gen 1:1

2. **Why did God make you and all things?**
   God made me to glorify him and enjoy him forever.
   (Ps 19:1; Jer 9:23, 24; Rev 4:11)
   Memory: 1 Cor 10:31

3. **How did God make you and all things?**
   God made all things out of nothing, by the Word of his power, in the space of six days, *and all very good.*
   (Gen 1:1–31)
   Memory: Gen 1:31

4. **What is special about God's creation of you?**
   God made me in his own image.
   (Gen 1:27; 9:6)
   Memory: Gen 1:27

5. **Who is God?**
   God is a spirit and does not have a body like man. He is infinite, eternal, and unchangeable.
   (John 4:24; 2 Cor 3:17; 1 Tim 1:17)
   Memory: Ps 86:8

6. **What is God like?**
   God is the first and best of beings. He is *holy, powerful, and good.*
   (Ps 147:5; Jer 32:17; Dan 4:34, 35; Eph 1:11)
   Memory: Isa 6:3

7. **Are there more gods than one?**
   No. There is only one true and living God.
   (Deut 6:4; Jer 10:10; Mark 12:29; Acts 17:22-31)
   Memory: Deut 6:4

8. **In how many persons does this one God exist?**
   God exists in three persons: the Father, the Son, and the Holy Spirit, equal in essence, power, and glory.
   (Matt 3:16, 17; John 5:23; 10:30; 14:9, 10; 15:26; 16:13-15; 1 John 5:20; Rev 1:4, 5)
   Memory: 2 Cor 13:14

9. **What are the decrees of God?**
   The decrees of God are his eternal purposes, whereby for his own glory he has ordained whatever comes to pass.
   (Eph 1:11-12)
   Memory: Dan 4:35

10. **How do you know there is a God?**
    The light of nature and the works of God plainly declare that there is a God, but *only his Word and Spirit effectually reveal him to me for my salvation.*
    (1 Thess 1:5-6; 2:13; 2 Tim 3:15, 16; James 1:18; 1 Pet 1:22-23)
    Memory: James 1:18

11. What rule has God given to direct you how you may glorify and enjoy him?
The Word of God, which is contained in the Scriptures of the Old and New Testaments, *is the only rule to direct me how I may glorify God and enjoy Him.*
(Job 11:7; Ps 119:104; Isa 8:20; Matt 22:29; 2 Tim 3:15–17)
Memory: 2 Tim 3:16–17

12. How can you glorify God?
I can glorify God by loving him and doing what he commands.
(Eccl 12:13; Mark 12:29–31; John 15:8–10; 1 Cor 10:31)
Memory: Deut 11:1

13. What is the greatest commandment?
The greatest commandment is to love the Lord my God with all my heart, soul, and mind.
(Deut 6:4–5; Mark 12:29–30)
Memory: Mark 12:30

14. How can you come to know God and what he has made?
The fear of the Lord is the beginning of knowledge.
(Prov 1:7)
Memory: Prov 1:7

15. What is sin?
Sin is any transgression against the law of God.
(1 John 3:4; Rom 3:20; James 2:9–11)
Memory: 1 John 3:4

16. Can you keep the law of God perfectly?
No. I am inclined by nature to hate God and my neighbor.
(Prov 20:9; Eccl 7:20; Rom 3:19, 20; James 2:10; 1 John 1:8, 10)
Memory: Rom 3:10

17. What are the results of sin?
Because of sin, all mankind lost communion with God and are under his wrath and curse, resulting in the miseries of this life, death itself, and the pains of hell forever.
(Deut 27:26; Rom 1:18; 2:2; Gal 3:10; Eph 5:6)
Memory: Rom 1:18

18. Is there any way to escape the punishment of God and be again received into communion with him?
God's justice demands that I make full payment, either through myself or *through a Redeemer.*
(2 Thess 2:13; Rom 5:21)
Memory: Isa 53:10-11

19. What kind of Redeemer must you seek?
I must seek a Redeemer who is truly human and also truly God.
(Isa 9:6; Heb 4:14-16)
Memory: Isa 9:6

20. Why must the Redeemer be a true and righteous human?
The Redeemer must be a true and righteous human because the justice of God requires that *only one with a human nature who has not sinned may pay for my sin.*
(Rom 5:12, 15; 1 Cor 15:21; Heb 2:14-16; 7:26-27; 1 Pet 3:18)
Memory: Heb 2:17

21. Why must the Redeemer also be true God?
The Redeemer must be true God *so that by the power of his divine nature he might bear the burden of God's wrath* and restore to me righteousness and life.
(Isa 9:5; Deut 4:24; Nah 1:6; Ps 130:3; Isa 53:5; 11; John 3:16; 2 Cor 5:21)
Memory: Acts 2:24

22. Who is that Redeemer who at the same time is true God and a true and righteous human?
My only Redeemer is the Lord Jesus Christ, the eternal Son of God, who became human and died to pay the penalty for sin.
1 Tim 2:5; John 1:14; 1 Tim 3:16; Col 2:9)
Memory: 1 Tim 2:5

23. How did Christ, being the Son of God, become human?
Christ, the Son of God became human by taking to himself true human nature, being conceived by the Holy Spirit and the virgin Mary.
(Matt 26:38; Heb 4:15; 7:26; Luke 1:31, 35)
Memory: Gal 4:4

24. How did Christ satisfy God's just wrath for sin?
Christ suffered the miseries of this life, the wrath of God, and *the cursed death of the cross.*
(Ps 22; Isa 53; Gospel records)
Memory: Phil 2:8

25. Why was it necessary for Christ to humble himself even unto death?
Christ humbled himself unto death because *the justice of God required* that satisfaction for my sins could be made in no other way than by *the death of the Son of God.*
(Matt 27:46; Phil 2:8)
Memory: Col 1:21–22

26. Did Christ stay dead?
No. Christ rose again from the dead on the third day.
(Luke 24:45–47; 1 Cor 15:3–4)
Memory: 1 Cor 15:3–4

27. How are you made a partaker of the redemption purchased by Christ?
I am made a partaker of the redemption purchased by Christ *through repentant faith in him* and his substitutionary atoning death.
(Mark 1:15; Luke 13:3,5; Acts 2:37–41; 16:30,31; 20:21; 26:20)
Memory: Eph 2:8–9

28. What is faith in Jesus Christ?
Faith in Jesus Christ is a saving grace, by which I receive and rest upon him alone for my salvation.
(John 14:6; Acts 4:12; 1 Tim 2:5; 1 John 5:11–12)
Memory: Gal 2:20

29. What is repentance unto life?
Repentance unto life is a saving grace, by which I turn from my sin to God, promising to strive after new obedience.
(Luke 19:8–10; Rom 6:1, 2; 2 Cor 7:9–11; 1 Thess 1:9–10)
Memory: 2 Cor 7:10

30. What benefits in this life come from repentant faith in Jesus Christ?
Those who repent and believe in Jesus Christ partake of justification, adoption, and sanctification.
(Ezek 36:26; Rom 8:30; Eph 1:5)
Memory: Rom 8:30

31. What is justification?
Justification is an act of God's free grace in which he pardons all my sins and accepts me as righteous in his sight only because of the righteousness of Christ imputed to me.
(Zech 3:1–5; Rom 3:24–26; 4:5; 5:17–19; 8:33; 2 Cor 5:21; Heb 8:12; Phil 3:9)
Memory: 2 Cor 5:21

32. What is adoption?
Adoption is an act of God's free grace in which I am received as a son of God with all its rights and privileges.
(John 1:12; Eph 1:5; 5:1; Gal 4:7, 31; 1 John 3:1–3)
Memory: Gal 4:7

33. What is sanctification?
Sanctification is the work of God's Spirit by which I am renewed after the image of God and am enabled more and more to die to sin and live to righteousness.
(John 17:17; Eph 2:10; 4:22–24; Phil 2:12–13; 1 Thess 5:23)
Memory: John 17:17

34. What do you believe about the Holy Spirit?
The Holy Spirit is true and eternal God together with the Father and the Son.
(Gen 1:1, 2; Matt 28:19; Acts 5:3, 4; 1 Cor 3:16)
Memory: John 14:16–17

35. What does the Holy Spirit do for you?
The Holy Spirit unites me to Christ, convicts me of sin, comforts me, and sanctifies me.
(Eph 2:8; 3:17; 1 Thess 1:6; 2 Thess 2:13)
Memory: 2 Thess 2:13

36. Since you have been saved by grace alone through Christ, without any merit of your own, why must you yet do good works?
I must do good works *because Christ also renews me by his Holy Spirit to be his image*, so that I might show thankfulness to God for his mercy.
(2 Cor 3:18; Rom 12:1–2; Eph 2:10)
Memory: Eph 2:10

37. What is prayer?
Prayer is an offering up of my desires to God for things agreeable to his will, in the name of Christ, with confession of my sins and thankfulness for his mercies.
(Gen 17:22; 18:33; Neh 1:4–11; 2:4; Matt 6:6; Rom 8:26, 27)
Memory: Ps 62:8

38. What is the church?
The church is an assembly of baptized believers in which the gospel is truly preached and the ordinances are rightly administered.
(Matt 18:20; Acts 2:42)
Memory: 2 Thess 2:13

39. What is the gospel?
The gospel is the good news that those who repent and believe in the death and resurrection of Christ for their sins will be forgiven.
(1 Cor 15:3–7; Rom 1:16)
Memory: Rom 1:16

40. To whom should you preach the gospel?
I should preach the gospel to all people in all nations to the end of the earth.
(Matt 28:19–20; Acts 1:8)
Memory: Matt 28:19–20

41. What has Christ commanded for the church's worship?
Reading, preaching, and singing the Word of God, prayer, baptism, and the Lord's Supper are all parts of the worship of God.
(1 Tim 2:1–2; 4:13; Col 3:16; Matt 28:19; 1 Cor 11:24–26)
Memory: 1 Cor 14:40

42. What is baptism?

Baptism is an ordinance of the New Testament, instituted by Jesus Christ, to be *a sign of the believer's fellowship with Christ* in his death, burial, and resurrection.
(John 3:23; Acts 2:41; 8:12, 35-38; Col 2:12)
Memory: Rom 6:4

43. What is the duty of those who are rightly baptized?

It is the duty of those who are rightly baptized *to join themselves to some visible and orderly church* of Jesus Christ.
(Acts 2:47; Heb 10:25)
Memory: Heb 10:25

44. What is the Lord's Supper?

The Lord's Supper is an ordinance of the New Testament, instituted by Jesus Christ, to be *a sign of the believer's communion with Christ and his church* through his broken body and shed blood.
(Mark 14:22-24; 1 Cor 11:23-29)
Memory: Luke 22:19-20

45. What benefits do believers receive from Christ at their death?

Believers are at their death made perfect in holiness and *immediately pass into the presence of God forever.*
(Heb 12:23; Phil 1:23; 2 Cor 5:8; Luke 23:43; 1 Thess 4:14; Isa 57:2; Job 19:26)
Memory: John 3:16

46. What will be done to the wicked at death?

The wicked will at their death *be cast into the torments of hell.*
(Ps 9:16-17; Luke 12:5; Rom 2:8-9,12; 2 Thess 1:8, 9; Rev 20:12-15)
Memory: Ps 9:16

47. Where is Christ now?

Christ ascended into heaven and sits at the Father's right hand.
(Rom 8:34; Col 3:1; Heb 1:3; 10:12; 12:2)
Memory: Eph 1:20-21

48. How does Christ's resurrection benefit you?
Christ's resurrection is a certain promise of my glorious resurrection.
(1 Cor 15:43; Matt 10:32; 1 John 3:2; 1 Thess 4:17)
Memory: 1 Thess 4:13–14

49. How does Christ's ascension into heaven benefit you?
Christ is my advocate in heaven before his Father and my certain promise that he will take me up to himself.
(1 John 2:1; Heb 4:15)
Memory: Rom 8:34

50. Will Jesus Christ come again?
Yes. Jesus Christ will come a second time in power and glory, which is the joy and hope of all believers.
(Matt 25:31–43; 2 Thess 1:7–10; 2 Tim 4:1)
Memory: Acts 1:11

51. What will happen to believers after Christ comes again?
Believers will live with Christ forever in a new heaven and a new earth.
(Isa 66:22; 1 Thess 4;16, 17; 2 Pet 3:10–13; Rev 21:1–4)
Memory: Rev 21:3

52. What is your only hope in life and death?
My only hope in life and death is that I am not my own but belong to God and to my Savior Jesus Christ.
(1 Cor 6:19–20; Rom 14:7–9; 1 Cor 3:23; Tit 2:14)
Memory: Rom 14:7–8

Study Guide Index

Memory Verse Index

Hymn Index

Study Guide

Week 1: Creation and Fall

Weekly memory verse:
Genesis 1:1 - "In the beginning, God created the heavens and the earth."

Weekly hymn:
"All Creatures of Our God and King"

Weekly catechism:
Who made you?
God made me.
What else did God make?
God made all things.

All Creatures of Our God and King

LASST UNS ERFREUEN

WORDS: Francis of Assisi, 1225; tr. William H. Draper, 1925

8.8.8.8.8 with refrain

MUSIC: *Geistliche Kirchengesäng*, 1623; arr. Ralph Vaughan Williams, 1906

Day 1: Creation

Genesis 1:1–2:3

Notes

Chapter 1, Verse 1. This verse describes part of what God did on the first day; he created the heavens and earth on the first day, but they were yet formless (v. 2).

Verse 3. Light. God created light also on the first day, even though he didn't create the physical sources of light until the fourth day. God was and is the eternal source of light.

Verse 4. Good. The word "good" can mean several different things. Here it does not likely refer to moral goodness but rather to ability to serve a particular function, or it could also mean beauty.

Verse 5. Day. In Hebrew, "day" with a number (as in "first day," "second day," etc.) always refers to a literal 24-hour period. God created the world in a literal six-day week.

Verses 11, 12, 21. Kind. God created all plants and animal species, showing that the theory that various creatures evolved across species lines in incorrect.

Verses 26, 27. Image. Adam and Eve were the only creatures God made in his own image, distinguishing them from all other creatures. The image of God includes self-consciousness, creativity, morality, and other communicable attributes of God that animals do not share with humans. *Dominion.* Since humans were the pinnacle of all of God's creation, he set them as rulers of the rest of creation. *Male and female.* Man and woman are equal in essence and value but distinct from and complementary to one another physically and relationally.

Verse 28. Be fruitful and multiply. God blessed Adam and Eve by giving them the ability to fill the earth with offspring, to cultivate and enjoy what he had made, and to rule over it all.

Chapter 2, Verse 2. Rested. God had no need of physical rest, yet he ceased from his creative work on the seventh day and established a seven-day cycle for human work, including the necessity for one day of rest each week.

Summary

Genesis 1 establishes God as the source, sustainer, and ultimate end of all things. As creator of all, God is King and has the right to do whatever he pleases with what he created for his own glory. Everything God made was perfect and good, but God created humankind as the pinnacle of all that he made, and thus as ruler of all under his supreme authority. Thus we are blessed with the privilege of cultivating and enjoying what God created, serving him in the capacity for which he created us, to his honor and glory.

Questions for Reflection

1. Why do you think God created the world in the order that he did?
2. What is our responsibility toward God as his creation?
3. What does it mean to have dominion over the earth, to subdue the earth, and to be fruitful?

Day 2: Adam and Eve

Genesis 2:4-24

Notes

Chapter 2, Verse 7. Formed. This is a more detailed, specific account of God's creation of Adam and Even on day six of creation. Unlike the other elements of creation, which God created out of nothing, he formed Adam from the earth, and thus when we die, we return to dust. However, he breathed into Adam the breath of life, and thus our souls live forever.

Verse 8. Eden. The location of the garden of Eden is not known, but it was likely in the Mesopotamian Valley, east of where Moses wrote this account.

Verse 9. Tree of life. This tree had a special ability to sustain eternal life. *Tree of knowledge.* This tree, forbidden for Adam and Eve to eat, was put in the garden as a test of whether they would choose good or evil.

Verse 15. Work it and keep it. This describes Adam's purpose. These two terms used together in the Old Testament most often refer to the duties of the Levitical priests in the Tabernacle/Temple. Adam's purpose was to serve as God's priest, communing with God in his holy sanctuary.

Verse 17. Die. The result of disobedience to God's command was separation, first spiritually, and eventually physically.

Verse 18. Not good. Adam was incomplete before the end of the sixth day until God created Eve, who as created from Adam and also in God's image was equal with him in essence and worth, was distinct physically from Adam and was a suitable helper for him.

Verse 24. One flesh. The fact that Eve was created from out of Adam establishes the basis for marital union.

Summary

God created a perfect, holy sanctuary in which he placed Adam, his priest whose purpose was to commune with God and obey his commands. He created Eve to complete Adam and assist him with his duties. These purposes and roles never changed. The purpose of all people is to worship God according to the commands that he has given in his sanctuary where he dwells.

Questions for Reflection

1. Why do you think God created Adam from the dust of the

earth instead of out of nothing?
2. Why do you think God created Eve out of Adam?
3. What does it mean for us today that Adam and Eve were created to worship and obey God?

Day 3: Fall

Genesis 2:25–3:24

Notes

Chapter 2, Verse 25. This verse describes the state of untested, innocent holiness in which Adam and Eve were created.

Chapter 3, Verse 1. Serpent. John identifies the serpent as Satan (Rev 12:9, 20:2). He tempts Eve to disobey God by questioning God's motives and authority, which is always the essence of temptation.

Verse 4. Her husband. While Eve was deceived into sinning, Adam ate of the fruit willfully.

Verse 7. The innocence that characterized Adam and Eve when they were created is now replaced by guilt and shame.

Verse 8. Walking. God's desire was to commune with his people in his sanctuary, but sin prevents free communion with God.

Verse 9. Where are you? This does not mean God didn't know where they were; it was simply a way to force them to explain why they were hiding from him and acknowledge their guilt.

Verse 15. This is the first proclamation of God's plan to send his Son to redeem mankind from their sin.

Verse 17. Cursed. Because of Adam's sin, all of mankind and all of creation fell under God's just curse.

Verse 21. Clothed. This is a foreshadowing of the atonement ("covering") for sin through the sacrificial death of a substitute that is necessary to restore broken communion with God.

Summary

God created Adam and Eve in order to commune with them in his sanctuary, but their disobedience broke that communion. Thus God cursed them, their posterity, and all of creation. But God did not leave us in our sin; he made a promise that he would one day crush the head of the serpent, representing sin, through an offspring of Eve—his only Son. He foreshadowed how this would take place when he killed an animal and covered their guilt with its skin. Sin breaks communion with God, but through the substitutionary atonement of the Son of God, restored fellowship is possible!

Questions for Reflection

1. Do you notice any similarities between Satan's temptation of Eve and his later temptation of Jesus in the wilderness (Matt 4:1-11)?
2. What consequences do we still experience today as a result of Adam's sin?
3. How did God fulfill his promise made in Genesis 3:15?

Day 4: Cain and Abel

Genesis 4:1-16; Proverbs 1

Notes

Genesis 4, Verse 4. Although the account here does not explicitly explain why God accepted Abel's offering and not Cain's, the New Testament seems to indicate that both inward heart motivation (Abel was "righteous," while Cain was "evil") as well as the sacrifices themselves (Abel's sacrifice was "more excellent" than Cain's) are in view (see John 3:12, Heb 11:4, and Jude 11). God cares about both the heart of the worshiper and that the worshiper presents what is excellent in obedience to God's clear commands.

Verse 14. Whoever. Eve must have birthed many children and enough time must have passed for the population of the earth to have increased considerably by this point.

Verse 15. Mark. While not clear what this mark was exactly, it must have been some sort of visible sign and warning that no one was to harm Cain in any way. This was an act of mercy by God in spite of Cain's sin.

Proverbs 1, Verse 1. Proverbs are short statements of wisdom. They are not necessary legal guarantees; rather, they are general principles that typically ring true.

Verse 2. Wisdom. Wisdom is not simply intellectual knowledge, but rather the ability to skillfully apply what one knows practically in life.

Verse 7. Fear. A proper imagination of God and reverence toward him precedes a right understanding of him. It is not enough to simply know who God is; a wise person has the appropriate heart affections toward him. *Fool.* A fool in Scripture is an unbeliever.

Summary

Knowledge of God alone is not sufficient for wise living that pleases him. Cain knew God and even spoke with him, but his self-interest and pride prevented him from obeying God and instead led him into horrendous sin. On the other hand, it is a proper fear of God that will lead us, like Abel, to reverence God and obey his clear instructions out of a true desire for fellowship with him. This is true wisdom.

Questions for Reflection

1. What clear instructions about worship has God given us in Scripture that should regulate how we approach him?
2. Why is knowledge of God alone insufficient for a life pleasing to God?
3. How can we resist temptation to sin, either from within our hearts or from others?

Day 5: Noah and the Flood

Genesis 6:1–8:19

Notes

Chapter 6, Verse 2. Sons of God. To whom this description refers is not clear; some believe it refers to angels, others think that it describes powerful human kings. Regardless, the point of these verses is to describe the increasing corruption on earth that leads to judgment.

Verse 4. Nephilim. The meaning of this term is also uncertain. It could refer to fallen angels or mighty, violent giants. Again, however, the primary emphasis is to describe the violence and injustice that characterized mankind at the time.

Verse 6. Regretted. This term describes the deep sorrow of God in response to the sinfulness of his creatures, not that it surprised him in any way.

Verse 19. Two of every sort. The ark had more than enough space to house two of each species of animal on earth, even by generous estimates.

Chapter 7, Verse 11. The water that covered the earth came from three sources: the "fountains of the great deep," the water canopy encircling the earth (the "windows of the heavens"; see 1:7), and the rain that fell over a period of forty days.

Summary

Sin deserves judgement. But God, who is rich in mercy, chooses to save those who trust in his promises and come to him in faith through the means that he has provided.

Questions for Reflection

1. What is the main lesson from the story of Noah and the flood?
2. What does sin deserve?
3. What is necessary to be rescued from judgment?

Week 2: Abraham and Isaac

Weekly memory verse:

Genesis 12:2 - "And I will make of you a great nation, and I will bless you and make your name great, so that you will be a blessing."

Weekly hymn:

"The God of Abraham Praise"

Weekly catechism:

Why did God make you and all things?
God made me to glorify him and enjoy him forever.

The God of Abraham Praise

WORDS: Moses Maimonides, 12th cent.; vers. Daniel ben Judah, 1404; para. Thomas Olivers, c. 1770, alt.

6.6.8.4.D

MUSIC: Hebrew melody, 17th cent.; adapt. Meyer Lyon, c. 1770

Day 6: God Establishes Human Government

Genesis 8:20–9:29; 11:1–9

Notes

Chapter 9, Verse 9. Covenant. God made this covenant not only with his people, but with "every living creature." This passage (8:20–9:17) is the establishment of God's common kingdom by which he rules over the earth through the means of human government, including the death penalty in cases of murder (9:6) based on the fact that people are created in the image of God.

Chapter 11, Verse 4. Top in the heavens. God established human government as the means through which he rules his common kingdom, but very quickly government was corrupted as a means to establish human autonomy and rebellion against God.

Verse 5. Came down. This is an ironic statement made by the narrator. The people wanted to build a high tower to heaven, but even then God, who is always high above all, had to "come down" to see what they had made.

Verse 9. Babel . . . confused. The Hebrew word translated "confused" is *Balel*, which sounds like the name of the city. Later this very city would be called Babylon (see Rev 17–18), the epitome of a worldly city.

Summary

God intended human government to be the means through which he would rule the common kingdom of the world. God intended human government to enforce his moral laws, protect the innocent, and punish evil. However, although human government was created by God, it regularly seeks to establish humanity as autonomous and self-sufficient. Thus God divided the people through confusing their languages, creating multiple people groups with their own governments.

Questions for Reflection

1. What did God intend for the purpose of human government?
2. Why was it wrong for the people to build the Tower of Babel?
3. Where did the different nations of the world come from?

Day 7: The Call of Abram

Genesis 11:26–12:20

Notes

Chapter 12, Verse 1. This is the initial introduction to the Abrahamic covenant, an everlasting, unilateral covenant God makes with Abram.

Verse 7. Land. Part of God's covenant with Abram is that his offspring would inherit the land of Canaan, a promise still yet to be completely fulfilled. *Altar.* Abraham worships in response to God's self-revelation and covenant.

Summary

God's covenant with Abram has ramifications for his offspring to this day, the promise having yet to be fulfilled. Yet the promise to bless all the nations of the world through Abram has and is being fulfilled through Jesus Christ, Abraham's seed, who offers salvation to all who believe in him.

Questions for Reflection

1. If God promised that Abram's descendants would inherit the land of Canaan forever, will he keep his promise?
2. What can Abram's response to God's covenant teach us about worship?
3. How have we non-Jews been blessed by the Abrahamic covenant?

Day 8: Lot

Genesis 13:1–14:16

Notes

Chapter 13, Verse 14. God reaffirms his promise to Abram that his descendants would inherit the land of Canaan.

Chapter 14, Verse 13. Hebrew. This is the first time this ethnic title is used. It means "descended from Eber" (see 11:15–17).

Summary

God reaffirmed his promise Abram after Lot chose the fertile land of the Jordan Valley. His defeat of Lot's captors confirms that God will indeed bless Abram and his descendants.

Questions for Reflection

1. What do you think motivated Lot to choose the land that he did?
2. What is revealed about Abram when he allows Lot to choose the land first?
3. What is revealed about Abram in his successful rescue of Lot?

Day 9: Blessing and Promise

Genesis 14:17-15:21; 16:1-16

Notes

Chapter 14, Verse 18. Melchizedek. This mysterious priest-king over Jerusalem has no biography or genealogy, leading later biblical authors to use him as a type of Christ (see Ps 110:4; Heb 7:17, 21). *Priest of God Most High.* This phrase indicates that Melchizedek did not worship one of the Canaanite pagan gods; rather, he worshiped the true God, the same God that called Abram (see v. 22).

Chapter 15, Verse 6. Believed. Abraham was justified, not by works, but by faith in the promises of God (see Rom 4:3, 9, 22; Gal 3:6; Jas 2:23).

Verse 7. Land. God's promise that Abram would inherit land is intricately tied with his covenant and confirmed in a formal ceremony (vv. 9-21).

Verse 12. Sleep. God put Abram to sleep because the covenant did not require any action on Abram's part; the covenant was completely unilateral—God would fulfill his promises regardless of what Abram or his descendants did.

Chapter 16, Verse 3. Hagar. It was a customary practice to marry a maidservant in the case of no male heir, but this demonstrated lack of faith in God's promise.

Verse 7. Angel of the Lord. This individual appears many times in the Old Testament and is often identified as the reincarnate Christ, one who is in some way both distinct from and identified with Yahweh.

Verse 12. Against. Ishmael's descendants are modern-day Arabs.

Summary

God will keep his promises, no matter how impossible they seem. Some of God's promises are dependent upon how we act, but others are unilateral, meaning that God will keep them no matter what we do.

Questions for Reflection

1. How can you be sure God will keep his promises?
2. Why is it important to believe the promises of God, no matter how impossible they seem?
3. What promises has God made to you?

Day 10: The Birth of Isaac

Genesis 18:1-15; 21:1-7

Notes

Chapter 18, Verse 3. Lord. Abraham recognized one of the three men as the true God.

Chapter 21, Verse 1. Visited. This conception and birth was clearly a miracle of God.

Verse 4, Circumcised. Cutting away the male foreskin was what God had commanded of Abraham's descendants as a sign of the covenant (see 17:11).

Summary

God can do anything, and we should trust that when he says he will do something, he will.

Questions for Reflection

1. Are there any promises God has made to you that seem impossible?

2. Why do you think God makes promises to us that seem impossible?
3. What can you do to be sure that you trust in God's promises no matter what?

Week 3: Lot

Weekly memory verse:

Psalm 8:1 - "O Lord, our Lord, how majestic is your name in all the earth! You have set your glory above the heavens."

Weekly hymn:

"Sing Praise to God Who Reigns Above"

Weekly catechism:

How did God make you and all things?
God made all things out of nothing, by the Word of his power, in the space of six days, and all very good.

Sing Praise to God Who Reigns Above

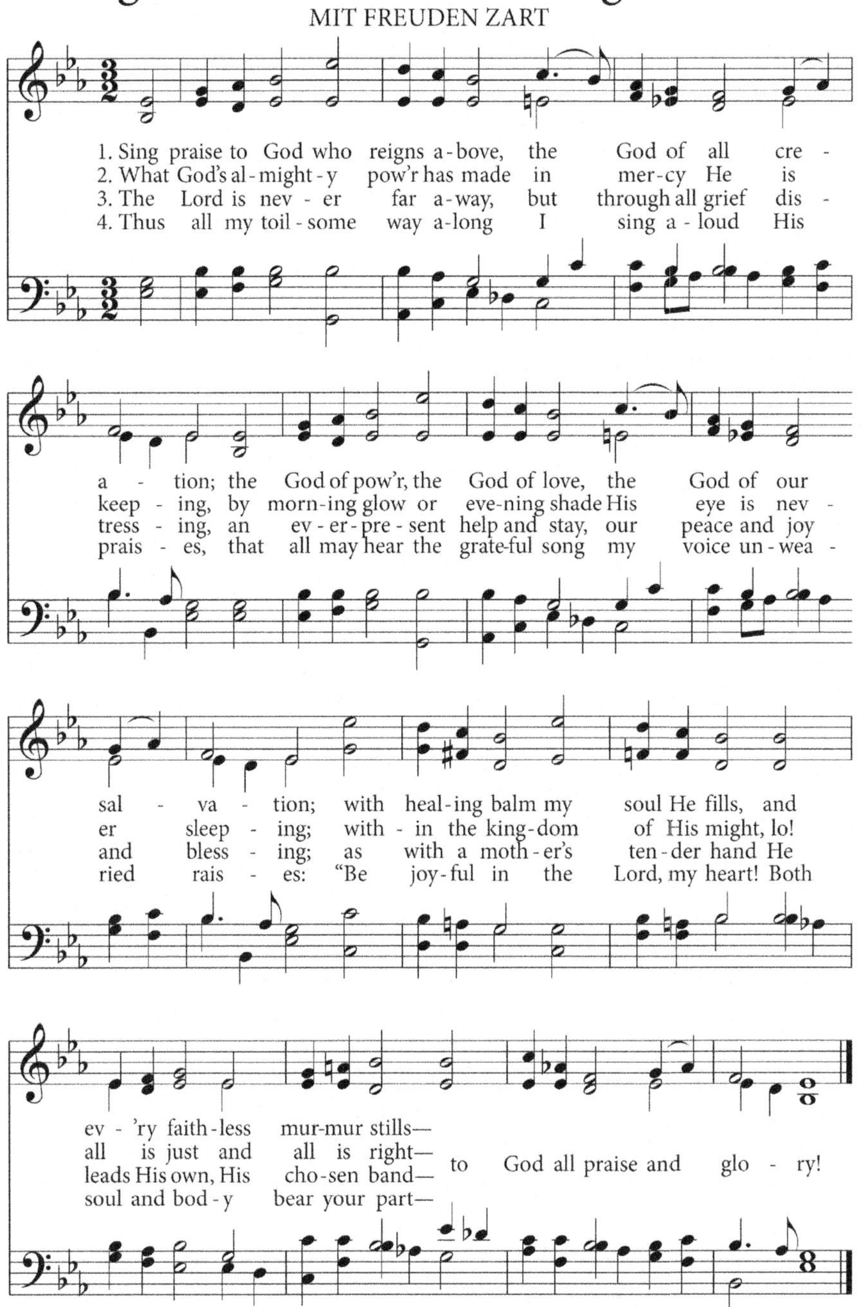

WORDS: Johann J. Schütz, 1675; tr. Frances E. Cox, 1864, alt. 8.7.8.7.8.8.7
MUSIC: Bohemian Brethren's *Kirchengesänge*, 1566

Day 11: God Rescues Lot

Genesis 18:16–19:29

Notes

Chapter 18, Verse 21. I will go down to see. This expression should not be taken to mean that God had limited knowledge; it is simply an expression that reveals the great care God gave in the decision to destroy the cities.

Summary

God is just, and he will punish sin. But he is also merciful; he rescues those who trust in him and do what he commands.

Questions for Reflection

1. What did God's rescue of Lot and destruction of Sodom and Gomorrah reveal about the nature and character of God?
2. What did Lot's actions reveal about his character, both for good and for evil?
3. What did Lot's wife's actions reveal about her character?

Day 12: The Way of the Righteous and the Wicked

Genesis 20; Psalm 1

Notes

Psalm 1, Verse 1. Blessed. This refers to God's redemptive favor toward the righteous.

Verse 6. Knows. This refers to more than simply knowledge; it describes the personal relationship God has with the righteous.

Summary

All people fall into one of two categories, righteous or wicked. These describe the nature and character of all people, those who follow God and live according to his law, and those who do not. The righteous will receive eternal blessing, but the wicked will perish forever.

Questions for Reflection

1. What does it mean to walk in the counsel of the wicked, stand in the way of sinners, or sit in the seat of scoffers?
2. What does it mean to delight in God's law?

3. What do the tree and chaff metaphors tell us about the righteous and wicked?

Day 13: Trust in the Lord

Genesis 21:8–21; Psalms 4–5

Notes

Genesis 21, Verse 17. Angel of God. This is the same individual as the Angel of the Lord, likely the pre-incarnate Son of God.

Psalm 4. To the Choirmaster. The superscriptions, or "titles" that precede 116 of the psalms were likely added shortly after their composition and contain reliable information about the author, context, and use of these psalms. Fifty-five psalms are given to the "Choirmaster," who was tasked with leading the singers and stringed accompaniment instruments in the Temple. King David wrote at least 75 of the psalms.

Verse 2. Selah. This term occurs quite often in the psalms, but its meaning is unknown. It is likely a musical term indicating a pause or an instrumental interlude.

Verse 4. Angry. The term here does not refer to expression of rage, but rather to trembling in fear of God in order that we may not sin. Our fear of God should be so strong that it motivates us to avoid evil.

Psalm 5. Flutes. While stringed instruments were the primary accompaniment instruments for singing in the Temple, other instruments, such as flutes, were used in social gatherings. Not all psalms were intended for use in the Temple.

Verse 1. Groanings. This psalm is the first example of a major category of psalms, the Lament. The purpose of psalms like these is to express a deep need and ask the Lord for his help, trusting that his way is always best.

Summary

No matter what the circumstances, in times of blessing and in times of pain, it is always best to trust in the Lord. He is the sovereign ruler of the universe, and nothing escapes his control. Therefore, we should trust in him to guide us, protect us, and comfort us in times of need. Only then will we be able to find rest and assurance.

Questions for Reflection

1. How does a proper fear of God motivate us not to sin?
2. How will trust in God give us rest and assurance?
3. What are some difficulties in your life for which you should trust the Lord?

Day 14: Confession and Grace

Psalms 6–7

Notes

Psalm 6. This is the first of the penitential psalms, in which God's servant confesses his sins to the Lord and finds grace and forgiveness.

Verse 2. Bones. This could indicate that David was afflicted physically, but in ancient times physical metaphors often indicated suffering of the whole person—body, mind, and spirit.

Verse 5. Sheol. This Hebrew term sometimes refers generally to death, as is likely the case here, and other times to a destination of punishment for the wicked.

Psalm 7. Benjaminite. This refers to an otherwise unknown event in the life of David.

Summary

God will always judge sin, but he offers grace and forgiveness to those who confess their sins before him. The psalms contain many examples of such confession, and God is always faithful to show mercy and deliver the one who acknowledges his guilt before him.

Questions for Reflection

1. Why must God always judge sin?
2. Are difficult life circumstances always the result of personal guilt, or could there be other reasons?
3. Why does God delight in showing mercy to the penitent?

Day 15: God's Goodness and Greatness

Genesis 23; Psalm 8

Notes

Psalm 8. This is a psalm of praise that also focuses quite a bit on creation and the dignity of man. Thus, it develops important Adamic theology that raises associations with the Last Adam, Jesus Christ (see. Heb 2:6–8).

Verse 1. Lord. The small caps indicates that this first title of the two in the verse is God's specially revealed name, Yahweh (Exod 3:14).

Verse 3. Fingers. God does not have a physical body, but psalmists often use anthropomorphic language. Here, "fingers" emphasizes the grandeur of the Creator God.

Verses 4–6. These verses are quoted often in the NT: 1 Corinthians 15:27, 28; Ephesians 1:22; Hebrews 2:5–10.

Verse 4. Son of man. This term refers generally to humanity, but it also has significant Messianic significance, and is Jesus's favorite title for himself in the NT.

Summary

A unique characteristic of the true God is that he is both good and great. If he were simply good but not great, he would have no power to project or to accomplish his will. If he were simply great and not good, he would be a powerful yet selfish despot. The true God is both good and great, creating all things and protecting those who cry out to him in need.

Questions for Reflection

1. What do the heavens, the moon, and the stars tell us about God?
2. What role did God give to humanity ("man") in relationship to the rest of creation?
3. Why should we praise the Lord?

Week 4: A Just God Justifies

Weekly memory verse:

Romans 4:5 - "And to the one who does not work but believes in him who justifies the ungodly, his faith is counted as righteousness."

Weekly hymn:

"Not What These Hands Have Done"

Weekly catechism:

What is special about God's creation of you?
God made me in his own image.

Not What These Hands Have Done

LEOMINSTER

WORDS: Horatius Bonar, 1861
MUSIC: George William Martin, 1862

SMD

Day 16: Justified by Faith

Genesis 22:1–19; Romans 4

Notes

Genesis 22, Verse 2. Moriah. Most scholars believe that this is the future site of Jerusalem, where Solomon would later build the temple (see 2 Chr 3:1).

Verse 5. I and the boy. Hebrews 11:17–19 states that Abraham was confident in God's promises concerning his son, and therefore believed that if Isaac died, God would raise him from the dead.

Verse 12. Now I know. God's test of Abraham was not for his own benefit as if he didn't know what Abraham would do; it was to demonstrate Abraham's faith in his promises.

Verse 13. Instead of his son. This is an important expression of substitutionary atonement.

Verse 16. Sworn. This is another key reaffirmation of the Abrahamic covenant, emphasizing its unconditional, unilateral nature, and focusing upon promises concerning land, seed, and blessing, which have yet to be completely fulfilled.

Summary

Abraham's life is a supreme example of justification by faith. Anyone who disobeys God's law in even the smallest measure falls under judgment, and thus no one can be justified through good works. Yet those who unreservedly trust in God's promises are declared righteous on the basis of the ultimate substitutionary sacrifice of atonement—Jesus Christ.

Questions for Reflection

1. Why did God test Abraham?
2. What important principle does the ram provided by God reveal?
3. What must each of us do in order to be declared righteous in God's sight?

Day 17: The Justice of God

Psalms 9–10

Notes

Psalm 9. Muth-Labben. This is likely the name of a tune.

Psalm 10, Verse 1. Why? It is appropriate to question why God withholds his justice as long as we follow the psalmist's example of also expressing confidence that God will indeed do what he has promised.

Summary

God is righteous and just, and he has promised that he will both punish evil and reward the good. Yet in this life it sometimes seems as if the good is punished and the evil is rewarded. This causes us to long for the righteousness and justice of God, and our appropriate response to these difficult circumstances is to trust that God will do what he has promised.

Questions for Reflection

1. What are some examples in your life of God rewarding good and judging evil?
2. What are some examples in your life of evil going unpunished?
3. What should be our response when we see wickedness go unpunished in this life?

Day 18: Isaac and Rebekah

Genesis 24

Notes

Verse 2. Thigh. This was an ancient Near Eastern customary way to make a solemn promise.

Verse 14. Camels. The hospitality customs of the day required giving water to people, but not to animals. The fact that Rebekah gave water also to the camels revealed her unusually hospitable character.

Summary

This story is the next step toward God fulfilling his promises to Abraham. Isaac needed a wife to continue the Abrahamic line, and Abraham desired that Isaac's wife be chosen from among his people rather than from the Canaanites. This arranged marriage was customary for the time, but even in these conditions, Isaac and Rebekah chose to love each other.

Questions for Reflection

1. Why did Abraham want Isaac to marry someone from among his people rather than from the Canaanites?
2. How does the blessing of Rebekah's sisters (v. 60) fit with the Abrahamic covenant?
3. What does this story reveal about love and marriage?

Day 19: Wisdom

Proverbs 2; Genesis 25:19-34

Notes

Proverbs 2. Heart. In the Old Testament, "heart" refers to the whole of a person—mind, will, and affections.

Genesis 25, Verse 20. Paddan-aram. This is located northeast of Canaan in upper Mesopotamia.

Verse 23. Younger. This prophecy ran contrary to the custom of the elder son receiving the family birthright.

Summary

Those who trust God and pursue righteousness must also pursue wisdom—the skillful application of knowledge. Wisdom comes from God alone to those to ask for it and incline their hearts toward truly knowing him.

Questions for Reflection

1. How does wisdom lead to understanding and knowing God?
2. Why is it so important to pursue wisdom?
3. What does the pursuit of wisdom help us avoid?

Day 20: God's Promise to Isaac

Genesis 26

Notes

Verse 1. Abimelech. This is likely a dynastic title for Philistine kings.

Verse 3. Bless. God reaffirmed with Isaac the covenant he had made with Abraham, emphasizing the same three elements of land, seed, and blessing.

Summary

God continued to fulfill the promises that he made to Abraham through his son, Isaac. Since the Abrahamic covenant was unconditional, even Isaac's sin did not prevent God from blessing him, even using pagans to accomplish that blessing. God will keep his promises to his people.

Questions for Reflection

1. How was Isaac's deception to Abimelech similar to and different from his father's deception?
2. In what ways did God use even unbelievers to bless his people?
3. What does this story tell us about the character and nature of God?

Week 5: Trust in the Lord

Weekly memory verse:

Proverbs 3:5-6 - "Trust in the Lord with all your heart, and do not lean on your own understanding. In all your ways acknowledge him, and he will make straight your paths."

Weekly hymn:

"Blessed Jesus at Thy Word"

Weekly catechism:

Who is God?

God is a spirit and does not have a body like man. He is infinite, eternal, and unchangeable.

Blessed Jesus, at Thy Word

LIEBSTER JESU

WORDS: Tobias Clausnitzer, 1663, sts. 1–3; *Geistreiches Gesang-Büchlein,* 1707, st. 4; tr. Catherine Winkworth, 1858, sts. 1–3; unknown, st. 4 — 7.8.7.8.8.8

MUSIC: Johann Rudolph Ahle, 1664; harm. Johann Sebastian Bach, 18th cent., alt.

Day 21: The One Who Finds Wisdom Is Blessed

Proverbs 3

Notes

Verse 1. Heart. In Hebrew thought, the heart refers to more than just emotions; it includes the totality of the human person: mind, spirit, will, and affections.

Verse 18. Tree of Life. This is a metaphor of blessings both in this life and the next.

Summary

Wisdom is foundational to all of life, so foundational that Solomon describes it as that with which God created the world. Wisdom should be the pursuit of all of God's people. In order to truly know God, we must involve the entirety of who we are in our pursuit of his wisdom.

Questions for Reflection

1. With a biblical understanding of "heart," what does it mean for our hearts to keep God's commandments?
2. What does God's discipline toward his people reveal?
3. How is wisdom more precious that material wealth?

Day 22: God's Sovereign Mercy

Genesis 27

Notes

Verse 4. Bless. Despite God's message to Rebekah that the older would serve the younger (25:23), the fact that Esau had given up his birthright for a meal (25:33), and Esau's terrible marriages (26:35), Isaac nevertheless determined to give him the birthright blessing, as was the custom.

Verse 27. Blessed. Jacob received Isaac blessing, but this came at great cost. Jacob never sees his mother again and endures a life full of family conflict due to his deception.

Verse 40. Break his yoke. The Edomites, descendants from Esau, continually fought against Israel in later history, occasionally freeing themselves from Israel's control.

Summary

Scripture later references this account of Isaac's blessing upon the younger son as an illustration that God's mercy is not based on family lineage, custom, or good works, but rather on the sovereign, wise choice of God himself (See Mal 1:2-3; Rom 9:13). Jacob certainly did not deserve the inheritance, but God chose to make him the heir and father of his people against normal expectations. God says, "I will have mercy on whom I have mercy" (Rom 9:15).

Questions for Reflection

1. Why do you think Rebekah wanted Jacob to have the blessing from Isaac?
2. Was it right for Rebekah and Jacob to deceive Isaac since God had told Rebekah that Jacob would receive the blessing?
3. If circumstances seem to be going against what we know God has promised, what is our responsibility?

Day 23: Jacob Marries Leah and Rachel

Genesis 28:1-29:30

Notes

Chapter 28, Verse 3. Bless. By this time Isaac had come to clearly understand that Jacob would continue the Abrahamic Covenant.

Verse 13. Land. God confirms to Jacob in a dream that he is the recipient of the covenant made with Abraham, including promise of a land, a seed, and blessing, just like his father and grandfather before him.

Chapter 29, Verse 17. Weak. This probably means that Leah's eyes were dull rather than brilliant and sparkling.

Verse 28. Gave. It appears that Laban gave Rachel to Jacob immediately following the week-long celebration of his marriage to Leah, before the seven years of additional labor.

Summary

Those who deceive will often themselves be deceived. It is fitting, and generally a biblical principle, that sins committed often come back around to those who commit them. Yet despite Jacob's sin and the temporal consequences he received, God did not abandon his unconditional promises to him and to his descendants.

Questions for Reflection

1. Why do you think Laban deceived Jacob and gave him Leah instead of Rachel?
2. What does Jacob's willingness to work seven more years reveal about his love for Rachel?
3. Did Jacob deserve to receive God's blessing and covenant?

Day 24: Jacob's Children

Genesis 29:31-31:3

Notes

Chapter 30, Verse 1. Lest I die. In ancient Near Eastern culture, a childless woman was considered worthless.

Verse 3. On my knees (some translations). A surrogate giving birth while sitting on the knees of the wife symbolized that she was giving birth on behalf of the wife.

Verse 37. Sticks. An experienced herdsman, Jacob apparently had skill in selective breeding, and also knew if he placed certain sticks that had been peeled into the drinking water of the sheep he wanted to breed, it would release a chemical that stimulated them to mate.

Summary

The story of Jacob bearing many children through four women and amid much controversy is a prime example of God using bad circumstances to actually accomplish his plan and keep his promises. God had promised Abraham, Isaac, and Jacob many descendants, and he begins to fulfill this promise by giving Jacob many children through a situation that was actually the result of Jacob's sin.

Questions for Reflection

1. On the basis of this story, do you think it is good for a man to have more than one wife?
2. What does the story of Jacob and the sheep reveal about the relationship between God's sovereignty and human responsibility?

3. What can this story teach us about the relationship between consequences of sinful action and the good promises of God?

Day 25: Jacob's Family Prepares to Leave

Genesis 31:4-55

Notes

Verse 11. Angel of God. This is the same as the Angel of the Lord, likely a pre-incarnate appearance of Christ.

Verse 19. Household gods. It is possible that Rachel stole these so that Jacob would be considered the head of the household after Laban's death and would receive the family inheritance.

Verse 53. Fear of his father Isaac. This was a specific title for the true God of Abraham, Isaac, and Jacob (see also v. 42). Jacob uses this official name to distinguish his God from the god by which Laban swore.

Summary

Once again, God protects his chosen people despite their sins and deceptions, even intervening and speaking to an unbeliever in order to accomplish his purposes. God will always keep his promises and always protect his people, regardless of the circumstances.

Questions for Reflection

1. How important were the household idols to Laban? Why?
2. In what ways does deception continue to be a problem for Jacob?
3. How does God demonstrate his sovereign care for his people in this story?

Week 6: God's Good Plan

Weekly memory verse:
Genesis 50:20 – "As for you, you meant evil against me, but God meant it for good."

Weekly hymn:
"What God Ordains is Always Good"

Weekly catechism:
What is God like?
God is the first and best of beings. He is holy, powerful, and good.

What God Ordains Is Always Good

WAS GOTT TUT

WORDS: Samuel Rodigast, 1675; tr. *The Lutheran Hymnal*, 1941

8.7.8.7.4.4.7.7

MUSIC: Servus Gastorius, 1681

Day 26: Jacob Wrestles with God

Genesis 32–33

Notes

Chapter 32, Verse 3. Edom. Edom was the territory of Esau, south of the Dead Sea. Hence, Esau's descendants are later called "Edomites."

Verse 24. A Man wrestled. This "man" may or may not have been the pre-incarnate Christ, but nevertheless, this all-night wrestling match epitomized Jacob's lifelong struggle with both God and men to receive the blessing of God. Ultimately, this event fundamentally changes Jacob, seen most clearly in a change of name ("Israel" means "he strives with God") and the limp he will carry with him until his death.

Chapter 33, Verse 20. El-Elohe-Israel. This means "God, the God of Israel." The term "El" was a general term for deity. God had not yet disclosed his unique name.

Summary

This story epitomizes the unusual and unexpected blessing of God upon Jacob as the heir to the Abrahamic covenant. God fulfills the promise he had made to Jacob at Bethel, protecting Jacob and returning him safely to Canaan. And Jacob's purchase of land and building of an altar in the same place where Abraham had first built one signifies the beginning of the fulfillment of the covenant, which has yet to be fully completed.

Questions for Reflection

1. What does Jacob's prayer to God in anticipation of meeting Esau reveal about him?
2. What does Jacob's wrestling with the representative of God all night signify?
3. Why do you think Esau forgave Jacob?

Day 27: God Renames Jacob

Genesis 35, 37

Notes

Chapter 35, Verse 1. Bethel. This is the place where God had confirmed the Abrahamic covenant with Jacob (28:13–15).

Verse 16. Ephrath. This is an ancient name for Bethlehem.

Chapter 37, Verse 3. Robe of many colors. The Greek translation of the Old Testament used this translation of Moses's phrase, although others prefer "a long sleeved robed." Either way, this is an ornate robe that indicated Joseph's favor in Jacob's sight as the future leader of the family.

Verse 25. Ishmaelites. These are descendants of Abraham's son, Ishmael, also called Midianites.

Verse 35. Sheol. This refers to the abode of the dead and could also be translated "grave."

Summary

God continues to confirm his blessing upon Jacob, including giving him a land and an offspring of royalty. Israel's many children mark the beginning of a great nation, which God will use to bless all the nations of the earth.

Questions for Reflection

1. Why do you think God changed Jacob's name?
2. What is the significance of the birth of Benjamin in what will later be Bethlehem?
3. What is important about the fact that both Jacob and Esau buried their father?

Day 28: Joseph Taken to Egypt

Genesis 39–41

Notes

Chapter 40, Verse 1. King of Egypt. This was likely Senusret II (1894–1878 BC).

Chapter 41, Verse 38. Spirit of God. The Egyptians certainly did not understand anything about the third person of the Trinity; this simply refers to Pharaoh's recognition that God was working in and through Joseph.

Summary

God providential care for his people strikingly characterized the story of Joseph. Instead of leaving his people to die of hunger in Canaan, God providentially arranges for seemingly terrible circumstances to come upon Joseph, which in the end work to save his people. What God ordains is always good for those who love him.

Questions for Reflection

1. Can God use even unbelievers to accomplish his purposes?
2. What does Joseph's story teach us about trusting God in the midst of even terrible circumstances?
3. What are some bad circumstances in your life that you have seen God use for your good?

Day 29: Joseph's Brothers Go to Egypt

Genesis 42-43

Notes

Chapter 42, Verse 6. Bowed down. Over 15 years had elapsed since Joseph's brothers sold him into slavery, and since he was dressed in Egyptian attire and likely standing a distance from them, it makes sense they did not recognize him.

Chapter 43, Verse 23. The God of your father. This statement by Joseph's steward may indicate that he had either come to faith in Joseph's God or at least knew much about him from Joseph.

Summary

So many promises of God come together in fulfillment in this story, including his promise to provide for his people and Joseph's dream of his brothers bowing before him. The story of Joseph in Egypt is one of the most striking testimonies to God's good providence.

Questions for Reflection

1. Why do you think Joseph tested his brothers?

2. What does Reuben's promise to Jacob reveal about him?
3. What does the way Joseph's brothers treated Benjamin reveal about them?

Day 30: God Meant it for Good

Genesis 44-46

Notes

Chapter 44, Verse 5. Divination. Joseph's special cup was apparently associated with divination, but this does not mean that Joseph himself participated in this pagan superstition.

Chapter 45, Verse 6. These two years. This would make Joseph 39 years old.

Verse 8. Father to Pharaoh. This is a title given to a person who, although unrelated to Pharaoh, performed a leadership role on his behalf.

Verse 10. Goshen. This land, in the northeastern area of Egypt, would have been fitting for grazing Jacob's herds. The Jews would dwell in this land for over 400 years.

Chapter 46, Verse 28. Judah. By this time Judah had replaced Reuben as the family leader.

Summary

In the mist of what seemed some of the most terrible of circumstances, God orchestrated the preservation of his people. What evil men meant for evil, God meant for good.

Questions for Reflection

1. What are the implications of the phase, "God meant it for good"?
2. Why must we be patient and trust God when we are experiencing bad circumstances?
3. Will we always know what good God intends to accomplish through bad circumstances?

Week 7: God Raises Up a Deliverer

Weekly memory verse:

Psalm 77:11 - "I will remember the deeds of the Lord; yes, I will remember your wonders of old."

Weekly hymn:

"God Moves in a Mysterious Way"

Weekly catechism:

Are there more gods than one?
There is only one true and living God.

God Moves in a Mysterious Way

WORDS: William Cowper, 1774
MUSIC: *Scottish Psalter*, 1615

CM

Day 31: A Father's Wise Instruction

Proverbs 4-5

Notes

Proverbs 4, Verse 4. Heart. It is instructive that the focus here is on the *heart* holding fast to the father's wise instruction instead of the *mind.*

Verse 23. Heart. In modern thought, the heart is often simply associated with feelings; however, in ancient Hebrew thought, the heart was the totality of what made a person and from which life itself flowed. Thus, as this verse emphasizes, the heart must be guarded diligently.

Summary

What we believe is very important, but it is not all that is important. At a fundamental level, life flows from our *hearts.* Therefore, we must diligently guard those things that influence our hearts.

Questions for Reflection

1. What kinds of things influence your heart?
2. How can you guard you heart from bad influences?
3. How can you know if your heart is being influenced in a negative way?

Day 32: The Birth of Moses

Exodus 1:1-2:10

Notes

Chapter 1, Verse 7. Increased. The growth of the nation of Israel grew from 70 men to 603,000 men 20 years of age and older, leading to the conclusion that the entire population was likely around 2 million (Num 1:46) by the time of the Exodus.

Verse 8. New king. This was likely one of the Hyksos kings of Egypt who reigned from approximately 1730 to 1570 BC.

Verse 22. Pharaoh. The timing of Moses's birth shortly after this decree leads to the conclusion that this Pharaoh was Thutmose I.

Chapter 2, Verse 5. Daughter of Pharaoh. Likely Hatshepsut.

Summary

God's provision for his people in Egypt allowed them to grow into a great nation as he had promised to Abraham. This led to further hardship, but God once again intervened and through his kind providence began to raise a deliverer.

Questions for Reflection

1. Do you think what the midwives did was right?
2. What did the midwives' action tell us about their respect for human life?
3. What value was it for Moses to be raised as the son of Pharaoh's daughter?

Day 33: God Hears the Cries of His People

Exodus 2:11–25; Psalm 90

Notes

Exodus 2, Verse 15. Midian. The Midianites descended from Abraham and Keturah (Gen 25:1–4). They lived on the eastern side of the Gulf of Aqabah in the Arabian Peninsula.

Verse 24. Heard . . . remembered. These are anthropomorphic descriptions of God, since God knows all things and never changes. They simply affirm that God was faithful to his covenant with Abraham in his dealings with the people of Israel.

Psalm 90. Moses. This may have been written during Moses's exile in Midian as an expression of trust and dependence upon God.

Verse 4. Watch in the night. Refers to a four-hour period of time.

Summary

Nothing escapes the knowledge of the Lord. God providentially arranged for the future deliverer of his people to be protected and raised in Pharaoh's court and then for him to spend time in exile in Midian. He had arranged for his growing people to find refuge in Egypt where they were able to flourish for a time, but now he has also arranged for them to be delivered and taken back to their promised land. God will always keep his promises, often through mysterious ways.

Questions for Reflection

1. What did Moses's killing of the Egyptian reveal about his relationship with the nation of Israel?
2. Why do you think God wanted Moses to spend time out of Egypt in Midian?
3. What characteristics of God can give us hope and confidence, even when we don't understand his ways?

Day 34: The Burning Bush

Exodus 3:1–4:18

Notes

Chapter 3, Verse 1. Horeb. This is another name for Mt. Sinai, which because of what takes place later after the Exodus, becomes known as "the mountain of God."

Verse 2. The Angel of the Lord. As before, this is God himself.

Verse 14. I am who I am. Here God discloses his unique, covenant name to Moses. God refers to himself using the Hebrew verb that means "to be" (*hayah*) and relates it to his divine name, Yahweh (v. 15). In most modern Bible editions, "LORD" in all caps indicates a translation of "Yahweh." The consonants from the Hebrew word *Yhwh*, combined with the vowels from one of God's other names, *Adonai*, form the English word, "Jehovah."

Summary

God puts in motion his plan to deliver his people and bring them into the promised land by revealing himself to Moses and calling him to lead the people out of Egypt. He discloses his unique, covenant name, Yahweh, and answers all of Moses's objections. God will use this weak man to lead the nation, but ultimately his supernatural acts will reveal that he is truly the one who delivers his people.

Questions for Reflection

1. Why do you think God commanded Moses to remove his shoes?
2. What does the name "I am who I am" reveal about God?
3. What does God reveal as the central purpose for the Exodus in 3:18?

Day 35: Moses and Aaron

Exodus 4:19-31; Psalm 77

Notes

Exodus 4, Verse 21. Harden. The tension between God's divine providence and human responsibility is one of the most difficult to reconcile in Scripture. Ten times in the story of the Exodus the text indicates that God hardened Pharaoh's heart, and ten times the text indicates that Pharaoh hardened his own heart. It is both true that God sovereignly acted in this affair and that Pharaoh was personally responsible for his actions.

Verse 24. Death. This incident reveals the seriousness God places upon the unique sign of the covenant, circumcision. Apparently Moses had not performed this sign with his own sons, and thus Zipporah quickly performed the procedure.

Psalm 77. This is a community lament in which God's people call out to him for help, making specific reference to God hearing his people's cries and delivering them through Moses and Aaron (v. 20). References to "the years of the right hand of the Most High" (v. 10), "redeemed your people" (v. 15), and "led your people like a flock" (v. 20) connect this psalm with the Exodus.

Summary

God promises to care for his people, and he will keep his promises. He sometimes moves in mysterious ways in accomplishing his will, but we can trust in him. When we call out to God in our distress, he hears us and answers, providing deliverance and comfort.

Questions for Reflection

1. On what basis can you trust the Lord, even in distress?
2. What responsibility to do you have toward God in this life?
3. Why is it important to regularly remember all the good that God has done in the past for his people?

Week 8: God Saves His People

Weekly memory verse:
Exodus 15:1 - "I will sing to the Lord, for he has triumphed gloriously; the horse and his rider he has thrown into the sea."

Weekly hymn:
"Guide Me, O Thou Great Jehovah"

Weekly catechism:
In how many persons does this one God exist?
God exists in three persons: the Father, the Son, and the Holy Spirit, equal in essence, power, and glory.

Guide Me, O Thou Great Jehovah

CWM RHONDDA

WORDS: William Williams, 1745; tr. Peter Williams, 1771

8.7.8.7.8.7.7

MUSIC: John Hughes, 1907

Day 36: Let My People Go

Exodus 5:1-6:13

Notes

Chapter 5, Verse 11. Straw. Straw was a necessary component for making bricks in ancient Egypt since it helped to bind the clay together.

Chapter 6, Verse 4. Covenant. God based his promise once again on the covenant he had made with Abraham.

Verse 12. Uncircumcised lips. This is an expression that refers to Moses's lack of eloquence.

Summary

God's promises are fundamentally rooted in his nature and character—he is a covenant-keeping God. God has providentially arranged for the circumstances of his people to be such that he will begin to powerfully display his nature and character through delivering them from bondage.

Questions for Reflection

1. Why did God providentially arrange for his people to be put in bondage, for their deliverer to be someone who lacked eloquence, and for Pharaoh to be so defiant?
2. How do seemingly unsolvable circumstances lead us to trust in God?
3. Have difficult circumstances in your life ever tempted you to distrust God's promises?

Day 37: The First Seven Plagues

Exodus 7-9

Notes

Chapter 7, Verse 1. Like God. Moses spoke with authority as God's representative before Pharaoh, and Aaron was his mouthpiece.

Verse 11. Magicians. These enchantments were part of the pagan religion of Egypt. It is unclear whether their magic was illusion, skill, or demonic influence.

Verse 14. Each of the ten miraculous plagues against Egypt specifically targeted one of their pagan deities, revealing that Yahweh was the true and living God.

Chapter 8, Verse 22. Goshen. This clearly indicates the supernatural nature of these plagues in that the land where the Israelites lived was spared.

Summary

Contrary to the claims of false religions throughout history, Yahweh is the one and only true and living God. The plagues against Egypt give a powerful demonstration of this fundamental truth.

Questions for Reflection

1. How did the plagues demonstrate that God is the one and only true and living God?
2. How did the failures of the magicians demonstrate the falsity of their pagan religion?
3. How did the responses of Pharaoh and his people increase their own guilt before God?

Day 38: The Passover

Exodus 10-12

Notes

Chapter 12, Verse 2. This month. The Passover event marked the beginning of Israel as an independent nation, and thus, the beginning of their religious calendar going forward. The month of Abib (March/April) was to be the first month of the year for Israel. Later, the month of Abib would become Nisan (see. Neh 2:1; Esth 3:7).

Verse 6. Twilight. By Israelite reckoning, a new day began at sunset. In the observation of the Passover, the lamb was to be sacrificed before sunset while it was still the 14th day of the month. This was the time at which Christ would later die (Luke 23:44-46).

Verse 14. Memorial. The detailed observance of the first Passover was to be observed as a liturgical memorial in Israel every year. In liturgical language, a "memorial" is a reenactment of an act of God on behalf of his people in such a way that people in future generations will be shaped by the event as if they had been there themselves, in this case, the redemption of Israel.

Verse 37. Six hundred thousand men. Based on this figure, a conservative estimate of the size of the nation at the time of the Exodus is around 2 million people.

Summary

With the final plagues against Egypt and the first Passover, God fulfilled his promise to redeem his people from their bondage. This event marked the most significant holy day for Israel, a day each year on which they would reenact God's redemption on their behalf, actively passing that experience down to future generations.

Questions for Reflection

1. Of what significance was it that the final plague targeted the firstborn sons in Egypt, including Pharaoh's own son?
2. What did the first Passover foreshadow with relation to Christ?
3. What does reenacting a work of God on behalf of his people do for those who participate?

Day 39: Crossing the Red Sea

Exodus 13-15

Notes

Chapter 15, Verse 1. Sang. This is one of three songs composed by Moses (see Deut 31:22; Ps 90). The hymn is divided into four stanzas, each ending with parallel ideas: (I) vv. 1b-5, (II) vv. 6-10; (III); vv. 11-16a; (IV) vv. 16b-18. Additionally, each stanza has three parts: An Introit (vv. 1, 6, 11, 16b); a Confession (vv. 2-3, 7-8, 12-12, 17); and a Narration (vv. 4-5, 9-10) or Anticipation (vv.14-16a, 18). Thus the progression of ideas through the hymn move from recounting the Lord's deeds in the past toward anticipating his help for the future.

Verse 21. Prophetess. Miriam is the first women to be given this title. She leads the other women in singing Moses's hymn and dancing with tambourines. This kind of folk dancing involved the women forming circles and spinning around as they sang and hit the tambourines.

Summary

God's ultimate power in delivering his people was displayed in the crossing of the Red Sea. There could now be no doubt for the people of Israel that God was with them and would do what he had promised. Their only appropriate response was a song of praise and trust in the Lord's power and promises.

Questions for Reflection

1. Why were the people so quick to complain against the Lord?
2. Does the fact that God used an east wind to make a path for Israel diminish the miraculous nature of the event?
3. What can we learn from Moses's song?

Day 40: Bread from Heaven

Exodus 16

Notes

Verse 1. Fifteenth day. Thirty days had passed since their departure from Rameses.

Verse 16. Omer. This was a little more than two quarts.

Verse 31. Manna. The Israelites coined a new term for this bread from heaven, which literally means, "What is it?"

Summary

God's grace and love for his people is so steadfast, that even in the midst of their unfounded complaints against him, the Lord hears their cries and provides for them. His promises to Abraham were unconditional, and he is going to keep those promises.

Questions for Reflection

1. What do the people's perpetual complaints against the Lord reveal about them?
2. What does the fact that God provided for their needs, even in the midst of their complaints, reveal about him?
3. What did the fact that no bread fell on the seventh day reveal about this day?

Week 9: Worshiping God at Sinai

Weekly memory verse:

Deuteronomy 6:4-5 - "Hear, O Israel: The Lord our God, the Lord is one. You shall love the Lord your God with all your heart and with all your soul and with all your might."

Weekly hymn:

"Immortal, Invisible, God Only Wise"

Weekly catechism:

What are the decrees of God?
The decrees of God are his eternal purposes, whereby for his own glory he has ordained whatever comes to pass.

Immortal, Invisible, God Only Wise

ST. DENIO

WORDS: Walter Chalmers Smith, 1867

11.11.11.11

MUSIC: Welsh hymn tune, from John Roberts's *Caniadau y Cyssegr*, 1839

Day 41: Journey to Sinai

Exodus 17-19

Notes

Chapter 17, Verse 7. Massah and Meribah. These names mean "testing" and "contending."

Verse 8. Amalek. Amalek was the grandson of Esau, and these are his descendants.

Verse 9. Joshua. This is the first appearance of the man who would lead Israel into the promised land.

Chapter 19, Verse 1. Third new moon. Israel spent approximately 11 months at Sinai (cf. Num 10:11).

Verse 5. If. While the Abrahamic Covenant was unconditional, the promises of blessing made in the Mosaic Covenant were conditioned upon their obedience to his Law.

Verse 24. Priests. Since the Law had not yet been given, no official priesthood had been established. These must have been the family representatives that served a priestly function for each clan.

Summary

On their journey to Sinai, God visibly displayed to the Israelites that he would materially provide for them as well as provide protection for them from their enemies by miraculously giving them water from a rock and by giving them an unlikely defeat over the Amalekites. God will always keep his promises and provide for his people. However, because of sin, even God's people tremble when they enter his presence and must be cleansed of their sin to enjoy full communion with him.

Questions for Reflection

1. What do you think Moses's use of his staff to accomplish many miracles signified?
2. Why did God make such a big deal about consecrating the people before they approached his presence?
3. Why couldn't the people touch the mountain?

Day 42: Israel at Mount Sinai

Exodus 20; Deuteronomy 6

Notes

Exodus 20, Verse 5. Generations. God will not punish children for the sins of their parents (Deut 24:16), but nevertheless the consequences of sin are often felt for many generations.

Deuteronomy 6, Verse 4. Hear. This important Jewish confession of faith is known as the *Shema* (Hebrew for "hear").

Summary

God promises to bless and care for his people, and he will do that unconditionally. However, the condition of the relationship between God and his people is dependent upon their obedience to what he commands. If they obey him, he will materially bless them; if they disobey, they will be punished. The essence of relationship with him, however is more than right beliefs and right actions; it is love for God.

Questions for Reflection

1. What do the Ten Commandments reveal about God?
2. What is the difference between the first and second commandment?
3. Why is loving God central to our relationship with him?

Day 43: The Golden Calf

Exodus 24, 32

Notes

Chapter 24, Verse 9. Saw God. Since God is a spirit and does not have a body like man, what these representatives of the people saw was actually a physical manifestation of his glory.

Chapter 32, Verse 1. Gods. This is the term *Elohim*, a generic name for deity. The Israelites were not actually asking to make an idol of a false god, but rather a visible representation of Yahweh himself (note that Aaron specifically calls the calf Yahweh in verse 5). They were attempting to worship Yahweh through a visible representation, something God had specifically forbidden in the second commandment.

Verse 4. Calf. This was a religious symbol borrowed from pagan religions that was intended to honor Yahweh by representing him as a powerful beast. This is a prime example of syncretism, the mixing of true worship with false worship.

Verse 6. Play. The pagan worship of Yahweh was accompanied by other typically pagan worship practices such as drunken, immoral rituals and celebration.

Verse 17. Noise. The music that accompanied the people's pagan worship of Yahweh was so loud and chaotic that it sounded to Joshua like war.

Summary

Those who draw near to the presence of God through obedience to the means that he has provided are able to see him and commune with him. But those who attempt to worship him through means that he has not prescribed, especially through means borrowed from pagan worship, will be several punished. God expects worship on his terms and according to his commands.

Questions for Reflection

1. What did the fact that the Hebrew leaders ate and drank in God's presence signify?
2. What do you think motivated the people to worship Yahweh through means borrowed from pagan worship?
3. Do you think God was too severe in his punishment of the people?

Day 44: Building the Tabernacle

Exodus 40

Notes

Verse 17. Second year. The Israelites built the tabernacle approximately one year after the Exodus from Egypt, while they were still at the foot of Mt. Sinai.

Verse 21. Ark. The Ark of the Covenant was a symbol of God's presence and, indeed, where the visible glory of the Lord dwelt. It was placed in the Holy of Holies, which was separated from the Holy Place in the tabernacle by a veil. Only the High Priest ever entered the Holy of Holies, and that only occurred one day per year on the Day of Atonement.

Summary

In his mercy and grace, God condescended to his people by creating a place where he could dwell in their midst. Even though his presence was in the tabernacle, however, the people's sin nevertheless prevented them from fully drawing near, and they had to be certain to follow his clear instructions for how to approach him. Today, God dwells in a new temple, the church.

Questions for Reflection

1. What does the fact that so much attention and care was given to building the tabernacle reveal about its importance?
2. Why were the people required to go to the tabernacle in order to worship the Lord?
3. Does God dwell in a tabernacle or temple today?

Day 45: Unauthorized Fire

Leviticus 10; Psalm 11

Notes

Leviticus 10, Verse 1. Unauthorized fire. Nadab and Abihu's sin was not that they were worshiping a false god, nor that they were explicitly disobeying a clear prohibition from God, but rather that they were adding to worship something God "had not commanded them."

Verse 6. Eleazar. One of Aaron's younger sons who lived and would be later named as the head of the high priestly line (see Num 25:10-13).

Verse 8. Wine. Since it was likely drunkenness that led to Nadab and Abihu's sin, Moses officially prohibits priests in tabernacle service from drinking alcohol.

Psalm 11, Verse 4. Temple. God's temple is in heaven; the earthly tabernacle and temple were mere shadows of the real temple, meant to visually picture the spiritual realities of the heavenly sanctuary of God (see Heb 8:5).

Summary

The worship of God must be pure and according to his commandments. Any adding of unauthorized practices to worship, whether for good or sinister motives, are rejected by God. He wants to be set apart as holy, and this means he has the prerogative to instruct his people as to how he wants to be worshiped.

Questions for Reflection

1. Why did God so dramatically punish Nadab and Abihu for offering unauthorized fire to him?
2. What does this incident teach about the negative effects of alcohol?
3. What can we learn from the fact that the earthly sanctuary was a picture of the true, heavenly temple?

Week 10: Wandering in the Wilderness

Weekly memory verse:

John 3:14-15 - "And as Moses lifted up the serpent in the wilderness, so must the Son of Man be lifted up, that whoever believes in him may have eternal life."

Weekly hymn:

"Be Thou My Vision"

Weekly catechism:

How do you know there is a God?

The light of nature and the works of God plainly declare that there is a God, but only his Word and Spirit effectually reveal him to me for my salvation.

Be Thou My Vision

SLANE

WORDS: 8th cent. hymn; tr. Mary Elizabeth Byrne, 1905; vers. Eleanor Hull, 1912, alt. 10.11.11.11
MUSIC: Irish folk melody

Day 46: Complaints Against the Lord

Number 11-12

Notes

Chapter 11, Verse 3. Taberah. A name that means "burning."

Verse 4. Rabble. This likely refers to non-Israelites who had accompanied Israel out of Egypt (see Exod 12:38).

Verse 17. Spirit. This was a special anointing of the Holy Spirit that was given to particular leaders in order to supernaturally equip them to fulfill God's task for them. It does not refer to a saving indwelling, as this same anointing is sometimes given even to unbelievers, and it can be taken away.

Verse 32. Ten homers. A homer was approximately 6 bushels.

Verse 34. Kibroth-hattaavah. A name that means "graves of craving."

Chapter 12, Verse 1. Cushite. Cush was the firstborn son of Ham (Gen 10:6-7), whose descendants became the Ethiopians. This wife of Moses likely refers to his second wife after the death of his first wife, Zipporah.

Verse 8. Mouth to mouth. Unlike with other prophets, God spoke to Moses directly instead of through visions and dreams. This indicated the special mediatorial relationship Moses had with God.

Verse 16. Paran. This was the region between Sinai and the promised land, thus this one verse summarizes the journey of Israel to Kadesh, on the northern border of Paran.

Summary

God promised that he would provide for his people, yet this did not stop them from complaining. Complaints against God reveal a lack of faith in him, and thus he punished it severely. Yet, in a beautiful display of his mercy and steadfast faithfulness toward his people, God chose to grant their request and provided them with meat in addition to the manna. And to question the special, anointed mediator between God and his chosen people was a particularly grievous sin.

Questions for Reflection

1. What does complaining against God reveal about our hearts?
2. Why did God provide the people with meat even though they had complained against him?
3. What are some ways you complain against God?

Day 47: Cries of the Faithful

Psalms 12–13

Notes

Psalm 12, Verse 1. Godly one is gone. This is clearly a hyperbolic statement, but it reveals David's perception that there are no righteous people left and sets the context for the rest of the psalm.

Verse 6. Pure . . . purified. David poetically contrasts the purity of God's words with the profanity of the wicked, but that same purity guarantees the purity of what he has promised.

Psalm 13, Verse 1. How long. This lament provides one of the simplest examples of a believer's appropriate response to turmoil. The psalm moves progressively from despair (vv. 1–2) through desires (vv. 3–4) to delight in the Lord (vv. 5–6).

Verses 4, 5. Rejoice . . . rejoice. The psalmist poetically contrasts the rejoicing of the wicked with his own confident rejoicing in the salvation of the Lord.

Summary

When it appears that no righteous people exist and that God's enemies are overwhelming, we must nevertheless trust in the steadfast, pure faithfulness of God. It is appropriate to cry out to the Lord in times of distress, but our knowledge of who he is must always lead us to confident trust in his promises.

Questions for Reflection

1. Have you ever felt that there were no other righteous people? How did you respond?
2. What about God gives us assurance and confidence that he will remain faithful to his people, even when it doesn't seem like it?

3. What should be our appropriate response in times of distress?

Day 48: Spies in Canaan

Numbers 13–14

Notes

Chapter 13, Verse 1. Send men to spy. Deuteronomy 1 makes clear that it was the people who originally requested that spies be sent into Canaan, but here the Lord affirms their desires.

Verse 16. Hoshea . . . Joshua. Moses changed the name "desire for salvation" to "the Lord is salvation."

Verse 20. Season of the first ripe grapes. This would have been midsummer.

Summary

Once again the people display their fundamental distrust in the Lord, despite their knowledge of his character and the fact of what he had already done on their behalf. On ten separate occasions the people had complained and questioned God's goodness, and now finally God judges the people for their sin, condemning them to die in the wilderness. Yet once again God displays his mercy by promising that their children will indeed enter the promised land.

Questions for Reflection

1. Why is the report of the ten spies called "bad" (13:32)?
2. Why is complaint against God such a terrible sin?
3. What did Joshua and Caleb's report reveal about them?

Day 49: Korah's Rebellion

Numbers 16–17

Notes

Chapter 16, Verse 32. Households. According to Numbers 26:11, the children were not part of those who were swallowed up.

Verse 46. Incense. Incense symbolizes intercessory prayer.

Verse 49. Died. This event is referenced as a warning in 1 Corinthians 10:10.

Chapter 17, Verse 4. The testimony. This refers to the Ten Commandments written on the stone tablets.

Verse 13. Comes near. This is a picture of drawing near to the presence of God, which permeates all of Scripture. It shows the truth that sin prevents anyone from drawing near without a mediator (in this case, Aaron, the High Priest) will die.

Summary

All of the complaining against God and his chosen servants comes to a climax in the rebellion of Korah, but God's swift judgment confirms that while his promises of blessing to those who obey will surely be fulfilled, so will his promises of judgment against those who rebel against him. His judgment is strong, but the people eventually learn the lesson that they must not challenge the mediators that God has chosen for them to be able to approach him.

Questions for Reflection

1. Why was rebellion against Moses and Aaron essentially a rebellion against God himself?
2. Do you think God was too harsh in his judgment of the rebels? Why or why not?
3. Why is a mediator necessary for a sinner to approach the presence of God?

Day 50: The Bronze Serpent

Numbers 20–21

Notes

Chapter 20, Verse 1. First month. Based on Numbers 33:38, this is now the fortieth year after the Exodus from Egypt. Miriam's death represents, in a way, the older generation that had all died in the wilderness.

Verse 14. Edom. The Edomites were descendants from Esau, the brother of Jacob (see Gen 36:10.

Verse 17. The king's highway. This was a central trade route that ran north and south and passed through the Edomite city of Sela.

Verse 20. Army. God had forbidden Israel from going to war with Edom (Deut 2:4–6), so Israel turned away.

Summary

Even though God had condemned the older generation to die in the wilderness, the younger generation apparently did not learn the intended lesson. Instead, they, too, complained against God and were punished. Yet this incident provided a beautiful picture of the redemption that was possible through faith in the one who was lifted up (John 3:14–15).

Questions for Reflection

1. Why were Moses and Aaron not allowed to enter the promised land?
2. Why do you think God provided the bronze serpent?
3. What does this incident tell us about the character of God?

Week 11: Preparing to Enter the Promised Land

Weekly memory verse:

Joshua 1:8 - "This Book of the Law shall not depart from your mouth, but you shall meditate on it day and night, so that you may be careful to do according to all that is written in it. For then you will make your way prosperous, and then you will have good success."

Weekly hymn:

"How Firm a Foundation"

Weekly catechism:

What rule has God given to direct you how you may glorify and enjoy him?
The Word of God which is contained in the Scriptures of the Old and New Testaments is the only rule to direct me how I many glorify God and enjoy Him.

How Firm a Foundation

FOUNDATION

WORDS: "K" in John Rippon's *A Selection of Hymns*, 1878 — 11.11.11.11

MUSIC: American folk tune, Funk's *Genuine Church Music*, 1832

Day 51: Balaam and the Donkey

Numbers 22:1–23:12

Notes

Chapter 22, Verse 3. Moab. The Moabites were descendants of Lot. Balak, the king, did not know that God had forbidden Israel from destroying Moab (Deut 2:9).

Verse 4. Midian. The Midianites were descendants of Abraham by Keturah (Gen 25:1–4).

Verse 5. River. This is the Euphrates River.

Summary

The humorous account reveals the fact that nothing can stand in the way of God's plan to bless his people—not false religions, not the enemies of God, and not even nature. God will work all things toward his purpose, and therefore God's people never need fear; we can always trust that God will keep his promises toward us.

Questions for Reflection

1. Why did Balak want Balaam to curse Israel?
2. Why do you think God chose to speak to Balaam?
3. Why do you think God used a donkey to speak truth to Balaam?

Day 52: The Wicked and the Righteous

Psalms 14–15, 105

Notes

Psalm 14, Verse 1. Fool. This designation refers not to intellectual capability but to moral failure.

Verse 3. None. Paul quotes this passage in Romans 3:10–12 as proof of the universal depravity of humankind.

Verse 7. Zion. This is the place where God's presence dwelt.

Psalm 15, Verse 1. Who. Psalm 15 contrasts with Psalm 14 by focusing on the righteous person rather than the wicked fool.

Verse 1. Tent. Like with "Zion," this "tent" or "tabernacle" represents the place of God's presence and blessing.

Summary

The difference between the wicked fool and the righteous person is ultimately a difference of belief—the fool rejects God, while the righteous pursues fellowship with God. But this fundamental difference also results in different ways of life—the fool is corrupt, while the righteous lives blamelessly. Beliefs always result in certain ways of life.

Questions for Reflection

1. What results from the fact that no one seeks after God on their own?
2. What is required for some people to seek after God?
3. What is the result of seeking fellowship with God?

Day 53: The Death of Moses

Deuteronomy 34; Psalm 16

Notes

Deuteronomy 34, Verse 4. You shall not go. God did not allow Moses to experience the promised land himself because of his unfaithfulness at Meribah (see Num 20:12).

Verse 6. Buried. Apparently God himself buried Moses.

Verse 9. Joshua. God had specifically designated Joshua to be Moses's heir (see Num 27:12-23).

Verse 10. A prophet like Moses. No prophet was greater than Moses until John the Baptist (Matt 11:11). The next time Moses appears is on the Mount of Transfiguration (Matt 17:13, Mark 9:4, Luke 9:10-31).

Psalm 16, Verse 10. This is a confident expression made by David but later applied to David's descendant, the Messiah by Peter (Acts 2:25-28) and Paul (Acts 13:35).

Summary

What God had promised through Moses—obedience brings blessing, but disobedience brings punishment—is fulfilled in Moses himself. Because of his unfaithfulness to God, God did not allow Moses to enter the promised land. Nevertheless, Moses was the greatest prophet who ever lived until John the Baptist. After John, the Prophet of whom Moses himself wrote appeared, Jesus the Messiah, the Redeemer who was not abandoned in the grave but rose again.

Questions for Reflection

1. Do you think God was too harsh to punish Moses for striking the rock instead of speaking to it?
2. In what ways was Joshua formally set apart as the new ruler of Israel?
3. What does it mean that in God's presence "there is fullness of joy"?

Day 54: Rahab and the Spies

Joshua 1:1–3:6

Notes

Chapter 1, Verse 4. Land. The borders of the land extend all the way to the Euphrates River in the far east, down to the Nile River in Egypt, and Lebanon in the north.

Verse 8. Book of the law. This refers to Scripture.

Verse 12. Manasseh. In Genesis 48, God gave Joseph a double blessing by giving his two sons, Ephraim and Manasseh, each their own tribe. Since the tribe of Levi wasn't given a portion of the land, due to their priestly function, this gave land to twelve tribes.

Chapter 2, Verse 11. He is God. This was a clear expression of Rahab's faith in the true God (see Heb 11:31; Jas 2:25).

Summary

God promised that he would give Israel the promised land, and he is finally beginning to fulfill that promise. The promise has never completely been fulfilled, however; Israel has never possessed all of the land. But God will indeed keep the promise he made to them; one day, they will possess the land from the Mediterranean Sea to the Euphrates River and from the Nile to Lebanon.

Questions for Reflection

1. Why was Joshua's admonition to meditate on God's Word so important?
2. What did Rahab's actions reveal about her?
3. What aspects of the Rahab story reveal God's control over the situation?

Day 55: Crossing the Jordan River

Joshua 3:7-5:12

Notes

Chapter 3, Verse 10. Drive out. God always has the right to judge sinners, and so his command to completely destroy all of the inhabitants of the promised land is just. What is amazing is why God allows sinners to go unpunished for as long as he does.

Summary

God continued to establish Joshua as Israel's new leader by performing the same kind of miracle that had established Moses—crossing a river on dry land. This marks the beginning of the invasion of the promised land.

Questions for Reflection

1. Why isn't God's command to kill all of the inhabitants of the promised land unfair?
2. Why are memorials, such as Israel's twelve stones by the river, important for passing on the history of what God has done for his people?
3. What did the ceasing of manna signify to the people?

Week 12: Invasion of the Promised Land

Weekly memory verse:
Job 19:25 - “For I know that my Redeemer lives, and at the last he will stand upon the earth.”

Weekly hymn:
“This is My Father’s World”

Weekly catechism:
How can you glorify God?
I can glorify God by loving him and doing what he commands.

This Is My Father's World

TERRA BEATA

WORDS: Maltbie D. Babcock, 1901 SMD

MUSIC: Traditional English melody; adapt. Franklin L. Sheppard, 1915

Day 56: The Fall of Jericho

Joshua 5:13-6:27

Notes

Chapter 5, Verse 13. A man. This is a Christophany—a pre-incarnate appearance of the Son of God.

Summary

If the people had any doubt that God would keep his promise and give them the land, this miraculous defeat of Jericho proved God's power. No natural explanation can account for what happened here. Only God's power could have destroyed the walls and protected Rahab and her household at the same time.

Questions for Reflection

1. Why do you think Christ appeared to Joshua?
2. Why do you think God commanded them to march around Jericho?
3. Why did God save Rahab and her family?

Day 57: The Sin of Achan

Joshua 7-8

Notes

Chapter 7, Verse 24. Sons and daughters. These must have been adult children who helped to cover their father's sin and were thus culpable of his actions.

Chapter 8, Verse 32. Wrote. By rewriting the law, Joshua was renewing the covenant Moses had made with Yahweh.

Summary

Achan's disobedience to God's clear commands resulted in his own punishment and consequences for his family. Sin is never only individual and private; it always results in pain for others as well, most of all God himself.

Questions for Reflection

1. What did God's punishment of Achan signify to the people?

2. What did the initial defeat and eventual victory show about the true cause of victory and defeat?
3. Why is there value in God's people renewing their covenant with him?

Day 58: Treaty and Conquest

Joshua 9-10

Notes

Chapter 9, Verse 15. Peace. This treaty with the Gibeonites was direct disobedience to the command God had given to destroy all the inhabitants of the land. Israel never fully obeys God, and this causes problems for them during their entire existence.

Chapter 10, Verse 11. Hailstones. These hailstones were clearly miraculous.

Verse 12. Sun. Some try to explain this away as simply a poetic expression or an eclipse, but taking all of verses 12-14 into account ("There has been no day like it"), it is best to simply view this at face value—this was another supernatural work of God.

Verse 13. Book of Jashar. This appears to be a book of songs recording the military victories of Israel.

Summary

God had promised the land to Israel and had clearly demonstrated his power and willingness to supernaturally fulfill that promise. God displayed this in his miraculous care for them in the wilderness, in parting the Jordan River, in defeating Jericho, and in sending hail and stopping the sun. Yet Joshua nevertheless fell into the trap of the Gibeonites and made peace with them in contradiction with God's commands and without consulting him in prayer. He should have trusted in God and not relied on his own, earthly wisdom.

Questions for Reflection

1. Why do you think Joshua made the treaty with the Gibeonites against God's commands?
2. What did God's sending of hail and stopping the sun reveal about him?

3. What are some ways you fail to trust God and instead trust in your own wisdom?

Day 59: Settling in the Land

Joshua 14, 23–24

Notes

Chapter 14, Verse 10. Eighty-five years old. Since Caleb was 40 years old at Kadesh Barnea (v. 7), and the Israelites wandered in the wilderness for 38 years, then conquering the Land must have taken seven years.

Chapter 24, Verse 8. Amorites. Sometimes this term refers to all the inhabitants of Canaan, and other times it refers to a particular tribe within the land.

Verse 29. One hundred and ten years old. This was approximately 1383 BC (see 14:7–10).

Summary

Joshua's retelling of Israel's history and renewal of the covenant with Yahweh reinforces the central biblical truth that obedience brings blessing, while disobedience brings punishment, even for the people of God. God will never forsake his everlasting promises, but he will chasten those whom he loves. Therefore, God's people must regularly recommit themselves to the Lord, choose whom they will serve, and affirm that they "will serve the Lord" (24:15).

Questions for Reflection

1. In what ways did the Israelites obey the commands of God? In what ways did they disobey?
2. What is the responsibility of one of God's people?
3. In what ways can you commit to God that you will serve him?

Day 60: Job

Job 1, 42; Psalm 49

Notes

Job 1, Verse 1. Job. The events of this narrative likely occurred during the patriarchal period, sometime between the Tower of Babel and either before or contemporaneously with Abraham. The book's author is unknown, but it could have been Moses (since Uz was adjacent to Midian), Solomon (because of similarity of content with Ecclesiastes), or one of the prophets (there are some reasons to believe this was written during or after the exile).

Verse 6. Sons of God. Refers to angels (see 38:7, Pss 29:1; 89:7; Dan 3:25).

Summary

God is sovereign and in control of all things, even the works of Satan. This should give us great confidence in God, motivating us to trust in him regardless of the circumstances. We may never know fully why God allows tragedies in our lives, but we can be sure that he has a purpose and that his ways are always good.

Questions for Reflection

1. Why did God allow Satan to bring tragedy upon Job?
2. Is it ever right to question God?
3. Has any tragedy ever occurred in your life, and you didn't know why God allowed it? How should you respond in such situations?

Week 13: Judges

Weekly memory verse:

Judges 3:9 – "But when the people of Israel cried out to the Lord, the Lord raised up a deliverer for the people of Israel, who saved them."

Weekly hymn:

"He Who Would Valiant Be"

Weekly catechism:

What is the greatest commandment?
The greatest commandment is to love the Lord my God with all my heart, soul, and mind.

He Who Would Valiant Be

ST. DUNSTAN'S

WORDS: John Bunyan, 1678; adapt. Percy Dearmer, 1906 — 6.5.6.5.6.6.6.5

MUSIC: Charles Winfred Douglas, 1917

Day 61: God Raises Up Judges

Judges 1-3

Notes

Chapter 1, Verse 6. Cut off. Cutting off a king's thumbs and big toes would have made him impotent in battle.

Chapter 2, Verse 1. Angel of the Lord. This is one of three pre-incarnate appearances of Christ in the book of Judges.

Verse 16. Judges. Judges were tribal leaders who God used to govern various portions of the nation.

Chapter 3, Verse 10. The spirit of the Lord. This is a special anointing of the Spirit of God upon a chosen leader to accomplish specific purposes. It is temporary and not necessarily given only to truly regenerate individuals.

Summary

The people of Israel failed to obey God's commands and even began to worship the false gods of the land because the former generation failed to pass on the knowledge of God and his works to their children. This is why it is so important that parents regularly teach their children about God and what he has done. Yet even in this condition, God answered his people when they cried out for help, sending them deliverers.

Questions for Reflection

1. Why did the people forget God and worship false idols?
2. Is God's use of people to accomplish his purposes necessarily dependent upon whether they are personally righteous?
3. Why does God answer his people's cries for help, even when they have sinned against him?

Day 62: Deborah and Barak

Judges 4-5

Notes

Chapter 4, Verse 4. Deborah. God raised up Deborah because of Barak's failure to lead.

Chapter 5, Verse 10. White donkeys. The unusual color of this animal made them valuable possessions for only those were who rich and influential.

Summary

This account, like many of the stories in Judges, is an example of God accomplishing his purposes and protecting his people even through individuals and circumstances that are contrary to his will and ways. God is sovereign, and he will do what he has promised even if no one obeys him.

Questions for Reflection

1. What did Deborah's leadership reveal about Barak's lack of character and courage?
2. Was Jael's action right and moral?
3. Why did God choose to bless something that was contrary to his moral will?

Day 63: The Call of Gideon

Judges 6

Notes

Verse 11. Angel. Once again, this "angel" is identified as Yahweh himself (see vv. 14, 16, 23, 25, 27).

Verse 37. Fleece. Gideon's requests for signs revealed his weak faith.

Summary

Gideon's question to the Lord reveals the mystery of God's providence in Judges. The oppression and sin of the people seemed to indicate that God had forsaken his people, and yet God was always there, fulfilling his promises and accomplishing his will, even when the people did not recognize it.

Questions for Reflection

1. When bad things happen, does this mean God is not present?
2. How should we respond when bad things happen to us?
3. Should we ask God for signs to prove that he will do what he has promised?

Day 64: Gideon's 300 Men

Judges 7-8

Notes

Chapter 7, Verse 5. Laps the water. There is no reason given for why this was used to distinguish the groups; it was just a way for God to divide the people.

Verse 18. The sword of the Lord and of Gideon. This revealed a trust in the power of God in combination with duty to obey him as he had commanded.

Verse 19. Set the watch. About 10 p.m.

Summary

God is sovereign, but he often uses people to accomplish his will. Divine sovereignty and human responsibility go hand in hand. Yet when God uses us, we should never assume that we are the ones who have actually accomplished the victory. To boast in what good we have supposedly done is to ignore God's hand behind it all.

Questions for Reflection

1. Who won the battle against the Midianites, Gideon or God?
2. If we accomplish something great for the Lord, who actually deserves the credit?
3. When we boast for what we have done for God, what does that reveal about us?

Day 65: Abimelech

Judges 9

Notes

Verse 5. Killed his brothers. This eliminated competition for rulership.

Verse 45. Sowed it with salt. This polluted the soil and water and made it impossible to grow anything.

Summary

This story once again reveals the sinfulness of God's people. They did not deserve God's protection or care; none of their conquests, victories, and eventual flourishing was a result of their righteousness or worthiness. It was only God's covenant with them and his faithfulness that grew them into a mighty, prosperous nation.

Questions for Reflection

1. Is there any indication in this passage that the people loved or desired to serve God?
2. Why did God continue to protect his people, even in the midst of their sinful lifestyles?
3. Why is God faithful to his promises?

Week 14: Samson

Weekly memory verse:

Psalm 17:8 - "Keep me as the apple of your eye; hide me in the shadow of your wings."

Weekly hymn:

"Jesus, Lover of My Soul"

Weekly catechism:

How can you come to know God and what he has made?
The fear of the Lord is the beginning of knowledge.

Jesus, Lover of My Soul

ABERYSTWYTH

WORDS: Charles Wesley, 1740
MUSIC: Joseph Parry, 1879

7.7.7.7.D

Day 66: Jephthah

Judges 10-12

Notes

Chapter 11, Verse 15. Did not take away the land. God had commanded the people to take complete possession of the land (Lev 15:23), but they did not, causing them all of their current problems.

Verse 29. Spirit. This is the special anointing of God for those he chose to lead his people.

Verse 30. Vow. This is another example of religious syncretism—the mixing of true religion with false. It was customary for pagan generals to make a vow to their god in return for military victory. The fact that Jephthah actually followed through and sacrificed his daughter further indicates his lack of faith in the true God and his promises.

Summary

God's faithfulness, even in the midst of his people's sin, is evidence of his mercy and love for his people. Yet he still chastens them, leaving them to suffer the consequences of their actions. The fact remains true, especially for God's people, that obedience will bring blessing, but disobedience results in suffering.

Questions for Reflection

1. What did God mean by, "I will save you no more" (10:13)?
2. Why did God raise up Jephthah to save the people even though they had forsaken him?
3. What does Jephthah's vow reveal about him?

Day 67: Samson's Birth

Judges 13-14

Notes

Chapter 13, Verse 5. Nazarite. This comes from the Hebrew word that means "to separate." Those taking this vow were set apart from the rest of the community in service to God.

Chapter 14, Verse 1. Philistines. It would have been strictly forbidden for any Jew, especially a Nazarite, to marry a Philistine woman.

Summary

The story of Samson is another prime example of God using someone to deliver his people who himself was not a worthy leader. Samson's victories were clearly accomplished only by the power of God, and Samson often reaps the results of his sinful actions. God can, and often does, use sinful people to accomplish his good plans.

Questions for Reflection

1. Why was Samson set apart by the Nazarite vow?
2. What significance was it that the flame of the altar and the angel of the Lord went up toward heaven (13:20)?
3. Why shouldn't Samson have married a Philistine woman?

Day 68: In the Shadow of Your Wings

Psalm 17

Notes

Verse 1, A Prayer. This is the first psalm simply titled "a prayer" (see also Pss 86, 90, 102, 142).

Verse 1. Just cause. David begins the psalm using metaphorical language from a law court to describe his plea before God.

Verse 8. Apple of your eye. This is a poetic expression that describes the pupil, a central and vital organ of vision. As one protects and values this organ, so God protects and values his people.

Summary

Our relationship to God as his people is one of just protection and care. God's justice ensures that he will always do right, punishing sin and rewarding righteous behavior, but we may not necessarily see this happen in our present lives; often even the unrighteous enjoy God's common grace, but we can be sure that from an eternal perspective, the wicked will be destroyed, and God will reward his people who are his greatest treasure.

Questions for Reflection

1. Why can we trust in God as our judge more than we can trust human judges?

2. What is communicated by the request, "hide me in the shadow of your wings" (v 8)?
3. Why do wicked people many times enjoy earthly benefits?

Day 69: Samson and the Philistines

Judges 15

Notes

Verse 8. Hip and thigh. This is an expression for violent slaughter.

Verse 14. Spirit of the Lord. This is an example of God's special, non-salvific anointing of an individual to accomplish a specific purpose, and further illustrates that God is behind all of Samson's strength and accomplishments in delivering the people from the Philistine oppression.

Summary

God continues to display his power and faithfulness to his promises by caring for his people, even using a vengeful, unrighteous man like Samson, and despite the fact that his own people didn't trust in him. It is a wonder and a blessing that God's faithfulness is not dependent upon any human response but is a direct reflection of his unchanging character.

Questions for Reflection

1. Was it right for Samson to burn the Philistine fields with the foxes?
2. Why did the men of Judah bind Samson?
3. Why did God anoint Samson with his Spirit?

Day 70: Samson's Defeat

Judges 16

Notes

Verse 5. 1,100 Pieces of silver. Since each of the five rulers pledged this amount, it was quite a large sum of money.

Verse 20. The Lord had left him. This reveals that it was not his long hair that gave Samson his strength, but rather the special anointing of the Lord. Cutting his hair was simply the final act that caused God to remove his Spirit's anointing power.

Verse 23. Dagon. This was an idol with the head of a fish and the body of a man.

Verse 28. Remember me. This prayer may indicate a heart of repentance.

Summary

Even though God used Samson to save his people, Samson's disobedience, arrogance, and vengeful spirit ultimately led to his destruction. Just because God uses a disobedient person to accomplish a good purpose does not absolve that person from his sin. God still holds responsible those who sin against him.

Questions for Reflection

1. How did Samson's sinful desire for wicked women lead to his defeat?
2. How did Samson's sin contribute to the Philistine's false worship (see v. 24)?
3. Do you think Samson was truly repentant at the end? Why or why not?

Week 15: Ruth and Boaz

Weekly memory verse:

Psalm 19:14 - “Let the words of my mouth and the meditation of my heart be acceptable in your sight, O Lord, my rock and my redeemer.”

Weekly hymn:

“The Heavens Declare Thy Glory, Lord”

Weekly catechism:

What is sin?
Sin is any transgression against the law of God.

Psalm 19

The Heavens Declare Thy Glory, Lord

UXBRIDGE

WORDS: **Psalm 19**; Isaac Watts, 1719 LM

MUSIC: Lowell Mason, 1830

Day 71: God's Revelation

Psalms 19-20

Notes

Psalm 19, Verse 1. Declare. Creation communicates something of God's glory and power in a general sense. This revelation is not enough to lead someone to salvation, but it is enough to leave them without excuse (see Rom 1:18-20).

Verse 3. Speech. Creation reveals God, not through literal words, but through other means.

Verse 7. Law . . . testimony. These terms refer to the written Word of God. God's Word communicates truths about him in a special sense. This revelation can lead someone to salvation.

Psalm 20. This psalm commemorates Israelite war, where God was considered the king, and the human king was his mediatorial general fighting on his behalf.

Summary

God has clearly revealed himself to us, both through what he has made and through his inspired Word. The general revelation given to us through creation displays God's glory and leaves us without excuse. The special revelation given to us through God's Word tells us who God is, what he requires of us, and what is necessary for forgiveness of sin.

Questions for Reflection

1. What does creation tell you about God?
2. Is the knowledge of God revealed in creation enough to lead you to salvation?
3. What does the Bible tell you about what God requires, about your sin, and about how to receive forgiveness of sin?

Day 72: Warnings Against Sin

Proverbs 6-7

Notes

Proverbs 6, Verse 1. Security. This warns against taking responsibility for another person's debt.

Verse 16. Six . . . seven. This is not meant to be an exhaustive list, but a representative list of the kinds of sins we should avoid. The two sequential numbers are meant to grab attention and communicate totality.

Verse 21. Bind. This was not necessarily meant to be literal, but it emphasizes the necessity to follow the wisdom of our elders in every circumstance of life.

Summary

The best deterrent against sin is giving careful attention to abide by the wise words of our elders. If we trust only in our own discernment, we may easily be led into sin. But if we always make the council of others our guide, we will be more likely to avoid sin and live a life of obedience to God's commands.

Questions for Reflection

1. What are lessons we can learn from ants?
2. In what ways can you apply the command to "bind" your parent's instructions on your heart?
3. How can you avoid the seven abominations to God?

Day 73: Wisdom's Call

Proverbs 8

Notes

Verse 22. His Work. Here wisdom claims credit for the agent through which God created all things at the beginning of time.

Verse 27. Circle. This Hebrew idiom seems to indicate a recognition that the earth is a globe.

Verse 29. Its limit. God apparently has specifically assigned shorelines across which the oceans may not pass.

Summary

Wisdom should be the primary pursuit of all of God's people, especially the young. Wisdom is the virtue through which kings rule justly and God's people live righteously. It is even that which God used to create all things. Wisdom should be treasured far above all earthly wealth.

Questions for Reflection

1. What is wisdom?
2. Why do you think Solomon chose to personify wisdom as a person in this proverb?
3. In what ways can you pursue wisdom?

Day 74: Naomi and Ruth

Ruth 1-2

Notes

Chapter 1, Verse 12. Too old. Naomi was probably over fifty years of age.

Verse 15. Her gods. The primary Moabite god, Chemosh, required child sacrifices (2 Kgs 3:27).

Verse 20. Naomi . . . Mara. "Naomi" meant "pleasant," while "Mara" meant "bitter."

Verse 22. Beginning of barley harvest. Normally the middle to end of April.

Chapter 2, Verse 1. Relative. Boaz could have been Elimelech's brother, or at very least in the same tribe.

Verse 2. Glean. According the Mosaic Law, the edges of a field were not to be harvested but were to be left for the needy. These needy ones did, however, need to work in order to harvest the grain for themselves.

Verse 20. Redeemer. According to Jewish tradition, a close relative, called a kinsman-redeemer, could redeem a family member who had been sold as a slave (Lev 25:47-49), land that had been owned by a family member but had to be sold during financial hardship (Lev 25:23-28), or the family name through marrying the widowed wife of a family member (Deut 25:5-10).

Verse 23. End of . . . harvest. This harvest period lasted for approximately two months, coinciding with the fifty days between Passover and the Feast of Weeks (i.e., Pentecost; Lev 23:15–16; Deut 16:9–12).

Summary

The providence of God over even the terrible circumstances of life is strongly communicated through the story of Ruth. God chose to redeem his people through famine, intermarriage with foreign women, death of husbands, and loss of property. God's ways are mysterious, but they are always good.

Questions for Reflection

1. Was it right or wrong for Mahlon and Chilion to marry Moabite women?
2. What did Ruth's loyalty to Naomi reveal about her?
3. Was it only coincidence that Ruth "happened" (2:3) to come upon Boaz's field?

Day 75: Ruth and Boaz

Ruth 3–4

Notes

Chapter 3, Verse 2. Winnowing. Harvesters would toss grain into the air in the late evening when winds were at their highest, separating the grain from the chaff that would blow away.

Verse 4. Uncover his feet. This was an ancient Near Eastern custom that indicated Ruth's desire to marry Boaz. This act would have been appropriate in this situation since Boaz was a generation older than Ruth (2:8) and thus would not have proposed marriage on his own.

Summary

God providentially chose to use the kinsman-redeemer tradition to rescue a Moabite woman and make her the mother of the kingly line of David, a line of kings from which would come *the* Redeemer, the Messiah.

Questions for Reflection

1. Why do you think God chose famine, unlawful marriages, death, and a Moabite woman to accomplish his plan?

2. What do Boaz's actions reveal about him?
3. When something terrible happens that seems to contradict God's promises, what should be your response?

Week 16: Samuel and Saul

Weekly memory verse:

Luke 1:46–48 – “My soul magnifies the Lord, and my spirit rejoices in God my Savior, for he has looked on the humble estate of his servant. For behold, from now on all generations will call me blessed.”

Weekly hymn:

“O Worship the King”

Weekly catechism:

Can you keep the law of God perfectly?

No. I am inclined by nature to hate God and my neighbor.

O Worship the King

LYONS

WORDS: Robert Grant, 1833

10.10.11.11

MUSIC: Attr. J. Michael Haydn, 18th cent.; arr. Joseph Martin Kraus, 1784

Day 76: Samuel's Birth and Calling

1 Samuel 1–3

Notes

Chapter 1, Verse 2. Two wives. Polygamy was never endorsed in Israel and was not God's intention, although it was tolerated (see Deut 21:15–17).

Verse 3. Year by year. Every Israelite man was required to attend three annual feasts at the sanctuary: Passover, Weeks, and Tabernacles (Deut 16:1–17).

Verse 22. Weaned. This would have probably been around age 3.

Chapter 2, Verse 1. Hannah prayed. Hannah's prayer is considered in Jewish and Christian traditions as an Old Testament canticle and is the basis for Mary's Magnificat (Luke 1:46–53).

Chapter 3, Verse 1. Boy. The Jewish historian Josephus suggests that Samuel was 12 years old here.

Verse 3. Lying down. Samuel was not likely sleeping in the Holy Place of the Tabernacle itself, but rather in a larger compound that housed the Tabernacle in Shiloh.

Summary

The similarities between Samson and Samuel are striking, but differences are also clearly apparent. Samuel grows to be a true servant of the Lord, a prophet, and a judge of Israel, leading them from the period of tribal lords to one unified monarchy. God's hand is evidently upon Samuel and remains so until his death.

Questions for Reflection

1. What did Hannah's oath and prayer reveal about her?
2. Why do you think Eli allowed his sons to continue their sinful lifestyles?
3. What did Samuel's response to God's call reveal about him?

Day 77: The Philistines Capture the Ark

1 Samuel 4; Psalm 21

Notes

1 Samuel 4, Verse 1. Philistines. These were not natives of Canaan, but rather "Sea Peoples" who immigrated and settled along the coast of southern Canaan. The Philistines plague God's people throughout Saul and David's reigns.

Verse 4. Ark of the Covenant. God never allows for the ark to be removed from the Holy of Holies and brought into battle. This may be another example of religious syncretism, led by Hophni and Phinehas, since pagan nations often carried religious talismans with them into battle.

Verse 22. Ichabod. This name means, "Where is the glory?"

Summary

Israel's religious syncretism comes to a climax in the capture of the ark and the deaths of Israel's primary priests. Samuel's prophecy had come true, and this establishes him as an important prophet and judge among the people.

Questions for Reflection

1. Why do you think Hophni and Phinehas brought the ark with them into battle?
2. Why do you think Eli died at the news of the deaths of his sons and the ark's capture?
3. Had God really left Israel as the people assumed with the ark's capture?

Day 78: The Ark Returned to Israel

1 Samuel 5:1-7:2

Notes

Chapter 5, Verse 2. Dagon. This Philistine god had the lower body of a fish and the upper body of a man. In Philistine theology, Dagon was the father of Baal and the head of the pantheon of gods (Judg 16:23).

Chapter 6, Verse 7. Cows. If these cows who were not trained to pull a cart and who were nursing calves walked away from the calves and pulled the cart toward Beth-shemesh, this would be a clear sign of supernatural intervention by God.

Verse 15. Stone. Even though this action may appear to be one of honoring and thanking the Lord, it was nevertheless in strict contradiction to what the Law required. The ark should have been covered and carried back to the tabernacle.

Verse 21. Kiriath Jearim. The ark remained in this city during the entirety of Saul's reign and much of David's reign until David brought it to Jerusalem (2 Sam 6:1–19).

Summary

The Philistines believed that their capture of the ark of God was a great victory, but God had other plans. He clearly demonstrates to them through demolishing their idol and sending plagues that he is the true God of all. Sadly, the Philistines seem to learn this lesson better than the men of Beth-shemesh, who disobey God's Law in how they handle the ark once it is returned.

Questions for Reflection

1. Did the Philistines' repentance and offering to God reveal their true belief in him, or something else? How do you know?
2. Why did God kill the men of Beth-shemesh?
3. Why do you think the ark remained in Kiriath Jearim for such a long time?

Day 79: The People Want a King

1 Samuel 7:3–8:22

Notes

Chapter 7, Verse 4. The Baals and the Ashtaroth. These are the primary fertility gods of the Canaanite pantheon.

Chapter 8, Verse 1. Old. Samuel was about 60 years old.

Verse 5. King. God had predicted this desire for a king in Deuteronomy 17:14, and he said he would allow it to occur.

Summary

The fact that the people of Israel wanted a king was not necessarily a problem. However, their motivation for wanting a king was evidence of their rejection of God as their supreme ruler and deliverer—they wanted to be like the other nations around them and they wanted a human leader to lead them in battle instead of the Lord. This lack of trust in God caused much trouble for the nation going forward.

Questions for Reflection

1. Why do you think the people refused to obey Samuel?
2. Why did the people want a king?
3. What results did Samuel say would come from choosing a king?

Day 80: Saul Chosen to Be King

1 Samuel 9-10

Notes

Chapter 9, Verse 3. Donkeys . . . were lost. This meant lost wealth.

Verse 12. High place. This was a place of sacrifice in Canaanite religion.

Verse 24. The leg. This was the choicest portion of meant that would typically be reserved for the priest according to the Law (Lev 7:28-36). The fact that Samuel gave it to Saul showed great honor for the new king.

Chapter 10, Verse 6. Spirit of the Lord. This was a special theocratic anointing of the Holy Spirit whereby God equipped Saul to be king. It was not the same as regeneration and could be removed.

Summary

God was gracious in that, even though it was wrong for the people to desire a human king in their distrust of God himself, God chose to give them what they requested. By all outward appearances, Saul was the ideal candidate to be king. Yet God had promised through Samuel that the people's desire for a human king would end up causing much pain.

Questions for Reflection

1. Why do you think God granted the people's request and gave them a king?
2. In what ways does Saul demonstrate humility in this passage?
3. Why was it important for Saul to receive an anointing from the Holy Spirit?

Week 17: Saul's Rise and Fall

Weekly memory verse:

1 Samuel 15:22 - "Has the Lord as great delight in burnt offerings and sacrifices, as in obeying the voice of the Lord? Behold, to obey is better than sacrifice, and to listen than the fat of rams."

Weekly hymn:

"Jesus Shall Reign"

Weekly catechism:

What are the results of sin?
Because of sin, all mankind lost communion with God and are under his wrath and curse, resulting in the miseries of this life, death itself, and the pains of hell forever.

Psalm 72

Jesus Shall Reign

DUKE STREET

WORDS: **Psalm 72**; Isaac Watts, 1719 LM
MUSIC: John Hatton, 1793

Day 81: Saul's Coronation

1 Samuel 11-12

Notes

Chapter 11, Verse 4. Gibeah. This was Saul's home town and the first capital city of the monarchy.

Verse 14. Gilgal. This town between Jericho and the Jordan River was a major religious center for early Israel.

Summary

By all outward appearances, Saul would be a strong leader and deliverer for the people of Israel. Yet Samuel still warns they people that their desire for a king is evidence of their distrust in God and their syncretism with the pagan nations. He urges them to follow after God and obey his commands alone.

Questions for Reflection

1. Why do you think Saul refused to kill the people who had rejected him as their king?
2. What significance was Samuel's statement "Here I am" (12:3) at the beginning of his address?
3. Why did Samuel recount the history of Israel?

Day 82: Saul's Disobedience

1 Samuel 13; Psalm 72

Notes

1 Samuel 13, Verse 9. Offering. Kings were allowed to sacrifice before the Lord (see 2 Sam 24:25; 1 Kgs 8:26-64), but Samuel had told Saul to wait for him seven days before offering a sacrifice (10:4). This was to test Saul, and Saul failed the test by asserting himself and offering the sacrifice on his own without Samuel's assistance as he had been commanded.

Psalm 72, Verse 1. King. This is a coronation psalm dedicated to Solomon at the beginning of his reign (1 Kgs 2). Although it is not referred to as such in the New Testament, the psalm contains several apparently messianic references (vv. 7, 17), and Isaac Watts applied it to the future earthly reign of Jesus Christ in "Jesus Shall Reign."

Verse 8. River. This refers to the Euphrates River, the eastern boundary of the promised land.

Summary

Saul's failure as a leader of God's people is evident very early in his reign with his disobedience to the clear command of God's chosen prophet. This leads God to choose one after his own heart, one who would stand at the head of a line of kings culminating in the Messiah himself, the God-man who will rule God's people perfectly.

Questions for Reflection

1. Why do you think Samuel commanded Saul to wait for him for seven days before offering a sacrifice?
2. Why do you think Saul disobeyed Samuel's command?
3. Why is a king who is both God and man the only successful fulfillment of God's promise to reign over his people on earth?

Day 83: Jonathan Defeats the Philistines

1 Samuel 14

Notes

Verse 2. Pomegranate cave. Pomegranate trees are common in Israel. This may have been large tree under which Saul was camped or a cave surrounded by trees.

Verse 18. Ark of God. The Greek translation of the Old Testament (the Septuagint) reads "ephod" here, which is more likely correct than "ark" since the ark remained in Kiriath Jearim until David later recovered it. The ephod, worn by Ahijah the priest (v. 3), contained sacred implements such as the Urim and Thummim used to determine the will of God. This fits what happens next in verse 19 better as well. "*Withdraw your hand*" refers to stopping the inquiry into the Lord's will.

Verse 21. Hebrews. These were Israelite deserters who had joined the Philistines.

Summary

Saul accomplished many military victories and expanded Israel's borders, but this account emphasizes his weak and unwise leadership. Saul's son, Jonathan, is clearly a better leader and blessed by God in battle. It is no accident that Jonathan and David become close friends.

Questions for Reflection

1. Why did Jonathan decide to fight the Philistines on his own?
2. How do we know that God won the battle on Jonathan's behalf?
3. What did Saul's oath reveal about him?

Day 84: God Rejects Saul

1 Samuel 15; Psalm 28

Notes

1 Samuel 15, Verse 2. Amalekites. These descendants of Esau were nomadic desert people.

Verse 12. Carmel. This is not the Mt. Carmel later associated with Elijah (1 Kgs 18:20ff).

Verse 24. I have sinned. This confession puts the blame on the people rather than on himself, revealing that he did not have a true heart of repentance.

Psalm 28, Verse 2. Lift up my hands. Outstretched hands in prayer was a sign of lament and pleading.

Summary

God's rejection of Saul becomes complete with Saul's second clear act of disobedience. Yet it was not Saul's actions alone that led to the rejection, for later David would sin in even greater ways. Rather, it was Saul's unrepentant heart and concern only for himself rather than the will of God that proved his unworthiness to rule God's people.

Questions for Reflection

1. What did Saul's refusal to kill all the people reveal about him?

2. What evidences in this passage show that Saul was concerned primarily for himself?
3. Why was Samuel so grieved?

Day 85: David is Anointed King

1 Samuel 16

Notes

Verse 10. Seven of his sons. Jesse had eight sons, including David. The fact that 1 Chronicles 2:13 says he had only seven sons is not necessarily a contradiction; one son may have died later and thus is not mentioned in Chronicles.

Verse 13. Anointed. David was anointed three times: once, here in the presence of his family, a second time before a tribal assembly (2 Sam 2:7), and finally before the nation (2 Sam 5:3).

Verse 13. Spirit of the Lord. Like with Saul, this is not regeneration but rather God's theocratic anointing of his chosen mediatorial leader in order to especially empower him to lead. This is the same anointing that David pleads with God not to take from him after his sin with Bathsheba (Ps 51:11). Since David now has God's blessing as chosen leader of Israel, this same anointing is removed from Saul (v. 14).

Verse 16. Lyre. This was the predominant instrument of Israelite worship.

Verse 23. Refreshed. This testifies to the power of music to affect people's emotions.

Summary

While the people of Israel chose Saul based on his external qualifications, God chose David on the basis of his character. God's choice of this mediatorial ruler provided the foundation for the ultimate mediator between God and man, the man Christ Jesus, who will one day rule over God's people on David's throne as the perfect fulfillment of what David foreshadowed.

Questions for Reflection

1. Did God tell Samuel to lie about his reason for going to Bethlehem in order to protect himself from Saul? Is it ever right to lie, even to protect life?
2. Why did the elders of Bethlehem tremble when they saw Samuel (v. 4)?
3. Why did Samuel assume God had chosen Eliab to be king (v. 6)?

Week 18: David and Saul

Weekly memory verse:

Psalm 18:1-2 - "I love you, O Lord, my strength. The Lord is my rock and my fortress and my deliverer, my God, my rock, in whom I take refuge, my shield, and the horn of my salvation, my stronghold."

Weekly hymn:

"Holy Trinity, Thanks and Praise to Thee"

Weekly catechism:

Is there any way to escape the punishment of God and be again received into communion with him?

God's justice demands that I make full payment, either through myself or through a Redeemer.

Holy Trinity, Thanks and Praise to Thee

SEELENBRÄUTIGAM

WORDS: Lorenz T. Nyberg, 1754
MUSIC: Adam Drese, 1665

5.5.8.8.5.5

Day 86: David and Goliath
1 Samuel 17

Notes
Verse 4. Six cubits. This was approximately 9 feet 9 inches feet tall.

Verse 25. His father's house. This would refer to an extended family of 50 to 100 people.

Verse 43. Gods. Goliath's gods were likely Dagon (1 Sam 5:2) and Ashtaroth (31:10).

Summary
Having already been anointed by Samuel as the true king of Israel, David now demonstrates God's blessing upon him through his courageous defeat of Goliath. This begins to establish David as the man after God's own heart who trusted in God and was the one God had chosen to both rule Israel and begin the royal line that would eventually bring the Messianic King.

Questions for Reflection
1. Why was Saul afraid of Goliath?
2. Why was Eliab angry at David?
3. What gave David confidence that he could defeat Goliath?

Day 87: David and Jonathan
1 Samuel 18; Psalm 18

Notes
1 Samuel 18, Verse 4. Robe. Jonathan willingly gave David all of the garments that signified his princely role since he recognized God's choice of David to be king.

Verse 13. Commander. Saul gave David command of a thousand troops as a way to exile him honorably.

Psalm 18. This psalm by David was written specifically in the context of David being delivered from Saul.

Summary

Saul's own family members demonstrated a recognition of God's choice of David to be king, yet Saul's jealousy and anger toward David only grew. This tension between Saul and David would continue and cause strife in the nation for some time. God's choice would be established, however, and would usher Israel into its most blessed period.

Questions for Reflection

1. Why did Jonathan love David? How did he show his loyalty and support for David?
2. Why was Saul jealous of David?
3. What was David's response when he was in danger?

Day 88: Saul Tries to Kill David

1 Sam 19; Psalm 59

Notes

1 Samuel 19, Verse 9. Harmful spirit. Saul's actions against David are not only due to his own personal jealousy, but they are also because of the Lord's judgment upon him.

Verse 13. Image. This was a household god, illustrating the fact that even the king's household was not immune from the idolatry that plagued Israel during this time.

Verse 23. Spirit of God. This was the last time Saul would receive the theocratic anointing from God.

Verse 24. Stripped off his clothes. Like Jonathan earlier, this removal of his royal garments signified God's rejection of Saul as king of Israel.

Psalm 59. This is another psalm written by David in the context of Saul's attempts to kill him.

Summary

The division between Saul and David increases, with Saul's own daughter demonstrating complete loyalty to David by deceiving her father. God's rejection of Saul is confirmed by his continual sending of a harmful spirit, and even when Saul receives God's anointing one final time, it is only in order to further establish God's rejection of him.

Questions for Reflection

1. In what ways does God display his rejection of Saul?
2. How does Michal show loyalty to David?
3. What did God's final anointing of Saul cause him to do?

Day 89: David Flees Saul

1 Samuel 20; Psalm 52

Notes

1 Samuel 20, Verse 25. Abner. This was Saul's cousin and chief military commander.

Verse 41. Bowed. This demonstrated David's respect and affection for Jonathan.

Summary

Although Saul made careful plans to kill David, his own son once again displayed loyalty to David and to the Lord by warning and protecting David. Over and over God confirms his choice of David by protecting him against all odds. David's ascendency to the throne is not easy, but God always accomplishes his purposes.

Questions for Reflection

1. In what ways did David and Jonathan display their close friendship?
2. Why do you think God made David's ascendency to his rightful throne so difficult?
3. How does David display trust in God even in the midst of threats upon his life?

Day 90: Saul Pursues David

1 Samuel 21–22; Psalms 34, 56

Notes

1 Samuel 21, Verse 4. Holy bread. This was consecrated for use in the tabernacle and was only to be eaten by priests. Ahimelech the priest received permission from the Lord to give the bread to David and his men considering the circumstances (22:10).

Psalms 34, 56. These psalms were written with reference to the events of 1 Samuel 21:10–15.

Summary

These events, filled with deception, disobedience to God's laws, unqualified priests, and treachery continue to illustrate the dysfunction of both the priestly and kingly offices of Israel during this time. Israel needed a God-chosen leader who would follow God's commands and lead the nation to repentance.

Questions for Reflection

1. Was it right for David to lie to Ahimelech?
2. What was the result of this lie?
3. How could David demonstrate such trust in God's goodness even when he was being pursued by both Saul and the Philistines?

Week 19: The Pursuit of David

Weekly memory verse:
2 Samuel 22:2-3 - "The Lord is my rock and my fortress and my deliverer, my God, my rock, in whom I take refuge, my shield, and the horn of my salvation, my stronghold and my refuge, my savior; you save me from violence."

Weekly hymn:
"Praise to the Lord, the Almighty"

Weekly catechism:
What kind of Redeemer must you seek?
I must seek a Redeemer who is a true and righteous human and who is at the same time true God.

Praise to the Lord, the Almighty

LOBE DEN HERREN

WORDS: **Psalm 103:1–6**; Joachim Neander, 1680; tr. Catherine Winkworth, 1863, alt.

MUSIC: *Stralsund Gesangbuch*, 1665

14.14.4.7.8

Day 91: David Spares Saul

1 Samuel 23–24; Psalm 57

Notes

1 Samuel 24, Verse 22. Swore. David fulfills this pledge in 2 Samuel 21:7 by sparing Mephibosheth's life.

Psalm 57. This psalm by David was written with specific reference to the events of 1 Samuel 24.

Summary

Even though God chose David to be King, David recognized Saul's legitimacy to be on the throne while he lived. Even Saul was deeply moved and impressed by David's actions, and this caused him to recognize God's hand of blessing upon David.

Questions for Reflection

1. Would David have been right to kill Saul?
2. Was David right to cut off a portion of Saul's robe?
3. What did David's oath to Saul reveal about him?

Day 92: David and Abigail

1 Samuel 25; Psalm 54

Notes

1 Samuel 25, Verse 16. Wall. David and his men had taken it upon themselves to protect Nabal's flocks while they were hiding in the wilderness, and now they expected due compensation.

Verse 28. Sure house. This indicates that Abigail recognized David as God's choice to be king, and this is why she acted the way that she did.

Psalm 54. This psalm was written in the context of David's time in the wilderness.

Summary

Abigail recognized God's hand upon David, and this caused her to both protect him from her evil husband and to plead with David to not do anything that would jeopardize his life or future reign. God continues to keep his promise that he will protect and bless his chosen one.

Questions for Reflection

1. Did David have the right to be compensated for his protection of Nabal's flocks?
2. Why do you think Nabal refused to pay David?
3. Would David have been right to kill Nabal and his men?

Day 93: David Lives Among the Philistines

1 Samuel 26–27; Psalm 37

Notes

1 Samuel 26, Verse 19. Go, serve other gods. By exiling David, Saul was in effect forcing him to abandon Yahweh worship since there was no way to worship God according to the Law outside of Israel.

Psalm 37. This is an acrostic poem, with each stanza beginning with the successive letters of the Hebrew alphabet.

Summary

God finally rewarded David for his trust and relieved him of the constant pursuit by Saul. David now enjoyed over a year of relative peace and prosperity, living among the Philistines and secretly raiding their various cities. He would never have trouble from Saul again.

Questions for Reflection

1. In what ways did God reward David for his trust and faithfulness?
2. Why do you think Achish gave David a city and trusted him?
3. What are some difficult circumstances you have faced in which you should trust God?

Day 94: Saul and the Medium of En-dor

1 Samuel 28; Psalm 83

Notes

1 Samuel 28, Verse 6. Urim. God regularly revealed his will through the use of the Urim, which was stored in the ephod of the high priest.

David was now in possession of the Urim since Abiathar had given him the ephod (23:6).

Verse 12. Cried. The fact that the medium cried out at the appearance of Samuel reveals that she knew that she could not really raise the dead and that God had miraculously allowed Samuel to actually appear.

Verse 13. God. The term translated "god" can also refer to something that looks like a god or otherwise spirit-being.

Summary
Saul reaches the climax of his failure in consulting the medium of Endor. He clearly knew that mediums were against God's Law since he himself had expelled them from the land. Yet in a desperate attempt to seek the help of God, Saul revealed his true heart by attempting victory through his own sinful means.

Questions for Reflection
1. What did the fact that Saul trembled in fear at the approaching Philistine army reveal about the effects of God's anointing earlier in his reign?
2. Why do you think God allowed Samuel to appear before Saul?
3. What did Samuel mean by "tomorrow you and your sons shall be with me" (v. 19)?

Day 95: David Fights the Philistines
1 Samuel 29-30

Notes
Chapter 29, Verse 8. Enemies. It is not clear here what David's plan was or whether he was doing right in the Lord's eyes. At one level, it appears that he was prepared to fight with Achish against Israel. On the other hand, he could have been plotting to betray Achish. Either way, he had not sought the Lord's will in this, but God providentially protected him from having to fight at all.

Summary
Despite some potentially unwise decisions on David's part, the Lord protected him and gave him victory, especially when he actively

sought the Lord's will. David, a man truly after God's own heart, sought strength in the Lord and ruled his men honorably, foreshadowing his just reign as the chosen king of Israel.

Questions for Reflection

1. Would it have been right for David to fight with Achish against Israel?
2. Would it have been right for David to pretend to fight with Achish, only to betray him?
3. What does it say about David's character that he distributed his spoils of war among the elders of Judah?

Week 20: David Becomes King

Weekly memory verse:
Psalm 20:7 - "Some trust in chariots and some in horses, but we trust in the name of the LORD our God."

Weekly hymn:
"Rejoice, the Lord is King"

Weekly catechism:
Why must the Redeemer be a true and righteous human?
The Redeemer must be a true and righteous human because the justice of God requires that only one with a human nature who has not sinned may pay for my sin.

Rejoice, the Lord Is King

WORDS: Charles Wesley, 1744, alt.
MUSIC: John Darwall, 1770

6.6.6.6.8.8

Day 96: The Death of Saul

1 Samuel 31; Psalms 76, 110

Notes

1 Samuel 31, Verse 2. Sons. Saul had four sons, three of which were killed in battle on this day.

Verse 4. Fell upon it. Saul's suicide was not an act of courage, but rather the ultimate evidence that he did not trust in the Lord.

Verse 6. All his men. It is unlikely this means that all 3,000 of Saul's men died on that day, especially considering 2 Samuel 2:8 indicates that Saul's own general, Abner, survived; more likely, this is a general sentiment that communicates the horrendous nature of the slaughter by the Philistines.

Psalm 110. This Messianic psalm is the most quoted psalm in the New Testament. It refers to the future reign of Christ on earth.

Summary

Saul displayed his ultimate self-interest and lack of trust in the Lord by committing suicide when he realized the battle against the Philistines was lost. This ended what was an almost universally disastrous reign, which God had promised when the people begged for a king. Now the stage is set for God's chosen one to take his rightful place.

Questions for Reflection

1. Why should Saul have trusted in the Lord rather than take his own life, even when he feared mistreatment by the Philistines?
2. Why do you think God allowed for such a terrible defeat?
3. How had God protected David by not allowing him to be part of this battle?

Day 97: David Anointed King of Judah

2 Samuel 1–2; Proverbs 9

Notes

2 Samuel 2, Verse 4. Anointed. Samuel had already anointed David in a private ceremony (1 Sam 16:3), but now he is officially recognized as king in Judah.

Verse 11. Seven years. Since Ish-bosheth reigned only for two years over the rest of Israel, it must have taken him five years to consolidate his power there.

Summary

With Saul dead, David begins to establish his reign over Israel. Yet this does not happen immediately. David first gains control only over the southern portion of Judah, while Saul's only surviving son, Ish-bosheth, establishes his rule over the rest of Israel. One day, the Messianic descendant of David will rule the whole earth from the same region.

Questions for Reflection

1. Why did David grieve over the death of Saul, despite the fact that Saul had wanted to kill him?
2. How did David's inquiry of the Lord contrast with Saul's?
3. How did David try to persuade the people to follow him rather than force them?

Day 98: David Anointed King of Israel

2 Samuel 3:1–5:4

Notes

Chapter 3, Verse 1. Long war. The transfer of power lasted at least as long as the two-year reign of Ish-bosheth.

Verse 13. Michal. Not only did Michal rightly belong as David's wife, but brining her to him, David would further gain sympathy with those within Saul's household.

Chapter 4, Verse 4. Mephibosheth. This brief introduction is included to indicate that Jonathan's son was not able to rule and thus not a threat to David.

Chapter 5, Verse 3. Anointed. This is David's third anointing and the one by which he establishes his rule over the entire nation.

Summary

After several years of war and consolidation of power, God finally establishes his chosen king over all of Israel. God had promised this would happen, but God often works through human means and in ways that might not seem to make sense to human observers. Yet God's plan is always right, and the way in which David takes power only helps to unify the nation under his reign.

Questions for Reflection

1. How did David show character and nobility in how he gradually gained rule over Israel?
2. Why did David request that Michal be brought to him?
3. What reasons do the elders of Israel give for why they have chosen to submit to David's rule?

Day 99: David Becomes King in Jerusalem

1 Chronicles 11:1-25

Notes

Verse 4. Jerusalem. Jerusalem was an ideal place for David to establish has his capital both politically and defensively. Politically it helped to unite the northern and southern tribes. The city was also easily defensible as it was surrounded on three sides by deep valleys.

Summary

God finally fulfills his promises to David and establishes him king over all the tribes of Israel. David wisely chooses Jerusalem as his capital city and begins his reign.

Questions for Reflection

1. Was it good for David to make the criterion for choosing his general whomever killed the Jebusites?
2. Why was David's choice of Jerusalem as his capital wise?
3. Why was every battle in Israel considered holy? Can the same be said of war today?

Day 100: David Brings the Ark to Jerusalem

1 Chronicles 13, 15:1-16

Notes

Chapter 13, Verse 3. Ark. The ark had been stored in Kiriath-Jearim for twenty years.

Verse 7. New cart. The Law required that the ark be carried by sons of Kohath using prescribed poles.

Chapter 15, Verse 16. Musical instruments. David carefully prescribed the musical instruments for the return of the ark, a large lyre, a small lyre (translated "harp"), and a set of hand cymbals that the musical leaders would use to keep the musicians together. These would later become the instruments prescribed for use in temple worship.

Summary

While David's motivation for bringing the ark to Jerusalem was noble, the fact that he did not consult the Lord or his Word first led to Uzzah's tragic death. It was not until David followed the Lord's clearly prescribed instructions for transporting the ark that God blessed his endeavor. God cares both about an individual's pure motives *and* obedience to his commands.

Questions for Reflection

1. What was David's motivation for bringing the ark to Jerusalem?
2. Was it harsh for God to kill Uzzah?
3. How did David demonstrate more care and commitment to God's commands the second time he brought the ark to Jerusalem?

Week 21: The Davidic Covenant

Weekly memory verse:

Luke 1:68–69 - "Blessed be the Lord God of Israel, for he has visited and redeemed his people and has raised up a horn of salvation for us in the house of his servant David."

Weekly hymn:

"Good Christians All, Rejoice and Sing"

Weekly catechism:

Why must the Redeemer be at the same time true God?
The Redeemer must be true God so that by the power of his divine nature he might bear the burden of God's wrath and restore to me righteousness and life.

Good Christians All, Rejoice and Sing

GELOBT SEI GOTT

WORDS: Cyril A. Alington, 1925
MUSIC: Melchior Vulpius, 1609

8.8.8.Alleluias

Day 101: God's Promise to David

2 Samuel 7–8

Notes

Chapter 7, Verse 4. Word of the Lord. While not called a "covenant" here, later in 23:5, this unconditional promise made to David is called "an everlasting covenant." It is a central passage in all of Scripture and is ultimately fulfilled in the Second Coming of Jesus Christ when he establishes his millennial kingdom on earth (Rev 19).

Verse 14. Father . . . son. These words are specifically applied to Jesus in Hebrews 1:5.

Verse 16. House . . . kingdom . . . throne. Luke 1:32–33 applies this promise to Jesus.

Summary

In a passage that is central to understanding all of Scripture, God establishes an unconditional, eternal covenant with David. He promises David blessings during his own lifetime, but also that his kingly line would be established forever. God begins to fulfill his promises to David with his son Solomon, but the covenant will not be fully fulfilled until David's descendant, the Messiah, will sit on David's throne in Jerusalem and rule over all things.

Questions for Reflection

1. What indications are in the covenant that God intends for it to be unconditional?
2. What promises to David does God make that will be fulfilled after David's death?
3. What promises have yet to be fulfilled?

Day 102: David Shows Mercy and Vengeance

2 Samuel 9–10; Psalm 23

Notes

Chapter 10, Verse 4. Shaved. This was an insult and sign of submission usually forced upon prisoners of war.

Psalm 23. Shepherd. The image of a shepherd is often applied to Jesus in the New Testament (John 10; Heb 13:20; 1 Pet 2:25, 5:4).

Verse 5. Table. To eat at someone's table was to indicate complete peace; thus, eating in the presence of one's enemies was amazing.

Summary

As David begins his reign, he shows incredible humility and mercy toward Jonathan's son, revealing a stark contrast with Saul. However, David's reign is continually characterized by war and strife, often as a result of David's own sinful choices.

Questions for Reflection

1. Why did David show mercy to Mephibosheth?
2. Why did Hanun disgrace David's men?
3. In what ways is God like a shepherd?

Day 103: David and Bathsheba

2 Samuel 11; Proverbs 10

Notes

2 Samuel 11, Verse 1. David remained. This was unusual for any king, especially David. Whether David had premeditated ulterior motives for staying behind or not, this phrase was meant to be a condemnation of David and foreshadowed his devastating sin.

Verse 8. Wash your feet. This was an unambiguous expression indicating to Uriah that he should go home to be with his wife.

Summary

David's sins of adultery and murder reveal him to be far from the perfect king God promised would one day rule over Israel. Nevertheless, God had promised David that he would never forsake him as he had Saul.

Questions for Reflection

1. In what ways did David try to cover his sin?
2. Was Bathsheba guilty of sin as well?
3. In what ways does David demonstrate folly instead of wisdom?

Day 104: David's Confession

2 Samuel 12; Psalm 51

Notes

2 Samuel 12, Verse 23. I shall go to him. This may refer to David's confidence that he would one day be reunited with his dead son, used by some as support for the idea that infants who die go to heaven. Alternatively, it could simply indicate David's recognition that he, too, will one day die, and that death is ultimately in the hands of God.

Psalm 51. This psalm was written by David as an expression of repentance after his sin with Bathsheba.

Verse 5. Conceive. This verse is evidence that life begins at conception since only sentient life could be described as being "in sin."

Verse 11. Presence . . . Spirit. Here David does not fear losing his salvation, but rather losing his special relationship with God as his chosen king who had received the special theocratic anointing of the Spirit.

Summary

David took responsibility for his sin and confessed it to the Lord with true contrition. God did not condemn David to death or take the kingdom away from him; nevertheless, sin always results in consequences even for those who are penitent.

Questions for Reflection

1. In what ways does David demonstrate true repentance?
2. What does David's response after his son's death reveal about him?
3. What are characteristics of true repentance as modeled in Psalm 51?

Day 105: Absalom Murders Amnon

2 Samuel 13; Proverbs 11

Notes

2 Samuel 13, Verse 37. Talmai. This king of Geshur, east of the Sea of Galilee, was grandfather of both Absalom and Tamar.

Summary

The consequences of David's sin continue with Amnon's sin and Absalom's murder of Amnon. This sets the stage for even greater, national consequences to come with Absalom's rebellion against his father and Israel's Civil War.

Questions for Reflection

1. Was Absalom right to have Amnon killed?
2. How did the death of Amnon resemble the death of Uriah?
3. What truths from Proverbs 10 are illustrated in the account of 2 Samuel 13?

Week 22: Absalom's Rebellion

Weekly memory verse:

Romans 3:23-24 - "For all have sinned and fall short of the glory of God, and are justified by his grace as a gift, through the redemption that is in Christ Jesus."

Weekly hymn:

"How Sad Our State"

Weekly catechism:

Who is that Redeemer who at the same time is true God and a true and righteous human?

My only Redeemer is the Lord Jesus Christ, the eternal Son of God, who became human and died to pay the penalty for sin.

How Sad Our State

SASHA

WORDS: Isaac Watts, 1707
MUSIC: Joan J. Pinkston, 1998

CMD

Day 106: Absalom's Return to Jerusalem

2 Samuel 14; Proverbs 12

Notes

2 Samuel 14, Verse 22. Favor. This demonstrates that Joab's motives were selfish.

Verse 26. Two hundred shekels. Absalom's cut hair weighed approximately five pounds.

Summary

David's graciousness and wisdom are on display as he allows Absalom to return to Jerusalem but requires him to live in his own house to learn repentance. However, rather than nurture repentance, it only creates further resentment in Absalom's heart and pushes him toward his rebellion.

Questions for Reflection

1. What was Joab's motivation for persuading David to allow Absalom to return?
2. Why did David allow Absalom to return but require that he live in a separate house?
3. What was Absalom's motive for wanting to be accepted into the king's presence?

Day 107: Absalom's Plot

2 Samuel 15; Psalm 3

Notes

2 Samuel 15, Verse 2. Judgment. It was customary to bring disputes to the king for judgment; Absalom took advantage of this practice by intercepting those who were on their way to the king and winning their loyalty through deception.

Verse 12. Ahithophel. This counselor of Absalom was Bathsheba's grandfather and may have wanted revenge on David.

Psalm 3. David wrote this psalm on occasion of fleeing from Absalom.

Summary

Having regained the king's favor, Absalom puts into motion a plot to overthrow the king by gradually winning the loyalty of the people. Key figures such as the priests, however, retain loyalty to the king and help him escape. The rebellion of Absalom is the ultimate consequence of David's sin years earlier.

Questions for Reflection

1. How did Absalom win the loyalty of many of the people of Israel?
2. What people displayed continued loyalty to David?
3. What was David's plan for Hushai?

Day 108: Absalom Takes Jerusalem

2 Samuel 16–17

Notes

Chapter 17, Verse 17. En-rogel. A spring less than a mile southeast of Jerusalem.

Verse 25. Amasa. This new general for Absalom was David's nephew.

Summary

Absalom takes Jerusalem and prepares for war against David and those loyal to him. In the providence of God, Absalom takes only half of Ahithophel's advice and instead follows the advice of Hushai, who is loyal to David. This allows David enough time to escape and prepare for battle.

Questions for Reflection

1. Was it right for Hushai to deceive Absalom?
2. How is God's providential hand clearly evident in what happens?
3. Why did Ahithophel kill himself?

Day 109: Absalom Is Killed

2 Samuel 18; Psalm 45

Notes

2 Samuel 18, Verse 18. No son. Since 14:27 indicates that Absalom had three sons, they must have all died before he built the monument.

Verse 33. My son. David's lament seems to be more inappropriately focused on himself than good for the kingdom.

Psalm 45. This psalm was likely written on the occasion of a royal wedding in the Davidic line.

Verse 6. Your throne. Since this king-groom was a member of the Davidic dynasty, it applies both to the immediate king and ultimately to the Messiah (Heb 1:8–9).

Summary

David's army ultimately defeats Absalom's army, but not without continuing devastation for David personally. Although this is a victory, David's earlier sin resulted in consequences that continued until his death. Yet God's covenant with him continues far beyond David's death and will be fulfilled in the ultimate coronation of the Messiah.

Questions for Reflection

1. Was Joab right to disobey the king and kill Absalom?
2. Was David's response to the death of Absalom right?
3. How do kings in David's line parallel the future reign of Christ?

Day 110: David Returns to Jerusalem

2 Samuel 19; Psalm 24

Notes

2 Samuel 19, Verse 13. Amasa. David replacement of Joab with Amasa, Absalom's general both secured the loyalty of Absalom's army and punished Joab for his disobedience to the king's commands.

Verse 43. Despise. This conflict lays the groundwork for future hostility and eventually the division of the kingdom.

Summary

David gradually regains the loyalty of the people and returns to Jerusalem. He once again demonstrates his graciousness and wisdom by forgiving those who rebelled against him. David is truly a man after God's own heart, even despite his sin and shortcomings.

Questions for Reflection

1. Was Joab's condemnation of David's mourning correct?
2. Why did David replace Joab with Amasa?
3. What seeds of dissention between the northern tribes and Judah are seen in this account?

Week 23: David's Reign

Weekly memory verse:

Psalm 27:1-2 - "The Lord is my light and my salvation; whom shall I fear? The Lord is the stronghold of my life; of whom shall I be afraid? When evildoers assail me to eat up my flesh, my adversaries and foes, it is they who stumble and fall."

Weekly hymn:

"Sun of My Soul"

Weekly catechism:

How did Christ, being the Son of God, become human?
Christ, the Son of God became human by taking to himself true human nature, being conceived by the Holy Spirit and the virgin Mary.

Sun of My Soul

HURSLEY

WORDS: John Keble, 1820 LM

MUSIC: *Katholisches Gesangbuch*, Vienna, c. 1774

Day 111: Sheba's Rebellion

2 Samuel 20; Psalm 25

Notes

2 Samuel 20, Verse 1. Sheba. Sheba was from Saul's tribe. He expresses here the sentiment of the northern tribes of animosity toward Judah, using words that are very similar to what would be said when the kingdom later divides.

Verse 4. Amasa. Amasa was Absalom's general with whom David had replaced Joab as his general.

Verse 6. Abishai. Since Amasa was unable to gather an army of Judah to end Sheba's rebellion, David appointed Joab's brother, Abishai, to do so. Joab and his men also accompanied Abishai, Joab intending to take vengeance on Amasa.

Verse 22. David was unable to depose Joab as general.

Summary

David is able to return to Jerusalem and reestablish his reign, but seeds of dissent have been planted in the northern tribes, which will eventually lead to a division of the kingdom. David's inability to control even his own general is evidence of strife within his administration.

Questions for Reflection

1. Why would the northern tribes have had animosity toward Judah?
2. What are some evidences that Joab intended all along to regain control as general of David's army?
3. What are some reasons David is experiencing so much difficulty in his reign?

Day 112: David's Final Battles

2 Samuel 21; Psalm 26

Notes

2 Samuel 21, Verse 1. Gibeonites. The famine was due to the fact that

Saul broke the covenant that had been made years earlier between Joshua and the Gibeonites (Josh 9:3–27).

Verse 8. Mephibosheth. This is a son of Saul, different from Jonathan's son, Mephibosheth, whom David spared.

Verse 9. Before the Lord. It is unclear why God allowed this superstitious ritual sacrifice to take place except that is stresses the importance of keeping covenants.

Summary
Turmoil continued in the kingdom through the end of David's reign. However, God protected David as he had promised and used David to secure peace that his son, Solomon, would enjoy.

Questions for Reflection
1. What does God think about covenants and promises?
2. How does Saul's actions toward the Gibeonites, breaking the covenant with them, contrast with David's protection of Jonathan's son, Mephibosheth?
3. Why do you think God allowed the Gibeonites to kill these descendants of Saul?

Day 113: David's Census
1 Chronicles 21; Psalm 27

Notes
1 Chronicles 21, Verse 1. Satan. Second Samuel 24:1 indicates that God moved David to number Israel, in contrast to this statement. This simply reveals that this was part of God's judgment upon Israel for some unspecified sin, and he used Satan to be a tool of that judgment. The census must have been evidence of pride in David's heart.

Verse 28. Threshing floor. This would later become the site of Solomon's temple.

Summary
This event reveals both David's fallibility and his heart for God. Out of pride he numbered the people, resulting in God's judgment, but out of humility he took responsibility for his actions and did what

was necessary to atone for his sin. God accepted David's confession and used this opportunity to have David purchase the land upon which Solomon would later build the temple.

Questions for Reflection

1. Was David responsible for numbering the people even though both God and Satan were involved?
2. What do you think motivated David to number the people?
3. Describe David's repentance for what he had done.

Day 114: Solomon Anointed King

1 Kings 1; Proverbs 13

Notes

1 Kings 1, Verse 1. Old. David was 70 years old.

Verse 2. Warm. In his old age, David's circulation prevented him from keeping warm, and thus he needed the body heat of others.

Verse 5. Adonijah. Adonijah was the fourth son of David and likely the oldest living son.

Verse 50. Horns of the altar. These were the four corners of the alter where priests would smear the blood of sacrifices. Adonijah was seeking the protection of God through this gesture.

Summary

As David neared the end of his life, God chose, through the prophet Nathan, Solomon to be the next king of Israel. In many ways this was an unlikely choice, similar to his father before him. Yet God chose him and protected the Davidic line through Solomon. Increasing tensions between Israel and Judah would later result in division, but for now the unity remained intact.

Questions for Reflection

1. Why do you think God chose Solomon to be king?
2. In what ways did God protect Solomon and the Davidic line through him?
3. How does Solomon reflect David's own heart of mercy in how he treats Adonijah?

Day 115: David's Death

1 Kings 2; Proverbs 14

Notes

1 Kings 2, Verse 7. Eat at your table. This was a position of honor that included a royal stipend.

Verse 10. City of David. i.e., Jerusalem.

Verse 11. Forty years. David reigned from approximately 1011-971 B.C.

Verse 17. Give me Abishag. This was likely an attempt by Adonijah to support his claim to the throne and start a revolt.

Summary

David's final exhortation to Solomon was counsel that would firmly establish Solomon as king by removing those who had been disloyal to David. Solomon follows the advice of his father, laying the foundation for what would be a very prosperous reign of peace. What was a political strategy was also part of God's plan to establish David's line in fulfillment of his covenant.

Questions for Reflection

1. Why did David advise Solomon to kill those who had been disloyal?
2. What was Adonijah's motivation in asking for Abishag to be his wife?
3. Was Solomon wise in following David's counsel?

Week 24: Solomon's Reign

Weekly memory verse:

2 Chronicles 7:14 – "If my people who are called by my name humble themselves, and pray and seek my face and turn from their wicked ways, then I will hear from heaven and will forgive their sin and heal their land."

Weekly hymn:

"Holy, Holy, Holy"

Weekly catechism:

How did Christ satisfy God's just wrath for sin?
Christ suffered the miseries of this life, the wrath of God, and the cursed death of the cross.

Holy, Holy, Holy

NICAEA

WORDS: Reginald Heber, 1826
MUSIC: John B. Dykes, 1861

11.12.12.10

Day 116: Solomon Prays for Wisdom

2 Chronicles 1; Proverbs 15

Notes

2 Chronicles 1, Verse 3. Gibeon. The tabernacle was still in Gibeon, while the ark was in Jerusalem.

Verse 9. Promise. This refers to the Davidic Covenant (2 Sam 7; 1 Chr 17).

Summary

In fulfillment of promises made to David, Solomon begins his reign and follows his father's example of allegiance to the Lord and his Law. Solomon leads the nation in the worship of Yahweh and shows humility in asking for wisdom from the Lord rather than wealth. God rewards Solomon by granting him a great kingdom.

Questions for Reflection

1. On what basis did Solomon make his request to the Lord?
2. What is wisdom?
3. What is foolishness?

Day 117: Solomon Builds the Temple

2 Chronicles 3-5

Notes

Chapter 3, Verse 2. Second month. It took 7 years, 6 months to complete the temple.

Chapter 4, Verse 2. Sea. This is the bronze laver, used for ritual cleansing (Exod 30:17-21).

Chapter 5, Verse 2. Ark. The ark was in a temporary tent that David had constructed in Jerusalem (2 Sam 6:17).

Summary

Solomon's first act as king was to initiate the building of the temple of the Lord in Jerusalem, a project that took seven years to complete. Careful attention was given to all the instructions God had given for the construction of the tabernacle. The temple was simply a larger, more elaborate, and permanent version of the tabernacle that God had prescribed for his worship.

Questions for Reflection

1. Why did Solomon give such careful attention to how God wanted the temple constructed?
2. What did the veil signify?
3. Why were sacrifices necessary?

Day 118: The Temple Dedication

2 Chronicles 6–7

Notes

Chapter 7, Verse 1. Fire. This happened at the dedication of the tabernacle as well (Lev 9:23–24) and signified God's acceptance of the sacrifice.

Verse 8. Feast. The dedication of the temple corresponded with the Day of Atonement and Feast of Tabernacles.

Verse 14. If my people. This is a promise given specifically to Israel, assuring them that if they follow the Law of God, he will bless them, but if they disobey, he will punish them. This does not nullify the Davidic covenant, however.

Summary

Solomon leads the people in a prayer of dedication for the temple and offers the appropriate sacrifices. God responds with approval, and the people celebrate with a great feast. This dedication ceremony pictures true worship: the people draw near to the presence of God through sacrifices of atonement that he has prescribed, he accepts them on that basis, and they commune with him in his presence.

Questions for Reflection

1. What were some of the main themes of Solomon's prayer of dedication?
2. How did God demonstrate his approval?
3. Did God's promise to punish the nation if they disobeyed him nullify the Davidic Covenant?

Day 119: Solomon's Reign

1 Kings 10-11

Notes

Chapter 10, Verse 1. Sheba. Sheba was located about 1,200 miles southwest of Jerusalem in Arabia.

Chapter 11, Verse 1. Foreign women. Solomon followed the traditional practice of kings in marrying daughters of foreign kings in order to establish peace with other natives. While this was politically savvy, it was in direct disobedience to the Law of God.

Verse 11. Covenant. This refers to the Mosaic Covenant, which was a conditional covenant unlike the unconditional Davidic Covenant.

Verse 38. A sure house. God promised to Jeroboam the same he had promised to David, if he obeyed God's Law.

Summary

Because both David and Solomon followed after the Lord, God blessed Solomon's reign, expanding the nation and giving him peace and unity. However, Solomon's marriage to many foreign wives caused him to forsake God later in his life, causing the nation to eventually forsake God and follow after idols.

Questions for Reflection

1. Why did God bless Solomon and the nation of Israel under his reign?
2. Why was it wrong for Solomon to marry pagan wives?
3. What does Solomon's sin later in his life reveal about wisdom?

Day 120: The Kingdom Divides

1 Kings 12-13

Notes

Chapter 12, Verse 15. By the Lord. In fulfillment of what he had promised to both Solomon and Jeroboam, God sovereignly ordained Rehoboam's foolishness. However, Rehoboam was nevertheless responsible for his own foolish choices.

Verse 16. David. This expression of rebellion by the ten northern tribes was the same as Sheba's failed rebellion in 2 Samuel 20.

Verse 21. Tribe of Benjamin. Benjamin's tribe divided in loyalty, with some of the northern towns joining the northern tribes, and some of the southern towns joining Judah.

Verse 27. Sacrifices. God had promised Jeroboam that if he followed the Law, God would bless him and give him a great kingdom. However, to obey the Law would mean that his people would be required to offer sacrifices in Jerusalem at the temple, which was in the southern kingdom. Jeroboam therefore made a politically savvy decision rather than trust and obey the Lord.

Verse 28. Calves of gold. Jeroboam did not intend to lead the people to worship false gods; rather, he was establishing a new way to worship Yahweh. The word translated "gods" in the text is the Hebrew term *Elohim*, which often referred to Yahweh. There are striking parallels between Jeroboam's act here and the golden calf of Exodus 32.

Summary

As punishment for Solomon's sin, God ordained the division of the kingdom, using both Rehoboam's and Jeroboam's foolishness to accomplish his punishment of the nation. While God promised Jeroboam that he would bless him if he obeyed the Law, Jeroboam chose to establish his own system of Yahweh worship, which led the people into eventual idolatry and destruction.

Questions for Reflection

1. Why was Rehoboam responsible for his sin even though it was part of God's sovereign plan to punish the nation?
2. Would God have blessed Jeroboam if he had allowed the people to offer sacrifices in Jerusalem?
3. Why is it wrong to worship God in ways that he has not prescribed?

Week 25: Elijah

Weekly memory verse:

Philippians 2:8 – "And being found in human form, he humbled himself by becoming obedient to the point of death, even death on a cross."

Weekly hymn:

"All Hail the Power of Jesus' Name"

Weekly catechism:

Why was it necessary for Christ to humble himself even unto death?
Christ humbled himself unto death because the justice of God required that satisfaction for my sins could be made in no other way than by the death of the Son of God.

All Hail the Power of Jesus' Name

CORONATION

WORDS: Edward Perronet, 1780; alt. John Rippon, 1787 CM

MUSIC: Oliver Holden, 1793

Day 121: The Fear of the Lord

Proverbs 16-18

Notes

Proverbs 16, Verse 10. Oracle. This is not an occultic oracle, but rather a decision made by a king based on divine relation.

Proverbs 17, Verse 19. Door high. This pictures one who is proud and displays his wealth with a large house with a huge front door.

Proverbs 18, Verse 16. Gift. This is not a bribe, but rather a legitimate present given to someone.

Summary

Solomon penned many wise words even though he himself demonstrated much foolishness in marrying many foreign wives and leading the nation into idolatry. It is only through truly fearing the Lord that one can retain wisdom.

Questions for Reflection

1. How can the fear of the Lord help us turn away from evil (16:6)?
2. What are some ways you have returned evil for good (17:13)?
3. Why is it important to listen before giving an answer (18:13)?

Day 122: Egypt Invades Judah

2 Chronicles 11-12; Proverbs 19

Notes

2 Chronicles 12, Verse 2. Shishak. This king of Egypt ruled from approximately 945-924 B. C. A record of this invasion was discovered on an Egyptian stone.

Summary

The invasion of Judah by Egypt foreshadows what is to come of the nation if they will not turn back to the Lord. God had promised them that if they obeyed him, he would bless them, but if they forsook him, he would send them into captivity. This final captivity does not happen for 200 years, but God is warning them by making them serve in Egypt for a time.

Questions for Reflection

1. How is Rehoboam's reign evidence of the lasting results of his father's sins?
2. How is God's mercy displayed in this account?
3. In what ways does the Egyptian invasion foreshadow what is to come for the nation?

Day 123: Kings of Judah and Israel

1 Kings 15–16; Proverbs 20

Notes

1 Kings 15, Verse 9. Asa. Asa was the first of a few good kings in Judah. There were no good kings in Israel.

1 Kings 16, Verse 15. Seven days. Zimri's reign was the shortest of any king of Israel.

Verse 25. More evil. While Jeroboam never intended the people to worship false gods, but instead attempted to create a new system of worshiping Yahweh so that the people would not go to Jerusalem, this inevitably led to idol worship. With Omri, Baal worship officially comes to Israel through the marriage of his son, Ahab, to Jezebel, the daughter of the neighboring kingdom of Phoenicia.

Summary

The record of kings in both Judah and Israel is almost entirely disastrous. While a few select kings in Judah fear the Lord and attempt reform, most of Judah's kings forsake God, and all of Israel's kings are evil. This reaches a climax in the reigns of Omri and Ahab, when full idolatrous Baal worship comes into Israel.

Questions for Reflection

1. What is required for a king to be considered good?
2. Why are there no good kings in Israel?
3. What does Israel's downfall reveal about the dangers of religious syncretism (mixing true worship with false worship)?

Day 124: Elijah

1 Kings 17; Psalm 29

Notes

1 Kings 17, Verse 1. Tishbite. Tishbite was a town east of the Jordan River.

Verse 3. Brook Cherith. Likely a seasonal brook that dried up in the hot season.

Verse 9. Zarephath. A town on the coast of the Mediterranean Sea controlled by Ahab's father-in-law.

Summary

God sends the prophet Elijah to confront Baal worship and to demonstrate that only Yahweh is the true and living God. He proclaims judgment of a drought upon Israel, and God confirms him as a true prophet through miraculously providing for his needs and by using him to raise the widow's son from the dead, something that Baal was supposed to have the power to do.

Questions for Reflection

1. Why did God send Elijah?
2. In what ways did God prove that he was God and Baal is not through Elijah?
3. Why did God allow Elijah to raise the widow's son from the dead?

Day 125: Elijah and the Prophets of Baal

1 Kings 18

Notes

Verse 3. Obadiah. This is not the minor prophet, but the chief servant of Ahab's court, probably second in command of the whole kingdom. Privately, he had continued to worship Yahweh, but he was a bit of a compromiser, afraid to stand up to the idolatrous king.

Verse 19. Mount Carmel. Elijah chose this mountain because it lay at the border of Israel and the neighboring nation of Phoenicia, Jezebel's native land. It was also known for frequent lightning strikes, so in a sense, Elijah was giving Baal, the supposed "god of storm," the "home field advantage."

Summary

An ultimate display that Yahweh was the true God, Elijah's encounter with the prophets of Baal is one of the most colorful stories in the Old Testament. Contrary to the pagan's chaotic worship in which they attempted to initiate an encounter with their god, Elijah prayed a simple request to God, based on God's own commands and initiative, in which he asked God to reveal that he was the true and living God. The result left no doubt.

Questions for Reflection

1. How did Elijah contrast with Obadiah?
2. Why did Elijah choose Mount Carmel?
3. How was the pagan worship different from how Elijah approached God?

Week 26: King Ahab

Weekly memory verse:

1 Corinthians 15:3-5 - "For I delivered to you as of first importance what I also received: that Christ died for our sins in accordance with the Scriptures, that he was buried, that he was raised on the third day in accordance with the Scriptures, and that he appeared to Cephas, then to the twelve."

Weekly hymn:

"Christ the Lord is Risen Today"

Weekly catechism:

Did Christ stay dead?
No. Christ rose again from the dead on the third day.

Christ the Lord Is Risen Today

WORDS: Charles Wesley, 1739
MUSIC: *Lyra Davidica*, 1708

7.7.7.7.Alleluias

Day 126: The Call of Elisha

1 Kings 19; Psalm 30

Notes

1 Kings 19, Verse 3. Beersheba. Elijah travels from the northern border of Israel south about as far away from Jezebel as he can get, to the southern border of Judah.

Verse 8. Horeb. This is another name for Mount Sinai, which was about 200 miles south of Beersheba.

Verse 15. Wilderness of Damascus. God is commanding Elijah to return once again to the north.

Summary

Discouraged that his actions did not lead to Jezebel's surrender and the end of Baal worship, Elijah flees to the southern border of Judah, and then on further south to Mount Sinai, where the people of Israel had met God long ago. Like Moses before him, Elijah received a message from God that strengthened him and commanded him to travel back to the north where he would anoint his successors who would complete what he had started.

Questions for Reflection

1. Was Elijah right to be discouraged?
2. Why did Elijah travel to Mount Sinai?
3. Why do you think Elisha killed his oxen?

Day 127: Ahab's Wars

1 Kings 20

Notes

Verse 26. Aphek. This was a town likely about three miles east of the Sea of Galilee.

Verse 34. Bazaars. Outside market places for the sale of Israelite goods.

Verse 35. Sons of the prophets. Likely an association of prophets who lived together.

Summary

Despite Ahab's sin and idol worship, God in his mercy chose to give him victory over invading enemies. Yet Ahab confirmed his own destruction by refusing to obey the Lord's commands even after God had helped him.

Questions for Reflection

1. Why do you think God chose to help Ahab?
2. How did God demonstrate that he is truly the only God?
3. What did Ahab's actions reveal about him?

Day 128: Naboth's Vineyard

1 Kings 21; Proverbs 21

Notes

1 Kings 21, Verse 3. The Lord forbid. God had forbidden Israelite families from permanently giving up ancestral property (Lev 25:23-28; Num 36:7-9).

Verse 27. Tore his clothes. A common expression of repentance or grief.

Summary

Both Ahab's and Jezebel's sin are manifested climactically in their conspiracy to kill Naboth and his sons in order to obtain his vineyard. As a result, God proclaims judgment upon them. Ahab sincerely repents, but Jezebel is judged, and Ahab's judgment comes later through his son.

Questions for Reflection

1. What did Ahab's actions reveal about him?
2. What did Jezebel's actions reveal about her?
3. Why did these acts finally bring judgement upon Ahab and Jezebel?

Day 129: Alliance Between Israel and Judah

2 Chronicles 18; Proverbs 22

Notes

2 Chronicles 18, Verse 1. Jehoshaphat. Jehoshaphat was king of Judah.

Verse 2. Went down. Samaria is north of Jerusalem, but the author uses "down" here to describe the king traveling down from the higher elevation of Jerusalem to the lower elevation of Samaria.

Verse 34. Died. First Kings 22:28 indicates that when Ahab died, the dogs licked up his blood, fulfilling part of the prophesy of judgement against Ahab given in 1 Kings 21:19, although the other part is later fulfilled in his son, Joram, who dies in the field of Naboth (2 Kgs 9:25-26).

Summary

Although Ahab and Jehoshaphat are able to establish relative peace between Israel and Judah, Jehoshaphat accomplishes this through an improper marriage of his son to Ahab's daughter, and Ahab eventually meets his promised ruin for his Baal worship.

Questions for Reflection

1. Why did Jehoshaphat establish peace with Ahab?
2. Was it right for Jehoshaphat to arrange for his son to marry Ahab's daughter?
3. Why does God allow Ahab to be killed in battle?

Day 130: Jehoshaphat's Reforms

2 Chronicles 19-20; Psalm 118

Notes

2 Chronicles 20, Verse 1. Moabites and Ammonites. These are descendants of Lot who lived east of the Jordan River.

Verse 2. Edom. Descendants of Esau who lived south of Judah.

Verse 10. Mount Seir. A landmark in Edom.

Summary

Despite Jehoshaphat's previous unwise alliances, he does what is right in the sight of the Lord and brings order to Judah not seen since the reign of Solomon. As a result, God protects Judah from invasion, and the king and his people respond with appropriate praise.

Questions for Reflection

1. Why didn't God judge Jehoshaphat for his wrong alliances?
2. In what ways does Jehoshaphat's prayer reveal his heart for God?
3. How do Jehoshaphat and the people respond when he delivers them from their enemies?

Week 27: The Start of Elisha's Ministry

Weekly memory verse:

Romans 10:9 – "If you confess with your mouth that Jesus is Lord and believe in your heart that God raised him from the dead, you will be saved."

Weekly hymn:

"My Faith Looks Up to Thee"

Weekly catechism:

How are you made a partaker of the redemption purchased by Christ?
I am made a partaker of the redemption purchased by Christ through repentant faith in him and his substitutionary atoning death.

My Faith Looks Up to Thee

OLIVET

WORDS: Ray Palmer, 1830
MUSIC: Lowell Mason, 1832

6.6.4.6.6.6.4

Day 131: Trust and Penitence

Psalms 31-32

Notes

Psalm 31, Verse 5. Into your hand. Jesus later quotes this verse during his crucifixion (Luke 23:46).

Psalm 32. This is one of seven penitential psalms, expressing confession of sin and forgiveness from God.

Summary

God hears the prayers of those who trust him, confess their sins, and find forgiveness through the means that he has provided. David presents the standard for these expressions of trust and confession to God.

Questions for Reflection

1. Why can we trust God?
2. When we sin, what should we do?
3. How can we find forgiveness from God?

Day 132: Elisha Succeeds Elijah

2 Kings 2; Psalm 33

Notes

2 Kings 2, Verse 3. Take away. This same expression was used to describe how Enoch was taken into heaven without dying (Gen 5:24).

Verse 23. Small boys. These are more likely young men in their early twenties (the same phrase is used to describe Solomon in 1 Kgs 3:7). Their jeering at him was not innocent; it was an expression of contempt for the prophet of the Lord.

Summary

The transition of ministry from Elijah to Elisha comes to completion when God takes Elijah to heaven miraculously without dying. Elisha takes up the mantle of Elijah's prophetic ministry. He is accepted by the other prophets, but rejected by others. Yet God confirms his ministry through miracle and judgment upon those who rejected him.

Questions for Reflection

1. Why do you think God took Elijah to heaven the way that he did?
2. What did Elijah's miracle at Jericho signify?
3. Why did God punish the young men so severely?

Day 133: Prayers of Lament and Praise

Psalms 35-36

Notes

Psalm 35, Verse 21. Aha, aha. This is a common way to taunt.

Psalm 36, Verse 1. No fear. Paul uses applies this phrase in Romans 3 to the whole human race.

Verse 11. Foot of arrogance. This likely alludes to a victorious military victor placing his foot upon the neck of the defeated general.

Summary

These psalms once again model appropriate ways to express lament and praise to the Lord. God will help us in time of trouble; therefore, we can trust in him, bring our burdens before him, and praise him for his always good answers to our needs.

Questions for Reflection

1. How should we view strong prayers in the psalms requesting that God destroy the psalmist's enemies?
2. Is it right to question God?
3. What is God's response toward sin?

Day 134: Elisha's Miracles

2 Kings 4; Psalm 38

Notes

2 Kings 4, Verse 14. No son, and her husband is old. This implied that there would be no heir and was a disgrace to her personally since she could not bear children.

Verse 23. New moon nor Sabbath. Both the first day of the month and the Sabbath would be typical days to visit a prophet.

Verse 42. Firstfruits. The firstfruits were supposed to be kept apart for God and the Levites. Even though Israel had forsaken the Law, this act demonstrates that there were still some righteous, God-fearing people in Israel.

Summary

God confirmed Elisha's ministry through miracles, many of which resembled the miracles of Elijah. While Elijah's ministry was often public and confrontational, Elisha's work was more local and met the needs of common folk. Nevertheless, it is clearly the same God at work in both, confirming his power and calling the people to worship him alone.

Questions for Reflection

1. Why do you think God chose to meet the needs of these otherwise seemingly insignificant people?
2. In what ways did Elisha's miracles resemble Elijah's?
3. How did God make clear that he was the one accomplishing the miracles and not Elisha himself?

Day 135: Naaman

2 Kings 5; Psalm 39

Notes

2 Kings 5, Verse 5. King. The king of Israel at this time was Jehoram.

Verse 14. Flesh. While modern leprosy attacks the nerves, this leprosy was a disease of the skin.

Verse 17. Earth. Ancient people believed that gods were bound to certain territories and could be worshiped only on ground in that land. Therefore, Naaman wanted to take some of the ground of Israel with him so that he could continue to worship the God of Israel.

Summary

The story of Naaman contrasts the apostacy and unbelief of most of the people of Israel with this pagan commander who, upon being healed by God, confesses Yahweh to be the one true and living God. Even Elisha's own servant, Gehazi, was more interested in material gain than the true worship of the Lord.

Questions for Reflection

1. In what ways did Naaman's view of Israel change after he was healed?
2. Why do you think God healed Naaman?
3. How were Gehazi's attitude and acts representative of the nation of Israel as a whole?

Week 28: Elisha's Continuing Ministry

Weekly memory verse:

Ephesians 2:8–9 – "For by grace you have been saved through faith. And this is not your own doing; it is the gift of God, not a result of works, so that no one may boast."

Weekly hymn:

"God, Be Merciful to Me"

Weekly catechism:

What is faith in Jesus Christ?

Faith in Jesus Christ is a saving grace, by which I receive and rest upon him alone for my salvation.

Psalm 51

God, Be Merciful to Me

REDHEAD

7. Not the formal sacrifice
hath acceptance in Thy eyes;
broken hearts are in Thy sight
more than sacrificial rite;
contrite spirit, pleading cries,
Thou, O God, wilt not despise.

8. Prosper Zion in Thy grace
and her broken walls replace;
then our righteous sacrifice
shall delight Thy holy eyes;
free-will offerings, gladly made,
on Thy altar shall be laid.

WORDS: **Psalm 51**; *The Psalter*, 1912 — 7.7.7.7.7.7
MUSIC: Richard Redhead, 1853

Day 136: Battle Against Syria

2 Kings 6:1–23; Psalms 40–41

Notes

2 Kings 6, Verse 1. Dwell. This could mean that the sons of the prophets lived together in a community, or it could simply mean "sit before," i.e., it could refer to the building where they met to be instructed by Elisha.

Verse 8. King of Syria. This could be either Ben-Hadad I or Ben-Hadad III.

Verse 23. Feast. A fest of this nature in the ancient Near East indicated the formation of a peace treaty.

Summary

God continues to confirm his hand of blessing upon Elisha as a true man of God. He uses Elisha to meet small needs as well as deliverance from Israel's enemies. In each case, it is clearly God who is performing the miraculous deeds, further emphasizing that he is the only true God.

Questions for Reflection

1. Why do you think God allowed Elisha to help recover the lost ax head?
2. How important are angels in God's plan?
3. Why did Elisha not allow Israel to kill the Syrian army?

Day 137: Siege by Syria

2 Kings 6:24–7:20

Notes

Chapter 6, Verse 25. Donkey's head. A donkey was an unclean animal, so the sale of the head of a donkey for an overvalued price illustrates the dire situation of Samaria.

Verse 28. Eat him. Moses had predicted that apostasy would lead to cannibalism (Deut 28:52–57).

Chapter 7, Verse 1. Seah . . . for a shekel. Compared to the earlier sale of a donkey's head and dove's dung for outrageous prices, this indicates Elisha's promise that the famine would end the next day.

Summary

Once again, God delivers the people of Samaria, not due to their trust in him, but rather at the hand of his prophet, Elisha. These deliverances despite the people's apostasy and distrust further condemn them and foreshadow the coming exile.

Questions for Reflection

1. Why did the king want Elisha dead?
2. What are some indications in this story of the absolute apostacy of Israel?
3. Why do you think God delivered Samaria despite their sin and distrust?

Day 138: The Shunamite Woman

2 Kings 8

Notes

Verses 1-6. This event likely occurred earlier chronologically, before the events of 5:1-7:20 (notice that Gehazi does not yet have leprosy as recorded in 5:27), but is included here by the author to thematically connect it to the theme of famine in 6:24-7:20.

Verse 2. Land of the Philistines. The land along the Mediterranean Sea, southwest of Israel.

Verse 7. Damascus. Elisha traveled here to obey the command God had given him at Horeb (1 Kings 19:15-16).

Verse 20. Edom. Edom had been under the control of the united Israel and of Judah since the division, but now Edom established its own independence. God had promised that the Messiah would control Edom (Num 24:18), so this revealed that none of the future kings of Judah could be the promised Messiah.

Summary

This chapter contrasts the faithfulness of the Shunamite woman and

Elisha, which brought them blessings, with the evil of Israel, Judah, and Syria, which resulted in turmoil. This continues to reveal the downward spiral of Israel and foreshadows its future demise as fulfillment of God's promised judgment.

Questions for Reflection

1. Why do you think God blessed the Shunamite woman?
2. What purpose did Elisha's trip to Damascus serve?
3. Why didn't God destroy Judah, despite its perpetual rebellion (8:19)?

Day 139: Hope in God

Psalms 42–44

Notes

Psalm 42. Psalms 42 and 43 were likely originally one psalm, indicated by thematic unity and the fact that while all of the psalms in this section have titles, Psalm 43 does not.

Verse 6. Jordan and of Hermon. This location in the north was the source of waters that flowed to the south.

Psalm 43. This psalm is a response to the lament of Psalm 42.

Psalm 44. This psalm is a national lament following an unidentified military defeat.

Summary

In the midst of difficult circumstances, small or great, we should express hope in our covenant-keeping God. Recognizing that God is the source of all blessing and all trouble, we can trust that his plan is perfect, that he will ultimately punish wrong and reward good, and that he will never forsake his promises.

Questions for Reflection

1. Is it wrong to question God during times of trouble?
2. What should always be our response when something bad happens?
3. What does it mean to hope in God?

Day 140: Cast Your Burden Upon the Lord

Psalms 50, 53, 55

Notes

Psalm 50. This is the first of the psalms ascribed to Asaph, one of the leaders of the Levitical musicians (1 Chr 15:19; 25:1–2).

Psalm 53. This psalm is almost identical to Psalm 14, except for verse 5, which celebrates a specific military victory. Romans 3:10–12 quote these verses extensively.

Psalm 55, Verse 22. Burden. This refers specifically to bad circumstances in which God's enemies are tormenting you.

Summary

Enemies of God are completely sinful; they do not seek him, and they torment God's people. Yet our response should always be one of trust in God's perfect will and prayer that he will fulfill his promises to punish evil and reward good. When we cast our burden upon the Lord, he will sustain us.

Questions for Reflection

1. How many people are sinners?
2. What does it mean to be an enemy of God?
3. What are some burdens that you should cast upon the Lord?

Week 29: Turn to God

Weekly memory verse:

Acts 3:19 – "Repent therefore, and turn back, that your sins may be blotted out."

Weekly hymn:

"How Blest Is He Whose Trespass"

Weekly catechism:

What is repentance unto life?

Repentance unto life is a saving grace, by which I turn from my sin to God, promising to strive after new obedience.

Psalm 32

How Blest Is He Whose Trespass

WIE LIEBLICH IST DER MAIEN

WORDS: **Psalm 32**; *The Psalter*, 1912

7.6.7.6.D

MUSIC: Johann Steurlein, 1575

Day 141: The Judge of the Earth

Psalms 58, 78

Notes

Psalm 58, Verse 3. From the womb. This indicates that all people are born sinners.

Verse 10. Bathe his feet. This is an expression indicating that the righteous will share in the victory accomplished by the Lord.

Summary

God is a just judge who will judge all sin. This eternal truth should motivate sinners to repent and turn to him lest they be consumed. It should also encourage the righteous that even though they are oppressed by the wicked and sin seems to go unpunished, God will inevitably fulfill his promise to judge sin.

Questions for Reflection

1. Are all people sinners from birth?
2. What does sin deserve?
3. What is the only way to escape judgment from God?

Day 142: Cry for Salvation

Psalms 60-61

Notes

Psalm 60. This psalm alludes to the events referred to in 2 Samuel 8:13 and 1 Chronicles 18:12 in which Edom attacked Judah while David and his army were in the north.

Psalm 61. This psalm is a personal lament that David roots in God's covenant.

Summary

When tragedy strikes on a large or small scale, the only right response is to cry to the Lord for salvation. Trust in self or other human means of rescue are futile. Only God is able to deliver us from trouble; he is our strong defense and salvation.

Questions for Reflection

1. In Psalm 60, why did the people think God had abandoned them?
2. What is meant by the phrase, "vain is the salvation of man" (60:11)?
3. Does God hear us when we cry to him? Why?

Day 143: Seeking God

Psalms 62-63

Notes

Psalm 62. Jeduthun. This was one of the original leaders of Temple music (1 Chr 25:1).

Psalm 63, Verse 1. Thirsts. David wrote this while in the wilderness, and thus this metaphor was fitting.

Verse 10. Jackals. These animals were scavengers who fed on dead bodies.

Summary

These psalms use rich metaphors to describe God's relationship to us and our need to seek earnestly after him. Relationship with God is not passive; his people must actively seek him through his Word and prayer, expressing need for him, dependence upon him, and praise for his goodness and grace.

Questions for Reflection

1. What does it mean to wait for God?
2. How is seeking after God like thirsting for water in a dry land?
3. What are some ways that you can seek God?

Day 144: Joash Repairs the Temple

2 Chronicles 24; Psalm 64

Notes

2 Chronicles 24, Verse 1. Joash. This is a variant of the name Jehoash, which 2 Kings uses.
Verse 4. Restore the house. The temple had been severely damaged

and much of the temple articles had been taken for use in Baal's temple during the reign of Athaliah (v. 7).

Summary

Joash did what was right in God's sight under the influence of the godly priest, Jehoiada, but after Jehoiada died, Joash followed the example of the kings before him and turned evil. Yet God does not allow sin to go unpunished, and Joash received the end he deserved.

Questions for Reflection

1. What kind of influence did Jehoiada have on Joash?
2. Why did Joash turn evil after Jehoiada's death?
3. How was Joash repaid for his evil choices?

Day 145: The Death of Elisha

2 Kings 13; Psalm 65

Notes

2 Kings 13, Verse 3. Ben-Haded. This is likely Ben-Hadad III, whose reign in Syria began about 801 B.C.

Verse 5. Savior. This "savior" was either Adad-Nirari, king of Assyria, whose attack on Syria freed Israel from Syria's control, Elisha, who led Joash to defeat the Syrians (vv. 15–19), or Jeroboam II, who later was able to expand Israel's land back into the area controlled by Syria (14:25–27).

Verse 14. Elisha. Nothing has been recorded of Elisha's activities for over 40 years.

Psalm 65, Verse 1. Zion. This is literally the hill in Jerusalem on which the temple was built, but it symbolizes the entire land God had promised to Abraham.

Verse 2. Shall all flesh come. This refers to the future millennial kingdom.

Summary

Despite Israel's continued sin against the Lord, God delivered them from the invading enemies on the basis of his everlasting covenant with Abraham that he would give the land to his descendants. God will fulfill that promise fully in the future millennial kingdom, when Israel will possess the land, and all nations will come there to worship God.

Questions for Reflection

1. Did God deliver Israel because of the goodness of the people?
2. Has God's promise to Abraham been completely fulfilled yet?
3. When will God complete the promise he made to Abraham?

Week 30: Jonah

Weekly memory verse:
Romans 6:23 - “For the wages of sin is death, but the free gift of God is eternal life in Christ Jesus our Lord.”

Weekly hymn:
“Jesus, Thy Blood and Righteousness”

Weekly catechism:
What benefits in this life come from repentant faith in Jesus Christ?
Those who repent and believe in Jesus Christ partake of justification, adoption, and sanctification.

Jesus, Thy Blood and Righteousness

GERMANY

WORDS: Nicolaus L. von Zinzendorf, 1739; tr. John Wesley, 1740 LM

MUSIC: William Gardiner's *Sacred Melodies*, 1815

Day 146: Jonah Flees God

Jonah 1–2

Notes

Chapter 1, Verse 1. Jonah. Jonah was a prophet of the northern tribes of Israel during the reign of Jeroboam II (ca. 793–758 BC), just prior to the ministry of the prophet Amos (see 2 Kgs 14:25).

Verse 2. Nineveh. This was a royal city of Assyria that traces back to Nimrod (Gen 10:11). It was destroyed by Nebuchadnezzar in 612 BC.

Verse 3. Tarshish. The location of this city is unknown, but the Greek historical Herodotus thought it was in southern Spain.

Summary

In a very unusual act, God commanded his prophet Jonah to preach salvation to a foreign city. Yet Jonah ran from God's will and was punished for his rebellion. Only a heart-felt prayer of repentance and submission resulted in his own deliverance by God.

Questions for Reflection

1. Why do you think God wanted Jonah to preach salvation to Nineveh?
2. Why did Jonah run?
3. In what ways did God show Jonah mercy in this account?

Day 147: Jonah Goes to Nineveh

Jonah 3–4

Notes

Chapter 3, Verse 6. King of Nineveh. This was likely either Adad-nirari III (ca. 810–783) or Assurdan III (ca. 722–755).

Chapter 4, Verse 3. Take my life. Jonah revealed his own sinful heart that actually had not changed even as a result of God's chastisement.

Summary

Jonah finally obeyed God and proclaimed the message from the Lord to Nineveh. God worked a miracle, and the people responded in repentant faith. As a result, God withheld his judgment. This whole event contrasts with Israel's lack of repentance and the inevitable judgment that was to come upon the nation, illustrated with Jonah's terrible response to Nineveh's repentance.

Questions for Reflection

1. Why did God withhold his judgment from Nineveh?
2. In what ways did the response of Nineveh contrast with Israel's current condition?
3. What did Jonah's response reveal about his heart?

Day 148: Let All Things Praise the Lord

Psalms 66–68

Notes

Psalm 66, Verse 4. All the earth. This acknowledges God's universal rule over all, but also foreshadows the future when all will worship God (Isa 66:23; Zech 14:16; Phil 2:10–11).

Psalm 67, Verse 1. Face to shine. When a king's face "shone" toward someone, this indicated his pleasure with that person and his intention to bless them.

Verse 3. Peoples. This refers to the Gentile nations, all of whom will one day worship the Lord.

Psalm 68, Verse 18. Ascended on high. Paul quotes this in Ephesians 4:8 with reference to Christ's triumphant ascension into heaven.

Summary

God's people worship the Lord now and receive rich blessings from him. One day, however, all things, including all the Gentile nations of the earth, will worship God perfectly.

Questions for Reflection

1. In what ways does God rule over all things now?
2. In what unique ways will God rule over all things in the future?
3. What should be the response of God's people to the promise that one day all things will worship God?

Day 149: Uzziah Reigns in Judah

2 Chronicles 26; Isaiah 6; Psalm 87

Notes

2 Chronicles 26, Verse 5. Zechariah. This is neither the priest mentioned earlier in 24:20, nor the prophet who wrote the book of Zechariah, but rather an otherwise unknown prophet.

Verse 16. Entered the temple. The Law forbade a king from taking the role of a Levitical priest (Num 3:10; 18:7).

Verse 22. Isaiah. This is not the inspired book of Isaiah the prophet, but rather some other book Isaiah the prophet apparently wrote.

Verse 23. Uzziah slept. This was the very year Isaiah the prophet had his vision of heaven (Isa 6).

Summary

Uzziah was a good king who did right in the sight of the Lord, and thus God gave him many victories. Yet those victories gave Uzziah pride so that he disobeyed the Lord by offering incense in the temple, and God punished him with leprosy. The same year Uzziah died, the prophet Isaiah was given a vision of heaven in which he saw the Ultimate King ruling and from whom he received forgiveness of sin and a message from the Lord.

Questions for Reflection

1. What caused Uzziah to grow proud?
2. Why was the fact that God only gave Uzziah leprosy actually an act of mercy?
3. On what basis were Isaiah's sins forgiven?

Day 150: Save Me, O God!

Psalms 69–70

Notes

Psalm 69, Verse 4. Hate me. Christ quoted this in reference to himself in John 15:25. Much of this psalm has application to Christ's earthly ministry.

Verse 9. Zeal for your house. This verse is quoted in John 2:17 and Romans 15:3.

Verse 21. Sour wine. This happened to Jesus on the cross (Matt 27:34).

Verse 22. Snare. This is quoted in Romans 11:9–10.

Verse 25. Desolation. This is quoted in reference to Judas in Acts 1:20.

Psalm 70. This psalm is nearly identical to Psalm 40: 13–17.

Summary

When God's people call for deliverance from God, he answers them. We might not always understand why God allows difficult circumstances to come into our lives, but he always has a perfect plan and will never let his people be completely overcome. There is no better example of this than in the life and death of Jesus Christ.

Questions for Reflection

1. In what ways does the New Testament apply Psalm 69 to Jesus Christ?
2. How can Jesus's life and death give us confidence in the midst of trouble?
3. What should we do when we are in the midst of trouble?

Week 31: The Fall of Israel

Weekly memory verse:
Romans 5:1 – "Therefore, since we have been justified by faith, we have peace with God through our Lord Jesus Christ."

Weekly hymn:
"O for a Thousand Tongues to Sing"

Weekly catechism:
What is justification?
Justification is an act of God's free grace in which he pardons all my sins and accepts me as righteous in his sight only because of the righteousness of Christ imputed to me.

O for a Thousand Tongues to Sing

AZMON

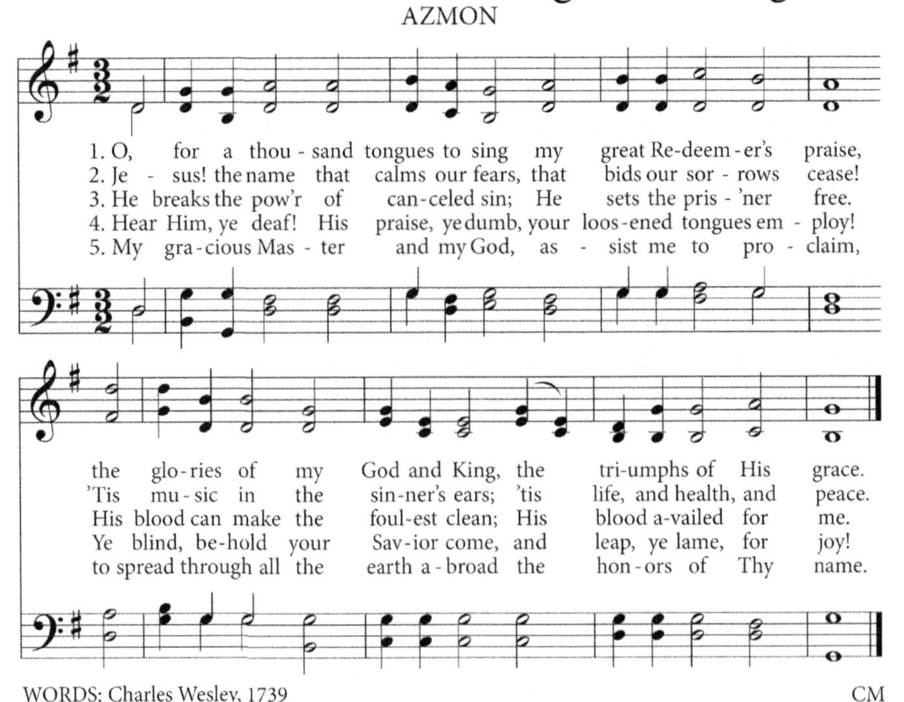

WORDS: Charles Wesley, 1739

CM

MUSIC: Carl G. Gläser, 1828; arr. Lowell Mason, 1839

Day 151: God Is My Strength

Psalms 71, 73

Notes

Psalm 71. This psalm expresses concern related to old age.

Verse 3. Continually. Psalm 71:1-3 is almost exactly the same as Psalm 31:1-3, with the exception that Psalm 71 adds the word "continually," emphasizing God's faithfulness to the aged author of the psalm.

Psalm 73. This psalm begins book three of the psalter and was written by Asaph.

Summary

Despite circumstances of old age or the trials of life, God remains faithful to his people. He may not deliver his people from every bad circumstance of life, but he will restore his people in the end and give them the strength to endure difficulties to his glory.

Questions for Reflection

1. In what ways has God been continually faithful to you?
2. How can the testimony of God's faithfulness to a person of old age be encouraging to us?
3. In what ways does God give us strength when we face difficult circumstances?

Day 152: Israel Falls

2 Kings 17; Psalm 74

Notes

2 Kings 17, Verse 6. Carried. According to Assyrian records, Assyria captured 27,290 Israelites and deported them to different locations in the empire. This occurred in 722 B.C.

Verse 19. Judah. The author includes Judah in his explanation for the exile, even though Judah's captivity would not occur for another 80 years.

Verse 24. Samaria. Samaria was resettled with foreigners, just as God had predicted (Deut 28). These people intermarried with Jews who had been left behind, become the Samaritans, who were later hated by New Testament Jews.

Summary

Israel's defeat was directly traceable to the sin of Jeroboam, which the nation never corrected. Out of convenience and pragmatism, Jeroboam had established syncretistic religious practices, mixing pagan worship with the truth worship of Yahweh. This had inevitably resulted in eventual idolatry, leading to the nation's ultimate demise.

Questions for Reflection

1. What led the people of Israel into idolatry?
2. In what ways do the problems of Israel resemble problems with Christian worship today?
3. Was God's punishment of Israel just?

Day 153: Hezekiah Destroys the High Places

2 Kings 18–19; Psalm 75

Notes

2 Kings 18, Verse 4. High places. Hezekiah was the first king of Judah to destroy the high places. Hezekiah's faithfulness to the Lord may have been the only thing keeping Judah from suffering the same fate that Israel had at the hand of Assyria.

Verse 17. The Tartan, the Rab-saris, and the Rabshakeh. Tartan is a title for the Assyrian general; Rab-saris was a palace official; and Rabshakeh meant "commander."

Verse 22. High places. The Rabshakeh wrongly assumed that Hezekiah's destruction of the high places limited the opportunity for the people to worship their God.

Chapter 19, Verse 2. Isaiah. This is the first reference in Kings to this important prophet. He had been ministering in Judah since the reign of Uzziah (Isa 6:1), 40 years prior.

Verse 31. The Zeal of the Lord. God promises a future messianic kingdom on the same basis as his promise of present deliverance of his people from Assyria.

Summary
In stark contrast to the syncretism and idolatry of Israel's kings, Hezekiah destroyed the high places and reestablished true worship at the Temple in Jerusalem. This pleased the Lord and provided Judah protection from the invading Assyrian armies.

Questions for Reflection
1. What differentiated Hezekiah's reign from the kings of the northern kingdom?
2. Why was Assyria successful in defeating Israel but unsuccessful in conquering Judah?
3. How does God's protection of Judah in this account give us hope for the establishment of the future messianic kingdom?

Day 154: God Delivers Jerusalem
2 Chronicles 32

Notes
2 Chronicles 32. This parallel account to 2 Kings 19 of Judah's deliverance emphasizes God's promise and protection of his people as a result of Hezekiah's faithfulness.

Verse 21. Angel. This is the Angel of the Lord, the pre-incarnate Son of God.

Summary
God protected his people, as he had promised, due to their faithfulness to him. This reveals a contrast to the present condition of the northern kingdom, but tragically, the southern kingdom of Judah would eventually also forsake the Lord and suffer the same destruction as Israel had.

Questions for Reflection
1. Why is it important to learn from the tragic mistakes of previous generations?

2. What does God's deliverance of Jerusalem from the Assyrians reveal about him?
3. In what ways have the previous generations of our own day forsaken God?

Day 155: Hezekiah Prays for Longer Life

2 Kings 20; Psalm 79

Notes

2 Kings 20, Verse 9. Shadow. This is the first mention in Scripture of a particular way of marking time, likely referring to some sort of sun-dial.

Verse 12. Envoys. Second Chronicles 32:31 indicates also that Merodach-baladan sent messengers because he was interested in what happened with the reversal of the sundial.

Summary

Hezekiah's faithfulness to the Lord is rewarded once again through the extension of his life despite his terminal illness. Yet his prosperity led him to flaunt his wealth before the Babylonians, leading Isaiah to prophesy the coming captivity a century later as a direct result of the corrupt leadership of Hezekiah's son and other descendants.

Questions for Reflection

1. Why did God agree to extend Hezekiah's life?
2. Why did Hezekiah show the Babylonians all of his wealth?
3. Will God keep his promise and send Judah into Babylonian captivity?

Week 32: Jeremiah

Weekly memory verse:
Jeremiah 23:5 - "Behold, the days are coming, declares the LORD, when I will raise up for David a righteous Branch, and he shall reign as king and deal wisely, and shall execute justice and righteousness in the land."

Weekly hymn:
"O Come, O Come, Emmanuel"

Weekly catechism:
What is adoption?
Adoption is an act of God's free grace in which I am received as a child of God with all its rights and privileges.

O Come, O Come, Emmanuel

VENI EMMANUEL

WORDS: Latin hymn, 12th cent.; tr. John M. Neale, 1851 — 8.8.8.8.8.8

MUSIC: Ancient plainsong, 13th cent.; adapt. Thomas Helmore, 1854

Day 156: Manasseh and Amon

2 Kings 21; Psalm 80

Notes

2 Kings 21, Verse 2. Evil. Although Hezekiah was one of the most righteous kings of Judah, and despite the fact that Hezekiah carefully prepared his son to be king, Manasseh turns out to be the most evil king in Judah's history, inevitably resulting in exile.

Verse 16. Innocent blood. This sin could have been child sacrifice, mistreatment of the weak, or persecution of God's prophets. It was likely a combination of all three.

Psalm 80. This psalm was likely written by someone in Jerusalem as he observed the defeat of the northern tribes in 722 BC.

Summary

God showed great mercy to his people during their history, often overlooking their idolatry and rebellion and providing them countless opportunities to turn back to him. Yet eventually their sin reached a climax wherein God's just justice required punishment. The evil reigns of Manasseh and Amon finally reach the point that God promises swift judgment.

Questions for Reflection

1. Why do you think Manasseh forsook God, even though his father raised him to be righteous?
2. In what ways did Manasseh's sin reach a point of horror unlike any king before him?
3. Did Judah's sin and God's promise of judgment nullify God's promises of future blessing for Israel?

Day 157: Josiah Repairs the Temple

2 Kings 22; Psalm 81

Notes

2 Kings 22, Verse 1. Reign. During Josiah's reign, Babylon defeated Assyria (612-609 BC), becoming the new superpower of the ancient Near East. Josiah was the last good king of Judah.

Verse 3. Eighteenth year. Josiah was twenty-six years old.

Verse 14. Huldah. Not much is known of this prophetess, and it was very unusual for God to speak to the nation through a woman in this way. Usually, God did something like this to condemn the lack of male leadership in the land (cf. Deborah, Judg 5).

Psalm 81. This psalm was likely intended to be used during the Feast of Tabernacles.

Summary
One final time in Judah's history, a righteous king leads the people back to following the Lord. Yet, the fate of Judah had already been established; because of the nation's pattern of idolatry against the Lord, judgment was inevitable. Yet because of king Josiah's righteousness, God spared him from having to witness the full judgment himself.

Questions for Reflection
1. In what ways did Josiah reveal his sincere desire to follow God's commands?
2. Why did the nation deserve judgment?
3. What did God's withholding judgment until Josiah's death reveal about him?

Day 158: Josiah's Reforms
2 Kings 23; Psalm 82

Notes
2 Kings 23, Verse 2. Book of the covenant. This was likely a reading of the entire Pentateuch, from Genesis 1 through Deuteronomy 34.

Verse 4. Bethel. Bethel was one of two places where Jeroboam had originally established syncretistic worship (1 Kgs 12:28–33); Josiah used the ashes of the burnt idols to desecrate the origin of false worship in the land.

Verse 10. Topheth. This title means "a drum" and designates the dominant instrument used during pagan worship, specifically child sacrifice (see Jer 7:31).

Summary

No king before or after Josiah, including David himself, was as righteous in following the Lord's commands and leading the people back to his worship. Josiah accepted nothing less than complete elimination of every false worship element and priest and complete obedience to every aspect of true worship, something that had never happened in Israel's history up to this point. It is remarkable that God had not judged the nation sooner.

Questions for Reflection

1. Why was Josiah so concerned to eliminate and even desecrate every remaining pagan high place and worship element?
2. Was Josiah just to execute false priests?
3. Why did God judge Judah despite Josiah's righteous reforms?

Day 159: The Call of Jeremiah

Jeremiah 1; Psalm 84

Notes

Jeremiah 1, Verse 2. Days. Jeremiah ministered from Josiah's reign (627 BC) to the last king of Judah, Zedekiah (586 BC).

Verse 3. Fifth month. Babylon would begin taking Judeans into captivity in the fifth month of 586 BC (July-August).

Verse 6. Youth. Jeremiah was 20-25 years old when he was called. This would make him 60-65 years old when Jerusalem fell and 85-90 when king Jehoiachin was released from prison in Jeremiah 52:31.

Summary

Jeremiah's role was to pronounce final judgment upon Judah, rendering him the title of "weeping prophet." Yet his prophecy also focuses on the need for repentance and the redemption that is possible for those who do. In the midst of sin's condemnation, hope always comes from the mercy and grace of God.

Questions for Reflection

1. Why did God send Jeremiah to call the people to repentance, even while they were being defeated and exiled?
2. Why did Jeremiah's words have authority, despite his youth

and inexperience?
3. What is significant about God's message that he knew Jeremiah even before he formed him (v. 5)?

Day 160: Jeremiah's Prophecy

Jeremiah 18–19

Notes

Chapter 18, Verse 12. Vain. Jeremiah's prophesy is full of apparent paradoxes. He calls them to repentance, but they cannot repent.

Verse 14. Crags of Sirion. This likely refers to the mountains of Lebanon, from which coon streams flowed. Israel had forsaken God's cool water for broken cisterns (2:13).

Chapter 19, Verse 1. Elders . . . priests. God chosen witnesses for the nation to observe his pronouncement of judgment.

Verse 6. Topheth. This word meant, "drum," and referred to the pagan worship practices that had come to characterize Judah.

Summary

Jeremiah called the people to repentance, even as they were facing impending judgment. God's mercy and grace are always on display, perfectly combined with his just judgment of sin. Jeremiah knew the people would not turn back to God and would be destroyed, and he even prayed for their judgment, but that didn't keep him from also proclaiming forgiveness for those who repent.

Questions for Reflection

1. What images do God and Jeremiah use to describe the people's sin and coming judgments?
2. Why did they use images to communicate the message to the people?
3. Who was ultimately responsible for the judgement upon the people's sin?

Week 33: Babylon Invades Judah

Weekly memory verse:
Psalm 86:11 – "Teach me your way, O Lord, that I may walk in your truth; unite my heart to fear your name."

Weekly hymn:
"Glorious Things of Thee Are Spoken"

Weekly catechism:
What is sanctification?
Sanctification is the work of God's Spirit by which I am renewed after the image of God and am enabled more and more to die to sin and live to righteousness.

Glorious Things of Thee Are Spoken

AUSTRIAN HYMN

WORDS: John Newton, 1779

MUSIC: Franz J. Haydn, 1797

8.7.8.7.D

Day 161: Daniel Taken to Babylon

Daniel 1; Psalm 85

Notes

Daniel 1, Verse 1. Third year. In 605 BC, Nebuchadnezzar initiates what would be the first of three invasions of Judah and deportation of some of its inhabitants. In this first deportation, he deported young noble men like Daniel (Belteshazzar), Hananiah (Shadrach), Mishael (Meshach), and Azariah (Abednego).

Verse 2. Shinar. Another name for Babylon.

Verse 4. Chaldeans. Another name for Babylonians.

Verse 8. Defile. The king's food and wine were dedicated to pagan idols, and thus consuming this food would have been religious compromise.

Verse 21. Cyrus. Cyrus was the king of Persia, who would conquer Babylon in 538 BC.

Summary

In fulfillment of Jeremiah's prophecies, Babylon began a series of invasions and deportations of Judah. Yet this first invasion provides examples of some of God's people who, despite the general apostasy of the nation as a whole, personally remained faithful to the Lord, even in the midst of exile.

Questions for Reflection

1. Was it right for Daniel to allow himself to be educated in the language and literature of the Chaldeans?
2. Would it have been right for Daniel to eat the king's meat and wine?
3. What makes some activities of unbelieving people acceptable for Christians, and other activities of unbelievers not acceptable?

Day 162: Nebuchadnezzar's Dream

Daniel 2; Psalm 86

Notes

Daniel 2, Verse 36. Interpretation. Nebuchadnezzar's dream pictures five empires that would rule over Israel: Babylon, Medo-Persia, Greece, Rome, and a revived Rome.

Verse 41. Toes. The ten toes represent rules during the period prior to Christ's second coming, when we will come and destroy them. *Iron.* This represents a revived Roman Empire.

Verse 44. Kingdom. This refers to the future millennial kingdom.

Verse 45. Stone. The stone is the Messiah, who will reign over the kingdom.

Summary

God uses Nebuchadnezzar's dream to picture a great statue that represents Israel's future. Five empires would rule over Israel: Babylon, Medo-Persia, Greece, Rome, and a revived Rome. But the dream also reveals that one day, the Messiah would come again and crush Gentile power, resulting in the establishment of his millennial kingdom on earth, and eventually the eternal kingdom.

Questions for Reflection

1. How many of the empires prophesied in Nebuchadnezzar's dream have already come and gone? Which are yet to come?
2. Has Christ yet definitively crushed Gentile rule and established his kingdom on earth?
3. What hope do we have that Christ will indeed one day rule on the earth?

Day 163: Jeremiah's Warning and Imprisonment

Jeremiah 24, 37

Notes

Chapter 24, Verse 1. Taken into exile. This is the second deportation of Judeans in 597 BC.

Verse 6. Bring them back. A remnant does return to Judah in 538 BC, but this promise has greater fulfillment yet to come when the Messiah unites his people in one nation in the Kingdom (see Rom 11:1-5, 25-27).

Chapter 37, Verse 13. Hananiah. Jeremiah had prophesied Hananiah's death (28:16), and so Hananiah's grandson is taking revenge on Jeremiah.

Summary

As Jeremiah had prophesied, Babylon continues to deport the people of Judah as God's punishment for their many years of rebellion and idolatry. Yet Jeremiah's warnings continue to go unheeded, and even Jeremiah suffers as a result of their continued rebellion. Yet one day, God has promised that a remnant would return, and his kingdom would be fully established.

Questions for Reflection

1. Why do the people continue refusing to repent, even as some of them are taken into captivity?
2. Was Jeremiah's ministry a failure?
3. How do we know God will keep his promise that one day a remnant will return, and he will establish his kingdom?

Day 164: The Fiery Furnace

Daniel 3

Notes

Verse 1. Image of gold. This statue, which was supposed to picture the greatness of Nebuchadnezzar, was 90 feet tall (likely including a large base) and 9 feet wide.

Verse 13. Since Daniel is not mentioned here, he must have been absent at the time. Surely he would have joined in refusing to bow had he been present.

Verse 25. A Son of the gods. The king apparently recognized the fourth man as a heavenly being. This possibly could have been the pre-incarnate Son of God.

Verse 28. God. Nebuchadnezzar was certainly not proclaiming allegiance to God as the one and only true God, but rather simply adding Yahweh to the pantheon of gods he worshiped.

Summary

Even in the midst of captivity, God reveals both that a remnant of people who are faithful to him still exists and that he remains faithful to those who follow his commandments. Not even fire had power over these people, demonstrating God's supernatural protection of his people.

Questions for Reflection

1. What may have motivated Nebuchadnezzar to construct the golden image and demand worship?
2. If only three Jews refused to bow to the image, what were other Jews who were present doing?
3. Why did God protect Shadrach, Meshach, and Abednego?

Day 165: The Fall of Jerusalem

Jeremiah 38–39

Notes

Chapter 38, Verse 6. Cistern. Cisterns were water reservoirs typically cut out from rock with a small opening at the top and a large, hollowed out inside for holding water.

Verse 27. Answered them. Jeremiah did not lie, but rather withheld details of the conversation, information to which they had no right.

Chapter 39, Verse 14. Gedaliah. This was a supporter of Jeremiah (26:24) who was also loyal to Nebuchadnezzar; thus he was named governor of those left in the land. He is later murdered in Chapter 41.

Summary

All of Jeremiah's prophesies finally come to completion in the final invasion of Jerusalem by Nebuchadnezzar. Jeremiah's proclamation of victory for Babylon is considered treason, and he is punished accordingly. Yet Jerusalem falls, the king's eyes are removed, and he and much of the remaining people are taken captive into Babylon, and Jeremiah is freed.

Questions for Reflection

1. Why did the people put Jeremiah in a cistern?
2. What evidence is in this passage demonstrating King Zedekiah's weakness and lack of character?
3. What in this passage shows God's care for his prophet?

Week 34: Babylonian Captivity

Weekly memory verse:

Ezekiel 37:27-28 - "My dwelling place shall be with them, and I will be their God, and they shall be my people. Then the nations will know that I am the Lord who sanctifies Israel, when my sanctuary is in their midst forevermore."

Weekly hymn:

"Jerusalem, My Happy Home"

Weekly catechism:

What do you believe about the Holy Spirit?

The Holy Spirit is true and eternal God together with the Father and the Son.

Jerusalem, My Happy Home

LAND OF REST

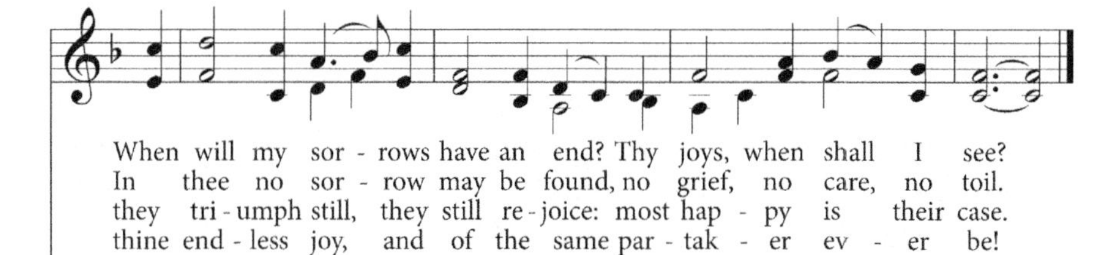

WORDS: F. B. P., 16th cent.; based on Augustine of Hippo, 5th cent. CM
MUSIC: Traditional American melody; arr. Annabel M. Buchanan, 1938

Day 166: Jeremiah Taken to Egypt

Jeremiah 43; Psalm 88

Notes

Jeremiah 43, Verse 1. Finished speaking. Jeremiah had warned the people in chapter 42 not to go to Egypt. Despite the fact that everything Jeremiah had prophesied to this point had come to pass, the people did not listen to him.

Verse 7. Tahpanhes. This is in the eastern delta region of Egypt.

Verse 11. Strike the land. This prophesies Babylon's invasion of Egypt in 568/67 BC.

Summary

God did not want his people to trust in their own strategies for safety or in the protection of other nations. Yet despite Jeremiah's warnings that the people not escape to Egypt for protection, they went anyway. God responded by using Jeremiah to prophesy that one day Babylon would destroy even Egypt. God's people could not escape the judgment due them.

Questions for Reflection

1. Why did the people want to go to Egypt?
2. Why didn't God want them to go to Egypt?
3. What was the result of the people's escape to Egypt?

Day 167: Jerusalem Captured and Burned

Jeremiah 52; Psalm 89

Notes

Jeremiah 52, Verse 1. Jeremiah. This is not the same man as the author of the book.

Verse 4. Ninth year. This chapter is another recounting of the fall of Jerusalem. So important is this event that it is recorded four times in the Old Testament (2 Kgs 25, 2 Chr 36:11–21, Jer 39:1–14, Jer 52).

Verse 28. Carried away. This is the third of four deportations to Babylon: 1) the first deportation in 605 BC marking the beginning of 70 years in exile, 2) the second in 597, 3) the third in 586, and 4) a final deportation in 582-61.

Verse 31. Jehoiachin. Jehoiachin had been taken to Babylon in 597. Here he is released from prison after Nebuchadnezzar's death, revealing God's faithfulness to the Davidic line.

Summary

Just judgment against Judah is recounted here. The city is destroyed, the Temple is burned to the ground, and all of the sacred implements are taken away. Nebuchadnezzar kills many of the leaders of Judah and takes others back to Babylon. God had remained faithful to his promise that if the people continue to rebel against him, he would send them into captivity. Yet God also remained faithful to the promise he had made to David by protecting the Davidic line in Jehoiachin.

Questions for Reflection

1. Was God just in judging Israel and Judah?
2. How was God able to both fulfill his promise of judgment upon Israel's rebellion while at the same time fulfill his promises to David?
3. How do we know God would continue to keep all of his promises?

Day 168: Israel in Exile

Ezekiel 37; Psalm 137

Notes

Ezekiel 37, Verse 1. Me. Ezekiel was a prophet to Israel during their captivity. He was taken captive at the age of 25 and called into ministry in 593 BC at the age of 30. This is one of Ezekiel's most well-known visions concerning Israel's future. It occurred the night before a messenger came with news that Jerusalem had been destroyed.

Verse 1. Bones. The dry bones in the vision picture the apparently dead Israel.

Verse 14. Spirit. God promised to one day revive dead Israel by putting his Spirit in them as a nation.

Verse 22. One king. The Messiah King will one day rule over a newly united nation of Israel in its land.

Verse 26. Covenant of peace. This is the New Covenant.

Summary
As a message of hope for Hebrew exiles, God gives Ezekiel a vision promising the full restoration of Israel in her land, newly united and cleansed from sin, and under the rule of the Davidic Messiah. Although Israel soon returns to its land, this prophecy will not be completely fulfilled until Jesus Christ comes again and rules over Israel for 1,000 years in the promised land.

Questions for Reflection
1. How would this vision give hope to Israel in Exile?
2. How does Jesus Christ begin to fulfill these promises in his first coming?
3. Which of these promises have yet to be fulfilled? When will they come to pass?

Day 169: Nebuchadnezzar's Conversion
Daniel 4; Psalm 91

Notes
Daniel 4, Verse 2. Most High God. This chapter begins and ends with Nebuchadnezzar's praise of God, and the middle gives the explanation for what led him to praise God.

Verse 9. Spirit. This should likely be translated "Spirit of the Holy God" in reference to the true God since no pagan worshipers believed their gods to be holy.

Verse 16. Beast. A disease later called lycanthropy causes a person to think he is an animal.

Summary
God demonstrates his ultimate power over all nations in converting the very man who defeated his people. After Daniel interprets the dream that prophesies what will happen, God smites Nebuchadnezzar with a maddening disease for seven years in response to his

pride. By the grace and mercy of God, Nebuchadnezzar confesses his sin to God and converts to the worship of Yahweh before his death.

Questions for Reflection

1. Why did God show mercy even to Nebuchadnezzar?
2. What are indications in Nebuchadnezzar's account of what happened that reveal he was likely truly converted?
3. What would this account have revealed to captive Israelites?

Day 170: The Handwriting on the Wall

Daniel 5, 9

Notes

Chapter 5, Verse 1. Belshazzar. This occurs in 539 BC, over two decades after his father, Nebuchadnezzar's death.

Verse 25. Writing. "Mene" means "appointed." "Tekel" means "weighed." "Peres" means "divided."

Verse 30. Darius. Possibly a title for Persian king Cyrus. Legend says that Persian troops dug trenches beneath the walls that diverted the river flowing into the city, thus gaining them quick passage into the palace.

Chapter 9, Verse 24. Seventy weeks. These are seventy weeks of years spanning the periods from Persian king Artaxerxes's decree to rebuild Jerusalem in 445 BC (Neh 2:1–8) to the Messiah's future kingdom. It prophesies 69 weeks (or 483 years) until Messiah would come, which was fulfilled at Christ's triumphal entry into Jerusalem in 30 AD, and a final 70th week, which some see as being fulfilled in a future seven-year Great Tribulation period.

Summary

God uses Persia to defeat Babylon as judgment for what they did to Israel. Yet God continued to protect Daniel and used him in Persia as well. Daniel prays for the peace and security of Israel, and God responds by giving Daniel a vision that promises a coming Messiah who would one day restore Israel's kingdom.

Questions for Reflection

1. How did Belshazzar demonstrate that he did not, like his father, convert to the worship of Yahweh?
2. Why did God allow Persia to defeat Babylon?
3. How does Daniel's vision give Israel hope?

Week 35: Return from Exile

Weekly memory verse:

Romans 8:5 - "For those who live according to the flesh set their minds on the things of the flesh, but those who live according to the Spirit set their minds on the things of the Spirit."

Weekly hymn:

"Spirit of God, Descend upon My Heart"

Weekly catechism:

What does the Holy Spirit do for you?

The Holy Spirit unites me to Christ, convicts me of sin, comforts me, and sanctifies me.

Spirit of God, Descend upon My Heart

MORECAMBE

WORDS: George Croly, 1867
MUSIC: Frederick C. Arkinson, 1870

10.10.10.10

Day 171: Daniel and the Lion's Den

Daniel 6; Psalm 92

Notes

Daniel 6, Verse 1. Darius. Probably a title for king Cyrus. God calls Cyrus his "shepherd" and "anointed" who would fulfill God's purposes (Isa 44:28, 45:1). *Satraps.* Administrators of Cyrus's kingdom.

Verse 8. The Law. According to Medo-Persian law, not even the king could revoke a decree that he made.

Verse 10. Prayed. The practice of praying three times a day had been established by David (Ps 55:16–17), and praying toward Jerusalem was according to Solomon's desire (1 Kgs 8:44–45).

Summary

God continued to protect and honor Daniel, even with his new captors in Persia. God apparently used Daniel and his faithfulness to motivate Cyrus around the same time as this event to allow the people to return to Jerusalem. Even in the face of death, Daniel remained loyal to God and his commandments.

Questions for Reflection

1. Why was Daniel made an important leader in Persia?
2. Why were the other officials jealous of Daniel?
3. Why did God protect Daniel from the lions?

Day 172: The Exiles Return and Rebuild the Temple

Ezra 1, 3; Psalm 93

Notes

Ezra 1, Verse 1. Cyrus. According to the Jewish historian, Josephus, Daniel read Isaiah's prophecy that Cyrus would allow the people to return to Jerusalem (Isa 44:28) to king Cyrus himself, which motivated Cyrus to make the proclamation. *Jeremiah.* Jeremiah had prophesied that Israel would return from exile after a 70-year captivity in Babylon (Jer 25:11; 29:10–14).

Chapter 3, Verse 1. Came up. The people return to Jerusalem in three waves. The first is in 538 BC under the leadership of Zerubbabel and Jeshua (Ezra 1-6), the second is in 458 under the leadership of Ezra (Ezra 7-10), and the third is in 445 under the leadership of Nehemiah (Neh 1-13). The first return is during Cyrus's reign, and the latter two are during Artaxerxes's reign.

Verse 12. Wept. The old men who still remembered Solomon's temple, which had been destroyed 50 years earlier, recognized that this second temple did not compare in splendor to the first.

Summary

In the sovereignty of God and in fulfillment of promises he had made through his prophets Isaiah and Jeremiah, God moves king Cyrus to allow the people to return to Jerusalem and rebuild the temple. He had preserved all of the sacred worship implements, and a group returned to begin rebuilding. God remains faithful to all of his promises, including promises of judgement and blessing.

Questions for Reflection

1. What does the fact that God used Cyrus to fulfill his promises reveal?
2. What shows that the returning exiles learned lessons from God's judgment?
3. How does God display his steadfast love in this account?

Day 173: The Temple is Dedicated

Ezra 6; Psalms 94-95

Notes

Ezra 6, Verse 2. Ecbatana. A city 300 miles NE of Babylon where Cyrus had a summer home.

Verse 3. Sixty cubits. This was bigger than Solomon's temple (see 1 Kgs 6:2).

Verse 10. Pray for the life of the king. This reveals that Cyrus's motive was self-serving.

Verse 15. Adar, in the sixth year. This would have been February or March of 516 BC. The book of Esther fits in the period between the completion of the temple and the second return of God's people under Ezra (Ezra 7–10) in about 458 BC.

Psalm 95. According to Hebrews 4:7, this psalm was written by David, likely for a celebration of the Feast of the Tabernacles, in which the people remembered God's provision during their wilderness wandering.

Summary

God kept his covenant with his people by protecting them and sovereignly arranging for their return to their land, including the rebuilding of the temple. Even though Cyrus had his own selfish motivation for allowing the people to return, it was God who truly turned the king's heart to accomplish his purposes.

Questions for Reflection

1. What does Cyrus's self-serving decision to allow the people to return to their land reveal about the sovereignty of God?
2. Why was it important that the first thing the people did was to rebuild the temple?
3. What does this event reveal about God's faithfulness to his promises?

Day 174: Ezra Restores Israel's Worship of Yahweh

Nehemiah 8–9

Notes

Chapter 8, Verse 1. Ezra. This is the first reference to Ezra the priest in the book of Nehemiah, but he had been serving since 458 BC (see Ezra 7–10).

Verse 3. Early morning until midday. This would have taken approximately six hours.

Verse 8. Gave the sense. This reading and explanation of Scripture provides the foundation for expositional preaching of God's Word.

Verse 18. Solemn assembly. This is the most common phrase used in the Old Testament to describe corporate worship services in the temple.

Summary

The people of Israel responded to God's faithfulness toward them by obeying what he had commanded them. They read his Law, the leaders explained what it meant, and the people responded with confession and worship. This is a great model for corporate worship: it is based on God's revelation, it leads to confession of sin and commitment to God, and it is filled with the reading and explanation of the Word of God.

Questions for Reflection

1. In what ways had the people of Israel learned their lesson for why they had been in exile?
2. How does this passage serve as a model for expositional preaching?
3. How does this passage serve as a model for corporate worship services?

Day 175: Worship the Lord in the Splendor of Holiness

Psalms 96–98

Notes

Psalm 96. Much of this psalm, along with Pss 97, 98, and 100, are found in 1 Chronicles 16 at the dedication of the tabernacle on Mt. Zion. It anticipates the time when God's temple will cover the whole earth (see Isa 25:9; 40:9–10).

Verse 1. New song. A "new song" is the song of the redeemed (see Rev 5:9; 14:3).

Verse 9. Splendor of holiness. Beauty finds its foundation in the nature of God himself.

Psalm 97, Verse 1. Reigns. Although the Lord reigns sovereignly over all things now, the psalmist anticipates the time when he will rule directly on the earth, which will happen at the Second Coming of Christ (see Matt 24; Rev 19).

Psalm 98. This psalm joyfully anticipates the time when God will rule over all the earth.

Summary

God sovereignly rules over all things, but we still anticipate the day when he will rule perfectly on earth. This will happen when Christ comes again in glory to judge the living the dead. All sin and unbelief will melt before him, and his people will gather to worship him in the beauty of his holiness in the temple of his presence, which will cover the whole earth.

Questions for Reflection

1. What does the rule of God on earth mean for the wicked?
2. What does the rule of God on earth mean for the righteous?
3. How might these psalms apply to us as we still await the coming of the Lord?

Week 36: The Birth of Jesus Christ

Weekly memory verse:
Psalm 100:1-2 - "Make a joyful noise to the Lord, all the earth! Serve the Lord with gladness! Come into his presence with singing!"

Weekly hymn:
"All People That on Earth Do Dwell"

Weekly catechism:
Since you have been saved by grace alone through Christ, without any merit of your own, why must you yet do good works?
I must do good works because Christ also renews me by his Holy Spirit to be his image, so that I might show thankfulness to God for his mercy.

Psalm 100

All People That on Earth Do Dwell

OLD HUNDREDTH

WORDS: **Psalm 100**; st. 1-4, William Kethe, 1561; st. 5, Thomas Ken, 1674 — LM

MUSIC: Louis Bourgeois, *Genevan Psalter*, 1551

Day 176: Worship the Lord Who Reigns

Psalms 99-101

Notes

Psalm 99, Verse 1. Upon the cherubim. This is a reference to the ark of the covenant, the symbol of God's presence in the Holy of Holies.

Verse 5. Footstool. A metaphor for the temple in Jerusalem, the place of God's earthly presence and reign.

Psalm 101, Verse 2. When will you come to me? This is a pleading for God's active work in David's rule over Israel.

Summary

The Lord reigns sovereignly over all things. His rule is always just and right, continually displaying his steadfast, faithful love to his people. What a privilege it is for God's people to worship this faithful, sovereign God. Recognition of this reality should cause us to live faithfully before him out of gratitude and praise to him.

Questions for Reflection

1. What does it mean that the Lord reigns?
2. What should be our response to the faithful reign of God?
3. What does it mean to "walk with integrity of heart" (Ps 101:2)?

Day 177: The Birth of John the Baptist

Luke 1

Notes

Verse 5. Herod. This is Herod the Great, the first in a line of Herods named in Scripture. He is probably Idumean, a descendant of Esau's line, the Edomites. *Division of Abijah.* The priesthood was separated into 24 divisions, each of which served twice a year (1 Chr 24:4-19).

Verse 9. Burn incense. Only a select few priests were allowed to enter the temple; since the altar of incense, just in front of the veil to the Holy of Holies, was kept burning at all times, a priest was chosen to enter every morning and evening to offer the incense.

Verse 31. Jesus. The name means "Savior."

Verse 36. Your relative. Since Mary was a descendant of David (3:23-28), and Elizabeth was a descendant of Aaron (1:5), they must have been related through Mary's mother, who apparently was a descendant of Aaron.

Verse 46. Mary said. Verses 46-55 are known as Mary's "Magnificat" after the first word in the Latin translation. This is one of the oldest biblical songs (called Canticles) that continued to be sung later in the church.

Verse 47. My Savior. Mary recognized her own sinfulness and need for salvation through her Son.

Verse 68. Blessed. Verses 68-79 is another song traditionally sung in the church, known as the "Benedictus."

Summary

Prophecies concerning the birth of John the Baptist and Jesus break into what had been silence from God since the time of Israel's return to Israel from captivity. God was now beginning to fulfill the promises that he had made to his people long ago concerning bringing them salvation. John the Baptist preceded the Messiah as a prophet of old.

Questions for Reflection

1. Why do you think God chose to deliver the news about John the Baptist to Zechariah in the temple?
2. What does Mary's *Magnificat* reveal about her?
3. How do both Mary's *Magnificat* and Zechariah's *Benedictus* connect Old Testament prophesies to what was beginning to happen?

Day 178: The Birth of Jesus Christ

Luke 2:1-39; John 1:1-18

Notes

Luke 2, Verse 1. Caesar Augustus. This is Caius Octavius, the heir of Julius Caesar. Octavius came to power as the first emperor of Rome in 44 BC. His reign over the entire Mediterranean region ushered in a great *Pax Romana*—a period of peace in the empire.

Verse 3. Own town. Each head of household had to return to the place of his tribe's origin for the census.

Verse 7. Manger. A feeding trough for animals. Where, exactly, Jesus was born is not stated explicitly in Scripture. He may have been born in a cave that was used to shelter animals.

Verse 8. Shepherds. Shepherds tended grazing sheep in the area all year round to provide sacrifices for the temple in nearby Jerusalem, so it is impossible to determine the time of year Jesus was born simply from this fact.

Verse 11. Christ. The Greek equivalent to "Messiah."

Verse 14. Glory to God. This is the third canticle in Luke's gospel that has traditionally been sung by Christians since the early church.

Verse 29. Now . . . depart. Known as the *Nunc Dimittis* from the Latin translation of these words, this is the fourth Lucan canticle.

Summary

After thousands of years of prophecy, God's promised Messiah finally came to earth in the most unexpected form—a baby. All of God's predictions concerning this coming were perfectly fulfilled including being born in Bethlehem (Mic 5:2) of a virgin (Isa 7:14). This was no ordinary baby, however; he would become the salvation of his people, a light for revelation to the Gentiles.

Questions for Reflection

1. Why was it important that Jesus be of the tribe of Judah and born in Bethlehem?
2. What does the angel's song (*Gloria*) reveal about Christ's coming?
3. What does Simeon's song (*Nunc Dimittis*) reveal about Christ's coming?

Day 179: The Visit of the Magi

Matthew 2; Psalm 102

Notes

Matthew 2, Verse 1. Wise men. These "magi" were probably magicians or astrologers from Persia. Although three gifts are mentioned later, the number of magi is not indicated in the text.

Verse 2. Star. This could have been something natural that God providentially used to guide the magi or a supernatural occurrence.

Verse 11. House. By now Mary, Joseph, and Jesus had moved into a house in Bethlehem, likely waiting for both mother and child to grow stronger before traveling. This may have occurred shortly after Jesus's birth or up to two years later (see v. 16).

Verse 15. Death of Herod. This was likely 4 BC. The family may have been in Egypt for a short time before being free to return.

Summary

The events of Jesus's birth and early life continue to fulfill Old Testament prophecy concerning the Messiah including the fact that he would be worshiped by Gentiles (Ps 72:10) and that children would die during this time (Jer 31:15). God miraculously protected his Son and his earthly family.

Questions for Reflection

1. Why do you think God led the magi to Jesus?
2. What did the gifts of the magi signify about who they thought Jesus was?
3. In what ways do these events fulfill Old Testament prophecies?

Day 180: Jesus in the Temple

Luke 2:40–52; Psalm 103

Notes

Luke 2, Verse 42. Twelve years old. One year prior to a boy's *bar mitzvah*, which would occur on his thirteenth birthday, he would participate in the Jewish feasts as part of his preparation.

Verse 49. My Father's house. This indicates that even at this young age, Jesus knew who he was and the mission his Father had given him to accomplish.

Verse 51. Was submissive. Jesus perfectly obeyed the Law from the time he was born, which enabled him to impute righteousness to sinners who believe in him.

Summary

When the Son of God came to earth, he did not give up his divinity, but he did truly take on human flesh. He grew and matured just like any other boy, and he fulfilled all that the Law required of a Jewish boy, including visiting Jerusalem, celebrating Jewish festivals, learning the Torah, and even obeying his parents. This all prepared him to be the perfect sacrifice for the sins of his people.

Questions for Reflection

1. Why did Jesus go to Jerusalem?
2. Was Jesus being disobedient to his parents by remaining in Jerusalem? How do you know?
3. What did Jesus's response to Mary reveal about him?

Week 37: Jesus's Early Ministry

Weekly memory verse:
John 3:16 – "For God so loved the world, that he gave his only Son, that whoever believes in him should not perish but have eternal life."

Weekly hymn:
"Of the Father's Love Begotten"

Weekly catechism:
What is prayer?
Prayer is an offering up of my desires to God for things agreeable to his will, in the name of Christ, with confession of my sins and thankfulness for his mercies.

Of the Father's Love Begotten

DIVINUM MYSTERIUM

WORDS: Marcus Aurelius C. Prudentius, 4th cent.; tr. John Mason Neale, 1851 8.7.8.7.8.7.7

MUSIC: Plainsong, 13th cent.

Day 181: The Baptism and Temptation of Jesus

Matthew 3:1–4:11; Psalm 104

Notes

Matthew 3, Verse 1. Wilderness of Judea. This was the region directly west of the Dead Sea.

Verse 2. Kingdom of heaven. Matthew uniquely uses this phrase, "heaven" being a poetic reference to God. The phrase "kingdom of God" is used everywhere else in Scripture.

Verse 3. The prophet Isaiah. Isaiah had prophesied the coming of John the Baptist in 40:3.

Verse 6. Baptized. The practice of baptism was already known in Judaism, as Gentile proselytes would be baptized to symbolize their entrance into the community. The Greek word *baptizō* means "to dip."

Verse 7. Pharisees and Sadducees. The Pharisees were a "separated" sect of pious, legalistic orthodox Jews. The Sadducees were wealthy Levites who denied the supernatural, rejected Jewish tradition, and only accepted the Pentateuch as authoritative.

Verses 16–17. Jesus . . . Spirit . . . voice from heaven. This is one of the clearest evidences in Scripture that the One God exists in three distinct persons—Father, Son, and Spirit.

Verse 4. It is written. All of Jesus's replies to Satan are quotes from Deuteronomy (8:3, 6:16, and 6:13–14).

Summary

John the Baptist prepared the way for the Messiah, just as had been foretold by the prophet Isaiah. Jesus fulfilled all the Law of God by being baptized and resisting a three-fold temptation of Satan—temptation that parallels the kind of temptation that led to Adam and Eve's fall. Jesus's perfect life made possible the imputation of righteousness to those who trust him.

Questions for Reflection

1. What Old Testament prophet would have come to mind in the Jewish people when they saw John and how he lived?

2. What was John's essential message?
3. What does Jesus's baptism and temptation reveal about him?

Day 182: The Wedding at Cana

John 1:19-2:12

Notes

Chapter 1, Verse 51. You will see. This likely alludes to Jacob's dream about a ladder from heaven in Genesis 28:12, indicating that the disciples would likewise receive supernatural confirmation from God concerning who Jesus truly was.

Chapter 2, Verse 2. Wine. The Greek term for "wine" could refer to the juice freshly squeezed from grapes, to boiled wine, to fermented wine, or to fermented wine diluted with water. Since Scripture clearly prohibits intoxication (Prov 23:31), there is every reason to assume that what Jesus made from the water was fresh grape juice.

Verse 4. My hour. This phrase refers to Jesus's death, resurrection, and exultation (see John 7:30, 8:20, 12:23, 27, 13:1, 17:1). Old Testament prophecies promised that in the future kingdom, wine would flow freely (Jer 31:12, Hos 14:17, Amos 9:13-14). Jesus was telling Mary that his death needed to happen before the blessings of the kingdom.

Summary

Jesus began his earthly ministry by calling his disciples and by performing his first miracle, turning normal water into wine. Jesus promised his disciples very early that they would receive confirmation from God that he was truly the Messiah, and the miracle at Cana was only the first of many confirmations of his deity and purpose.

Questions for Reflection

1. How did Jesus's disciples know that he was the Messiah?
2. What did the fact that Mary went to Jesus for help reveal about what she thought of him?
3. How did the miracle at Cana confirm that Jesus was the Messiah?

Day 183: Jesus Speaks with Nicodemus

John 2:13–3:21; Psalm 106

Notes

John 2, Verse 15. Drove them all. The cleansing of the temple marked the beginning of Jesus's public ministry and affirmed the importance of pure worship. Jesus cleansed the temple a second time at the end of his ministry (Matt 21:12–17, Mark 11:15–18, Luke 19:45–46), further emphasizing how important true worship was to Jesus.

Verse 21. His Body. The New Testament uses the temple as a metaphor for Jesus, for individual Christians (1 Cor 6:19), and for the church (1 Cor 3:16–17, Eph 2:19–22).

Chapter 3, Verse 3. Born again. In the Greek this phrase can mean both, "born again" and "born from above." Jesus meant the latter, but Nicodemus clearly interpreted it as the former.

Verse 5. Water and the Spirit. The Greek construction here means "spiritual water." Jesus is stressing the need for spiritual cleansing.

Summary

Although the Jews obeyed the letter of the Law, their worship was ultimately corrupt. Jesus displayed his anger toward such corruption by cleansing the temple, and his encounter with Nicodemus revealed what a right relationship with God required. In order to gain eternal life with God, a person must be born from above and spiritually cleansed, which happens only when one believes in Jesus.

Questions for Reflection

1. Why did Jesus cleanse the temple?
2. Why must we be born from above?
3. What brings spiritual cleansing from sin?

Day 184: The Woman at the Well

John 4:1–42

Notes

Verse 4. Samaria. Samaria was the capital city of the northern kingdom after the nation split (1 Kgs 16:24). Later, the term came to describe the whole region. When Assyria invaded in 722 BC, they left some Jews in the region and brought other non-Jews into Samaria. This led to the Samaritans becoming a mixed group of Jews and non-Jews by intermarriage along with a syncretistic religion. For all of these reasons, the Samaritans came to be despised by pure Jews.

Verse 20. This Mountain. The Samaritans had developed their own worship practices on Mt. Gerizim.

Verse 23. Spirit and truth. These are the two interconnected components of biblical worship. "Spirit" refers to the immaterial, inward response of a person's heart, and "truth" refers to the correct object (God) and content of biblical worship. Worship is a spiritual response to God as a result of understanding biblical truth about God.

Summary

Worship is a spiritual response to God as a result of understanding biblical truth about God. Jesus's encounter with the Samaritan women gave him an opportunity to emphasize this essence of worship. With his coming, death, and resurrection, the essence of worship makes a specific location, like a mountain or temple, unnecessary when approaching God in worship. God is seeking those who will worship him in spirit and truth.

Questions for Reflection

1. Why was the fact that Jesus asked the woman for a drink so unusual?
2. Why did the woman ask Jesus about the proper way to worship?
3. What does it mean to worship in spirit and truth?

Day 185: Jesus Rejected at Nazareth

Luke 4:14–44; Isaiah 61

Notes

Luke 4, Verse 15. Synagogues. These centers of worship and teaching originated either during or shortly after the Babylonian captivity, when Nebuchadnezzar destroyed the temple. Even after the temple was rebuilt, they continued to be places where Jews would regularly gather in each town.

Verse 17. Scroll. It was customary in a synagogue service for a portion of Scripture to be read and then explained to the people. Jesus read from Isaiah 61.

Verse 23. Capernaum. Scripture does not give much information about what Christ did during his time in Capernaum, but John's gospel does mention his visit there (2:12; see also 4:46–54).

Isaiah 61, Verse 2. Day of vengeance. When Jesus read this passage in the synagogue, he stopped reading in the middle of verse two since the rest of the passage refers to his second coming, not his first.

Summary

Although Jesus's miracles confirmed that he was the Anointed One and his authoritative teaching astounded people, many of his own people rejected him. This was no surprise to God; he had predicted such a rejection in the Old Testament, a rejection that was indeed necessary so that Jesus could die in the place of sinners.

Questions for Reflection

1. What did Jesus mean when he said that Isaiah 61:1-2a was being fulfilled?
2. Why did Jesus mention Elijah helping the widow of Zarephath and Elisha healing Naaman?
3. Why did the people want to kill Jesus?

Week 38: Jesus's Ministry in Galilee

Weekly memory verse:

Colossians 1:18 - "And he is the head of the body, the church. He is the beginning, the firstborn from the dead, that in everything he might be preeminent."

Weekly hymn:

"When Morning Gilds the Skies"

Weekly catechism:

What is the church?
The church is a community of believers in which the gospel is truly preached and the ordinances are rightly administered.

When Morning Gilds the Skies

LAUDES DOMINI

WORDS: Sebastian Portner's *Katholisches Gesangbuch*, 1828;
tr. Edward Caswall, 1858

MUSIC: Joseph Barnby, 1868

6.6.6.6.6.6

Day 186: Jesus Heals Many in Galilee

Mark 1:21-45; Psalms 108-109

Notes

Mark 1, Verse 21. Capernaum. An important fishing village on the north shore of the Sea of Galilee, which Jesus used as his center of ministry while in Galilee.

Verse 29. The house of Simon and Andrew. Simon Peter, Andrew, James, and John were all from the nearby town of Bethsaida (John 1:44); they may have relocated to Capernaum when Jesus established his ministry there.

Psalm 108. David combined parts of two of his other psalms, Psalm 57 and 60, to compose this psalm.

Summary

Early in his ministry, Jesus began to cast out demons and heal many. This confirmed that he was truly the Messiah since Old Testament prophecies had predicted that after the Messiah came, there would no longer be any sickness. The complete fulfillment of such promises will not occur until Jesus returns to set up his Kingdom, but during his first coming he gave a foretaste of these Kingdom blessings in order to demonstrate who he truly was.

Questions for Reflection

1. What do the demon's statements reveal about demons' beliefs concerning Jesus?
2. Why did Jesus heal people while he was on earth?
3. Why do God's works on behalf of his people deserve praise?

Day 187: The Sermon on the Mount

Matthew 5-7

Notes

Chapter 5, Verse 1. Sat down. This was the normal teaching posture for a rabbi. This discourse, the first of five recorded in Matthew, is Christ's exposition of the true meaning of the Mosaic Law, which both condemned the legalism of the Pharisees and revealed the impossibility of perfect obedience, leading those who wished to enter Christ's Kingdom to rely solely on him for salvation.

Verse 3. Blessed. This word literally means "happy." It refers to a deep, long-lasting well-being enjoyed by the faithful.

Verse 17. Fulfill. Jesus fulfilled the Law by perfectly obeying it, establishing the positive righteousness necessary for sinners to be reconciled to God.

Verse 18. Not an iota, not a dot. These are two of the smallest markings in Hebrew writing.

Verse 32. Except on the ground of sexual immorality. There is much debate over what, exactly, this indicates. Some suggest this allows for divorce when one spouse has committed adultery; others argue that this does not allow for divorce, rather, it simply indicates that divorce does not cause adultery if adultery has already been committed.

Summary

Jesus taught that the Law requires perfect obedience in order for someone to enter his Kingdom. Yet in his thorough exposition of the true meaning of the Law, Jesus also reveals that it is impossible for any human being to perfectly obey it. Jesus, as the Son of God, was the only human ever able to fulfill the Law, and thus entrance into his Kingdom is possible only for those who receive his righteousness.

Questions for Reflection

1. What message did this discourse present for the Pharisees?
2. What message does this discourse present for those who wish to enter Christ's Kingdom by obeying the Law?
3. What is the only way to enter the Kingdom of Christ?

Day 188: Jesus Heals a Paralytic

Mark 2:1-12; Psalms 111-112

Notes

Mark 2, Verse 1. Home. This was likely Peter's home.

Verse 4. Roof. Homes at this time had flat roofs made of dried clay that were placed on supporting beams. Thus, it was easily removed to allow room to lower the paralytic.

Psalm 111. This psalm and the next are acrostic poems, with each of the its 22 lines corresponding to the 22 letters of the Hebrew alphabet.

Psalm 112, Verse 9. Horn. The horns of an animal signified strength.

Summary
Although forgiveness of sin does not always result in physical healing in this life, such healing will be a reality in the life to come. By both forgiving the paralytic's sins and healing him, Jesus was foreshadowing the blessings of his Kingdom. Forgiveness of sin, and future healing, are possible only by faith in Jesus Christ.

Questions for Reflection
1. What did the paralytic's friends' actions reveal about what they thought of Jesus?
2. Why did Jesus heal the paralytic?
3. Why did the people think Jesus had blasphemed God?

Day 189: Praise the Lord for Delivering Us
Psalms 113-116

Notes
Psalm 113. This psalm begins a series of six psalms known as the "Egyptian Hallel." "Hallel" is Hebrew for "praise." These psalms were associated with the Exodus from Egypt and thus traditionally sung as part of the celebration of Passover.

Psalm 114. This psalm has the most direct connection to the Exodus.

Summary
God demonstrates his grace, mercy, and steadfast love through what he has done, and each of these are marvelously displayed through the Exodus from Egypt. By recounting these things, we are led to praise the Lord as if we had been there ourselves.

Questions for Reflection

1. Why did the people of Israel regularly recount the events of the Exodus?
2. How does the Exodus from Egypt display the power of God?
3. How does the Exodus from Egypt display the grace and mercy of God?

Day 190: Jesus Raises the Dead to Life

Luke 7:1-17; Psalm 117

Notes

Luke 7, Verse 6. Not worthy. A Jew who entered a Gentile's house was considered unclean.

Verse 11. Nain. A town south east of Nazareth.

Verse 14. Touched the bier. Jews would have considered this defiling.

Summary

Not only does Jesus perform healing miracles, demonstrating that he is Messiah, but he literally reverses death itself. This begins to show the people that God himself is at work.

Questions for Reflection

1. What do the centurion's actions reveal about him?
2. Based on the centurion's actions, what is faith?
3. Why did fear seize the people after Jesus raised the boy to life?

Week 39: Jesus Heals and Forgives

Weekly memory verse:

Romans 1:16 - "For I am not ashamed of the gospel, for it is the power of God for salvation to everyone who believes."

Weekly hymn:

"Jesus! What a Friend for Sinners"

Weekly catechism:

What is the gospel?

The gospel is the good news that those who repent and believe in the death and resurrection of Christ for their sins will be forgiven.

Jesus! What a Friend for Sinners

HYFRYDOL

WORDS: J. Wilbur Chapman, 1910 — 8.7.8.7.D

MUSIC: Rowland H. Prichard, c. 1830

Day 191: Jesus Forgives a Sinful Woman

Luke 7:36-50; Psalm 120

Notes

Luke 7, Verse 37. Woman. There are many similarities between this account and when Mary, the sister of Martha and Lazarus, anointed Jesus (Matt 25:6-13; Mark 14:3-9; John 12:2-8), but this is a different woman, apparently a prostitute, and this event occurred in Galilee rather than Bethany. There is also little reason to identify this woman as Mary Magdalene (Luke 8:2), as some have argued. *Alabaster Flask.* Alabaster was a type of marble that was carved into a container for expensive ointments and perfumes. The container had to be broken to use the ointment.

Verse 41. Denarii. A denarius was a typical wage for a day's labor.

Verse 44. Water for my feet. It was customary for a host to wash his guest's feet, so this was a considerable oversight.

Verse 47. For she loved much. As the parable makes clear, her love is a result of unconditional forgiveness, not the other way around.

Psalm 120. Psalms 120-136 are known as "The Great Hallel," almost all of which are "Songs of Ascent" (Pss 120-134), songs Jews would sing as they ascended to Jerusalem for annual feasts.

Summary

God is able and willing to forgive any amount of sin, no matter how great, if sinners simply come to him in faith, calling out to him in their distress, and repenting of their sins. In fact, he loves to forgive great sinners because it glorifies him and those who have been forgiven much respond with deep love toward him.

Questions for Reflection

1. Why were the Pharisees upset about what the woman did?
2. In what ways did the woman demonstrate repentance and faith in Jesus?
3. Why does forgiveness from great sins result in great love for Christ?

Day 192: Jesus Speaks in Parables

Mark 4:1–34; Psalm 121

Notes

Mark 4, Verse 2. Parables. These were common forms of teaching in Judaism. Jesus began teaching in parables during the latter part of his ministry to both conceal the truth from the unbelieving crowds, to whom he would give no explanation, and make the truth clearer for his disciples, to whom he often later gave the interpretation privately (see Mark 13:10–17).

Verse 11. Secret. Literally, "mystery." A mystery refers to something hidden previously but now revealed in the New Testament.

Verse 20. Bear fruit. These are the only people who are truly converted in Jesus's parable. Each of the others ultimately reject the gospel, even those who have an initial emotional response that later proves to be superficial.

Summary

Up to this point in his ministry, Jesus had clearly proclaimed the need for repentance, and yet most of the people either rejected him outright or proved to be attracted only superficially to what they could get from him. Thus Jesus began to speak in parables as a way to conceal the truth from these unbelievers lest the truth further condemn them. At the same time, parables provided a powerful tool for making the truth clear to his own disciples.

Questions for Reflection

1. Why did Jesus speak in parables?
2. Does high emotion and outward enthusiasm prove that someone is truly a follower of Christ?
3. What proves that someone has truly accepted the gospel?

Day 193: Jesus Displays His Power

Luke 8:22–39; Psalm 107

Notes

Luke 8, Verse 22. The lake. This was the Sea of Galilee.

Verse 26. Gerasenes. A small town on the east shore of the Sea of Galilee.

Verse 27. A man. Matthew refers to two men; perhaps one of them was more dominant.

Psalm 107, Verse 3. Gathered in. This indicates that this psalm is likely post-exilic.

Summary

Jesus's miracles confirmed that he was Messiah and demonstrated his power over both the physical world and the spiritual world. For believers, this creates trust and confidence in Christ. For unbelievers, this creates fear.

Questions for Reflection

1. What was the disciples' response when Jesus calmed the storm?
2. What was the response of the demon-possessed man when Jesus cast out the demons?
3. What was the response of the people of Gerasenes?

Day 194: Worshiping in God's House

Psalms 122–124

Notes

Psalm 122, Verse 1. House of the Lord. The place where the presence of God dwelt and where the people drew near for worship. This was an appropriate expression for those ascending to Jerusalem for one of the annual worship festivals.

Verse 4. Decreed for Israel. God prescribed that the people ascend to Jerusalem for the feasts of Passover (Unleavened Bread), Weeks (Pentecost), and Booths (Deut 16:16).

Summary

Like Jews ascending to Jerusalem to worship in the house of the Lord, so Christians should delight in gathering as the house of God, the church (1 Tim 3:15). Christians should give as much priority and attention to faithful worship in the church as the Jews were supposed to give to worship festivals in the temple, for this is where we meet with God in a unique way to hear from his Word and respond with appropriate affection.

Questions for Reflection

1. What characterized a Jew's attitude as he ascended to Jerusalem for worship?
2. What are similarities between Jewish worship in the house of the Lord and Christian worship in the church, the house of God?
3. In what ways should we demonstrate worship in the church as a priority and joy?

Day 195: Jesus Restores Life and Heals the Sick

Matthew 9:18–32; Psalms 125–126

Notes

Mark 9, Verse 18. Ruler. This was Jairus (Mark 5:22; Luke 8:41), a ruler in the synagogue.

Verse 23. Flute players. This was customary for times of mourning.

Verse 24. Sleeping. Similar to what Jesus said about Lazarus, he is speaking metaphorically (John 11:11, 14).

Summary

Not only did Jesus display power over the physical earth and spiritual powers, he also demonstrated his power over death and disease. He confirmed that he was truly the Son of God and that those who have faith in him would be immediately healed of their spiritual death and disease, eventually to experience physical life and health for all eternity.

Questions for Reflection

1. What healed the woman?
2. Why did Jesus restore the girl's life?
3. What healed the blind men?

Week 40: True Repentance and Faith in Christ

Weekly memory verse:

John 6:40 - "For this is the will of my Father, that everyone who looks on the Son and believes in him should have eternal life, and I will raise him up on the last day."

Weekly hymn:

"I Sought the Lord"

Weekly catechism:

To whom should you preach the gospel?
I should preach the gospel to all people in all nations to the end of the earth.

I Sought the Lord

PEACE

WORDS: Jean Ingelow, 1878
MUSIC: George W. Chadwick, 1893

10.10.10.6

Day 196: Jesus Declares His Deity

John 5

Notes

Verse 1. Feast. John often organizes his narrative around specific Jewish feasts, but this is the only case in which he does not specifically name which feast was taking place.

Verse 2. Sheep gate. This was likely a small gate in the north wall of Jerusalem, near the northeast corner (see Neh 3:1, 31, 12:39).

Verse 3. Lay. This pool may have been fed by intermittent natural springs that caused the water to stir, and it may also have contained minerals that had medicinal value.

Verse 18. Equal with God. This passage is one of the clearest declarations of Jesus's deity. He claims to be equal with God in his person, works, power, judgement, and honor.

Summary

Jesus is God, which he clearly displayed through his miracles and declared through his teaching. Therefore, Jesus had the authority to forgive sin, heal the sick, and even supersede even the Law. Those who believe in him will receive eternal life, but those who reject him will be condemned.

Questions for Reflection

1. Why were the Jews upset with Jesus?
2. What are some ways Jesus declared his deity?
3. What are some ways Jesus displayed his deity?

Day 197: Jesus and His Apostles are Rejected

Mark 6:1-29; Psalm 127-128

Notes

Mark 6, Verse 11. Shake off the dust. This was a gesture that symbolized rejection of further contact based on the people's reaction toward them and their message.

Verse 13. Herod. This was Herod Antipas, the ruler of Galilee, son of Herod the Great.

Summary

Jesus brought a message of forgiveness for those who would repent and believe in him, and yet most of the people rejected his message and that of his apostles, even though their message was confirmed by many miracles. The result of such rejection was condemnation.

Questions for Reflection

1. Why did the people of Nazareth reject Jesus even though they were astonished by his teaching?
2. What did the response of the people to the apostles' message reveal about most of the people of Israel?
3. How are Herod's acts further illustrative of the rejection of the Jews?

Day 198: Jesus Feeds the Multitudes

John 6:1-21; Psalms 129-130

Notes

John 6, Verse 10. Five thousand. This was the number of men; adding women and children, the total may have been near 20,000.

Verse 19. Walking. This miracle further confirmed Jesus's deity and power over the physical world.

Psalm 130. This psalm encapsulates one of the most complete expressions of true repentance in all of Scripture, and the promise of forgiveness for those who do repent.

Summary

Despite the large crowds that followed Jesus, the feeding of the multitudes is another case of the people rejecting Jesus for who he really was. They clearly followed him out of desire for physical satisfaction or political revolution. Jesus wanted them to repent and believe.

Questions for Reflection

1. In what ways did the people demonstrate that they did not truly believe in Jesus as the Son of God?

2. Why were the people attracted to Jesus?
3. What are some aspects of true repentance found in Psalm 130?

Day 199: Jesus Is the Bread of Life

John 6:22-71

Notes

Verse 22. Crowd. This is the same crowd that Jesus had fed the day before.

Verse 53. Eat . . . drink. Jesus is speaking figuratively here, rather than literally. He is also not speaking of the ordinance of communion here, which he had not yet instituted. He is drawing a parallel between the necessity of eating and drinking for physical life with the necessity of accepting his death on the cross for spiritual life.

Summary

Jesus's second encounter with the crowd in Galilee further confirms their ultimate rejection of him as the Son of God. Even though he had displayed his power to them and declared to them his deity, they nevertheless demanded greater signs. Jesus was clear: those who would repent and believe in him would receive eternal life, yet because of the obvious hardness of their hearts, only those whom the Father drew would do so.

Questions for Reflection

1. How did the people demonstrate that they did not truly believe in Jesus?
2. What did Jesus mean by insisting that his people must eat his flesh and drink his blood?
3. How did the apostles' own reactions demonstrate the fact that God must work to bring people to faith in him?

Day 200: Jesus Predicts His Death and Resurrection

Mark 8:27-38; Psalms 131-132

Notes

Mark 8, Verse 29. This is finally a clear declaration of faith in Jesus as the Messiah.

Verse 30. Tell no one. As had already been clear, Jesus knew that the Jewish people who were attracted to him were so only out of a desire for political deliverance. In contrast, God's plan for Jesus was the cross, which brought spiritual deliverance.

Summary

Despite all of Jesus's teachings and displays of power, most of the people of Israel simply desired physical prosperity and political freedom, and thus they ultimately rejected Jesus as the true Messiah. Only a small few, epitomized in Jesus's apostles, truly believed that he was the Son of God.

Questions for Reflection

1. How did Peter's confession clearly demonstrate faith in Christ?
2. Why did Jesus need to suffer and die?
3. How is true belief in Christ described in this passage?

Week 41: The Light of the World

Weekly memory verse:

2 Corinthians 4:6 – "For God, who said, 'Let light shine out of darkness,' has shone in our hearts to give the light of the knowledge of the glory of God in the face of Jesus Christ."

Weekly hymn:

"O Splendor of God's Glory Bright"

Weekly catechism:

What are the ordinances of the church?

Baptism and the Lord's Supper were specially instituted by Christ to represent the benefits of union with him by visible and outward signs.

O Splendor of God's Glory Bright

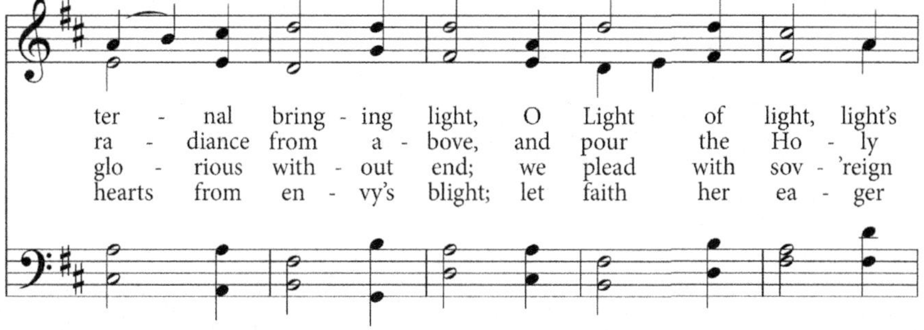

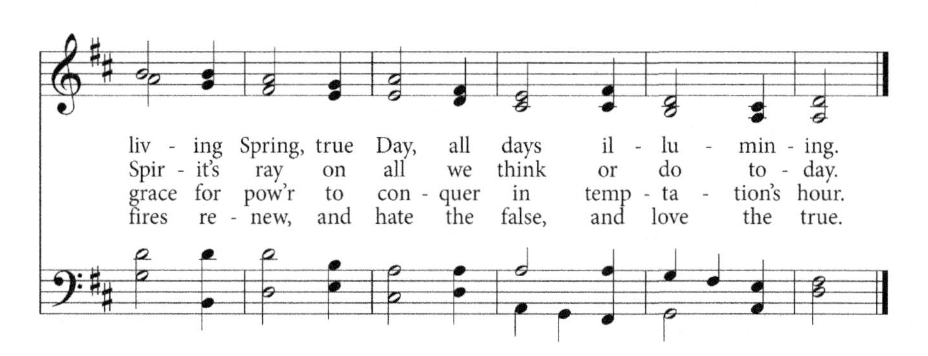

5. O joyful be the passing day
with thoughts as pure as morning's ray,
with faith like noontide shining bright,
our souls unshadowed by the night.

6. Dawn's glory gilds the earth and skies,
let Him, our perfect Morn, arise,
the Word in God the Father one,
the Father imaged in the Son.

WORDS: Ambrose of Milan, 4th cent.; tr. composite — LM
MUSIC: Trier manuscript, 15th cent.; adapt. Michael Praetorius, 1609

Day 201: The Transfiguration

Mark 9:1–29; Psalm 133

Notes

Mark 9, Verse 1. See the Kingdom of God. This refers to what comes next in the narrative of all three synoptic gospels, the Transfiguration, which provided a foretaste of the glory he will display at his second coming.

Verse 2. High mountain. Most likely Mt. Hermon, the highest mountain in the region. *Transfigured.* This word means, "to transform." Jesus displayed his divinity in a special way to the three disciples.

Verse 4. Elijah with Moses. Moses symbolized the Law, and Elijah symbolized the prophets, the two divisions of the Old Testament.

Verse 5. Three tents. Peter wanted to build three booths because he believed the Kingdom was coming at that moment, and he knew Zechariah's prophecy that in the Kingdom all the nations would come to Jerusalem each year to celebrate the Feast of Booths (Zech 14:16).

Verse 13. Elijah has come. The disciples were confused, trying to reconcile Malachi's prophecy that Elijah would come before the Day of the Lord (Mal 3:1, 4:5) with what they had just seen. Jesus declared that the prophecy had indeed been fulfilled in John the Baptist, who was representative of Elijah.

Summary

Jesus's Transfiguration provided a preview of the Kingdom of Christ that would be fully established at a later time. It fully confirmed that Jesus was the Messiah, the Son of God, affirmed verbally by God the Father. Jesus did this to reassure his disciples in the context of the increasing rejection of his Messiahship by the people of Israel and his own teaching concerning his impending suffering. None of what was about to happen, Jesus was showing them, would nullify the promises concerning the coming Kingdom. In fact, the events soon to follow would ensure the Kingdom.

Questions for Reflection

1. Why did the disciples need reassurance at this point in Jesus's ministry?

2. What did the Transfiguration confirm for the disciples?
3. How can this story help give us confidence in promises for the future that have yet to come to pass?

Day 202: Teachings of Jesus

Matthew 17:24-27; Luke 9:37-50

Notes

Matthew 17, Verse 26. Sons are free. Kings customarily did not charge their own sons tax, and so as God's Son, Jesus was technically exempt from the temple tax.

Luke 9, Verse 48. Child. Jesus used a child as a symbol of humble trust, which was a key characteristic of followers of Christ.

Summary

Greatness in the Kingdom of Christ is not attained by status or good works. Rather, Christ desires followers who will trust him completely and demonstrate the humility of a child. This is key to understand in light of the reality of the glory and majesty of the King just displayed on the Mount of Transfiguration. Yet even Jesus humbled himself and became a servant, which qualifies him to be the greatest in the Kingdom.

Questions for Reflection

1. Why was Jesus willing to pay the tax, even though he was technically exempt from paying it?
2. What stimulated the debate among the disciples about who would be greatest in the Kingdom?
3. In what ways did Jesus himself exemplify the kind of humility he requires of his followers?

Day 203: Temptation and Forgiveness

Matthew 18:7-35; Psalm 134

Notes

Matthew 18, Verse 8. Cut it off. This is hyperbole, exaggeration to make an important point.

Verse 10. Their angels. The pronoun here is collective, which signifies that angels guard believers in general, not that each believer has a personal guardian angel.

Verse 15. Sins against you. This becomes the basis for discipline within the church.

Verse 21. Seven times. Jewish rabbis taught that God only required forgiveness three times, so Peter thought he was being generous.

Summary
Jesus's teaching provided much important instruction regarding holy living that continues to apply to his followers. Christians today must flee temptation, removing anything that might cause them to sin. They must be careful not to cause others to sin through their actions. And they must be willing to forgive others who sin against them, just as they have been forgiven much.

Questions for Reflection
1. What are some areas in your life where you need to be careful about temptation to sin?
2. What are some areas in your life where you might cause others to sin?
3. How much should you be willing to forgive others who sin against you?

Day 204: Opposition to Jesus Increases
John 7:1-8:30

Notes
Chapter 7, Verse 2. Feast of Booths. This was the most popular of the three main Jewish feasts, meant to remind the people of their wilderness wanderings and used as a celebration of the ingathering of the harvest. It was often associated with both water and light, which Jesus uses as examples for his teaching (vv. 37-38, 8:12).

Verse 3. Brothers. Jesus's brothers were James, Joseph, Simon, and Judas (Matt 13:35). James later became the pastor of the Jerusalem church and wrote the NT epistle that bears his name, and Judas wrote

Jude. His brothers did not believe in him until after his resurrection (Acts 1:14; 1 Cor 15:7).

Summary

Jesus always knew that he would need to suffer and die in order to accomplish forgiveness for sins, but at this point in his ministry, he began teaching this subject more fully as the people's rejection of him increased. Many marveled at his teaching and believed in him, but many did not, including his own brothers, because they expected that the Messiah would come in glory and revolution.

Questions for Reflection

1. Why did Jesus enter Jerusalem secretly?
2. In what ways did Jesus use the occasion of the Feast of Booths to teach about who he was?
3. Why did Jesus's teaching cause some to believe and some to reject him?

Day 205: Jesus Heals a Man Born Blind

John 9

Notes

Verse 2. Who sinned. It was commonly assumed at the time that physical ailments were always caused by personal acts of sin.

Verse 7. Pool of Siloam. This pool was southeast of Jerusalem. Water used in the Feast of Booths was drawn from this pool.

Summary

Jesus's healing of the man born blind provides both one of the most picturesque examples of what happens when someone believes in Christ and an important exacerbation of the opposition to Jesus by the religious leaders of Jerusalem. Those who believe in Christ, who is the light of the world, receive spiritual sight; those who reject him are condemned in their spiritual blindness.

Questions for Reflection

1. Why were the religious leaders upset about Jesus healing the blind man?

2. In what ways did Jesus use this healing to teach important spiritual truths?
3. How is blindness an accurate picture of unbelief?

Week 42: Parables of the Kingdom

Weekly memory verse:

Luke 19:10 - "For the Son of Man came to seek and to save the lost."

Weekly hymn:

"Come, Christians, Join to Sing"

Weekly catechism:

What is baptism?

Baptism is an ordinance of the New Testament, instituted by Jesus Christ, to be a sign of the believer's fellowship with Christ in his death, burial, and resurrection.

Come, Christians, Join to Sing

MADRID

WORDS: Christian H. Bateman, 1843

MUSIC: Traditional Spanish melody; arr. David Emlyn Evans, 1927

6.6.6.6.D

Day 206: Traveling to Jerusalem

Luke 17:11-18:14

Notes

Chapter 17, Verse 14. Priests. The lepers would have had to be declared ceremonially clean by priests before rejoining society.

Verse 37. Corpse. Jesus's point in this passage is that the final judgment will come quickly and will be clearly evident to all when it comes.

Chapter 18, Verse 14. Justified. This is a legal term that means to be declared righteous. Those who believe in Christ are declared righteous by God because of Christ's righteousness imputed to them.

Summary

On his way to Jerusalem, Jesus both taught and illustrated the necessity of faith for forgiveness of sin and the fact that judgement would one day come upon those who did not believe. His deliverance of his people was not presently coming through political revolt, as many of the Jews believed. Rather, his suffering provided the means for spiritual deliverance, and one day he would return to bring judgement for those who failed to believe and full deliverance for his people.

Questions for Reflection

1. What was significant about the fact that the thankful leper was a Samaritan?
2. Why did Jesus need to suffer in order to bring complete deliverance for his people?
3. What was Jesus's point in the parable of the unjust judge?

Day 207: The Parable of the Good Samaritan

Luke 10:25-42

Notes

Verse 27. He answered. The lawyer summarized the Law exactly as Jesus had done on a previous occasion (Matt 22:37-40).

Verse 35. Two denarii. Two days' wages.

Verse 38. Village. This was Bethany, two miles east of Jerusalem, near the Mount of Olives.

Summary

Jesus emphasized that love for God and love for others is the core of our responsibility. Jesus turned the lawyer's self-righteous question on its head by insisting that perfect obedience to the Law meant showing kindness to anyone in need, even those normally considered enemies. He also taught, however, that while serving others is important, worshipping at Jesus's feet was even greater.

Questions for Reflection

1. Is it possible to perfectly keep all of God's Law?
2. Why were the Samaritan's actions so remarkable?
3. Does focus upon loving Christ mean we do not need to serve others?

Day 208: Invitation to Christ's Banquet

Luke 14; Psalm 135

Notes

Luke 14, Verse 2. Dropsy. An illness where fluid is retained in the body, sometimes caused by kidney failure or even cancer.

Verse 15. Eat bread. This man had a commonly held believe that only Jews would be at the heavenly feast. Jesus responded by illustrating that Gentiles would also be invited.

Verse 24. My banquet. Jesus's point was that Israel, which had been previously invited, largely rejected him, and so the invitation would be extended to those whom Jews normally considered unclean and unworthy.

Verse 26. Hate. Jesus is speaking with hyperbole. He does not mean that his followers must literally hate their family members, but rather that in comparison to their love and devotion for him, their love for family members would seem like hatred.

Summary

The Jews thought that by virtue of their heritage, they would automatically be given honor and exclusive rights to God's blessings. Jesus insisted, however, that those who rejected him, despite their ethnicity, would be left to judgment. Rather, only those who gave up everything to follow him would receive eternal blessing, even including Gentiles.

Questions for Reflection

1. Why were the Pharisees watching Jesus closely?
2. Why did the Jews think that they alone would enjoy God's blessings?
3. What did Jesus say was required to receive God's blessings?

Day 209: Parables of the Lost Sheep, Coin, and Son

Luke 15; Psalm 136

Notes

Luke 15, Verse 8. Coin. Literally, "drachma," a typical day's wage.

Verse 11. Two sons. This parable has general applicability to any sinner who repents, but it also applies more generally to the Pharisees' self-righteousness, represented by the elder son.

Psalm 136. For his steadfast love endures forever. This repeated refrain indicates that this psalm was likely sung responsively or antiphonally.

Summary

God eagerly desires to forgive repentant sinners, and in fact, Christ specifically came to seek and to save those who are lost. In contrast to the self-righteous Pharisees, those who recognize their own sin and come to God in repentance receive a welcome reception into God's arms.

Questions for Reflection

1. What do the parables of the lost sheep and coin reveal about God's desire to save lost sinners?

2. What does the parable of the lost son reveal about what is necessary in order to receive salvation?
3. What does the illustration of the elder son reveal about the Pharisees?

Day 210: Parables about the Kingdom

Matthew 13:44-52, 25:1-46

Notes

Chapter 13, Verse 44. Hidden. These two parables both teach that the Kingdom is hidden from most people, but those to whom it is revealed are willing to give up everything to possess it.

Verse 52. What is new and what is old. Jesus is saying that the disciples should not reject old truths just because he has given them new revelation; rather, they should understand the new revelation in light of the old, and the old in light of the new truth they have been given.

Chapter 25, Verse 15. Talents. A talent is a measure of weight, not a particular currency.

Verse 31. His glorious throne. This refers to Christ's earthly reign, and the judgment in view here precedes that reign and involves those still alive at his coming.

Summary

The promised Kingdom of God is something hidden from those who do not believe in Jesus Christ, but to those who do believe, it is the greatest possible treasure. When Christ comes again to rule his Kingdom, he will separate those who believe from those who don't. Those who believe will inherit the Kingdom, but those who do not will receive eternal punishment.

Questions for Reflection

1. How valuable is the Kingdom of God?
2. Does God judge based on how much we have or how faithful we are with what he has given us?
3. What determines who will inherit Christ's Kingdom?

Week 43: Holy Week

Weekly memory verse:

John 11:25 – "Jesus said to her, 'I am the resurrection and the life. Whoever believes in me, though he die, yet shall he live.'"

Weekly hymn:

"My Song Is Love Unknown"

Weekly catechism:

What is the duty of those who are rightly baptized?

It is the duty of those who are rightly baptized to join themselves to some visible and orderly church of Jesus Christ.

My Song Is Love Unknown

LOVE UNKNOWN

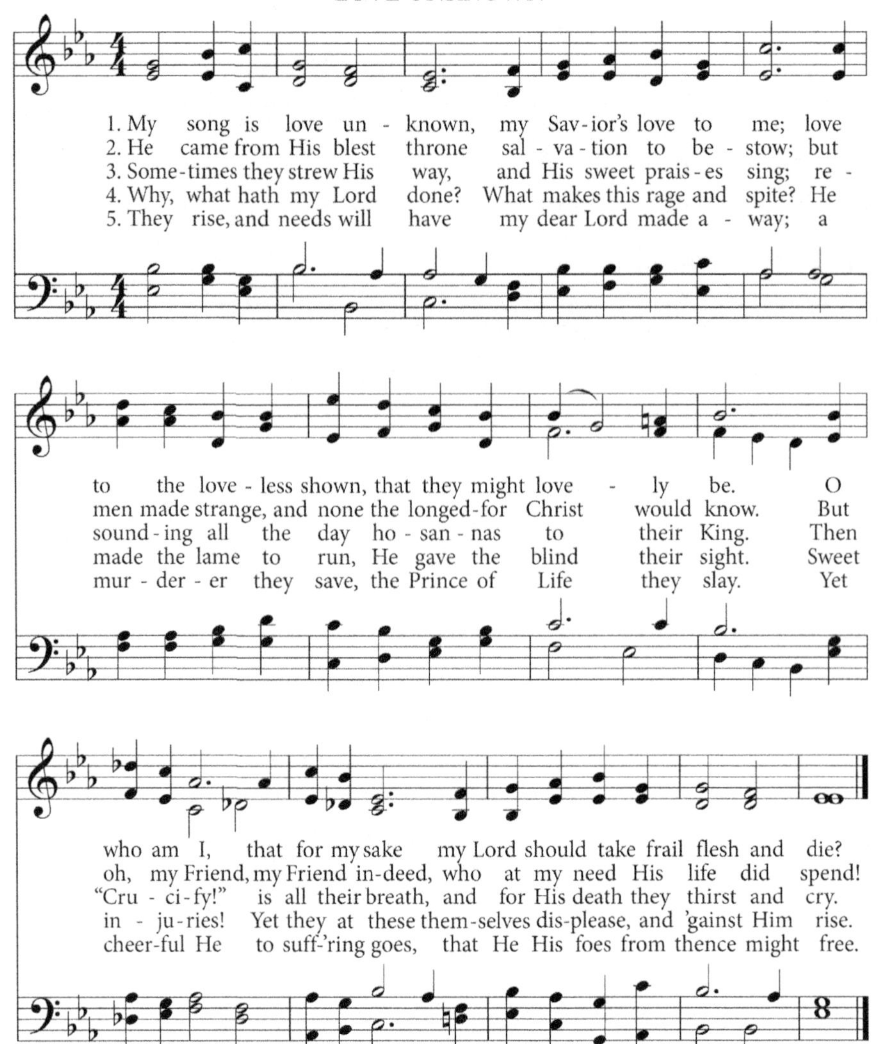

6. In life, no house, no home
   my Lord on earth might have;
   in death, no friendly tomb
   but what a stranger gave.
   What may I say? Heav'n was His home,
   but mine the tomb wherein He lay.

7. Here might I stay and sing,
   no story so divine;
   never was love, dear King,
   never was grief like Thine.
   This is my Friend, in whose sweet praise
   I all my days could gladly spend.

WORDS: Samuel Crossman, 1664
MUSIC: John Ireland, 1918

6.6.6.6.4.4.4.4

Day 211: Jesus Raises Lazarus from the Dead
Luke 16:19–31; John 11

Notes
Luke 16, Verse 20. Lazarus. This is not the same Lazarus who later dies and is raised by Jesus (John 11). However, this is the only person named in Jesus's parables, and therefore this is likely a true story rather than one made up to teach a lesson.

Verse 22. Abraham's bosom. A figurative expression that refers to heaven.

Verse 23. Hades. This refers to the place of the wicked prior to their final judgment. Some assume this parable indicates that the realm of the dead is one place with two parts, one for the righteous and the other the unrighteous, which was a common rabbinic teaching of the time. However, Scripture teaches that the righteous immediately enter the presence of God upon their death (see 23:43, 2 Cor 5:8, Phil 1:23).

Verse 29. Moses and the prophets. The Old Testament Scriptures.

John 11, Verse 49. Caiaphas. Caiaphas was appointed High Priest by the Roman prefect, Valerius Gratus, in AD 18.

Summary
The highpoint of Jesus's earthly ministry was the very public raising of Lazarus from the dead. Through this miracle, Jesus confirmed his deity and emphasized his power over death. What Jesus did in this case of physical death is what he does to the spiritually dead who believe in his sacrificial atonement on their behalf.

Questions for Reflection
1. How does the raising of Lazarus confirm what Abraham said to the rich man in Jesus's parable about the fact that if people don't believe the Scriptures, then they will not believe even if someone rises from the dead?
2. Why did Jesus wait before traveling to Bethany?
3. Why did Jesus raise Lazarus from the dead?

Day 212: Zacchaeus and Blind Bartimaeus

Matthew 20:20–28; Mark 10:46–52; Luke 19:1–10

Notes

Matthew 20, Verse 23. You will drink my cup. James was later beheaded (Acts 12:2), and John was imprisoned on Patmos (Rev 1:9).

Mark 10, Verse 46. Jericho. Jericho was located 15 miles northeast of Jerusalem.

Luke 19, Verse 2. Tax collector. Tax collectors were Jews hired by Romans to collect taxes, and they were often corrupt, taking more money for personal profit.

Summary

Christ clearly taught and exemplified that the greatest in his Kingdom would be those who served others. He demonstrated this through his healings, and Zacchaeus manifested this by the fruit of his repentance.

Questions for Reflection

1. Why did James and John desire great honor in the Kingdom?
2. According to Jesus, what is required for those who wish to follow him?
3. How do we know that Zacchaeus was truly repentant?

Day 213: The Triumphal Entry

John 12:1–11; Matthew 21:1–11; Luke 19:39–40

Notes

John 12, Verse 5. Three hundred denarii. A full year's wages.

Matthew 21, Verse 8. Spread their cloaks. This was a traditional display of homage for royalty.

Verse 9. Hosanna. This is a transliteration of the Hebrew expression from Psalm 118:25 that means "Save us now." The date of Jesus's triumphal entry was Nisan 9, AD 30, exactly 483 years after the prophecy of Artaxerxes that there would be seventy weeks between the rebuilding of Jerusalem (445 BC) and the first advent of the Messiah (Dan 9:24–26).

Summary

Jesus's triumphal entry into Jerusalem marked his official and very public claim as the promised Messiah. He had taught this and demonstrated this by miracles during his public ministry, but this final act left no question and led to the final plots for Jesus's death.

Questions for Reflection

1. How did Mary's act unintentionally predict Christ's coming death?
2. What did the people's acts reveal about what they thought of Jesus?
3. What did the Pharisees' rebuke reveal about what they thought of Jesus?

Day 214: Jesus Cleanses the Temple a Second Time

Mark 11:12–12:12

Notes

Chapter 11, Verse 14. May no one. Fig trees were often types of the Jewish Nation (Hos 9:10, Nah 3:12, Zech 3:10), and therefore Jesus's curse of this fig tree was a lesson concerning Israel's fruitlessness and rejection of him.

Verse 15. Temple. This is the second time Jesus cleansed the temple (see John 2:14–16), revealing his deep desire for pure worship.

Verse 23. This mountain. Jesus did not mean this literally; rather, this was a reference to a common metaphor used to describe great rabbis who could solve difficult problems.

Summary

Knowing his death for sins was coming quickly, Jesus even more publicly displayed his displeasure with the Jews and their rejection of him as well as their corrupt worship. He rebuked the religious leaders and continued to prepare his disciples by strengthening their faith.

He knew that he would soon be rejected, but that in that rejection, he would become the cornerstone.

Questions for Reflection

1. Why did Jesus drive out the money changers from the temple?
2. What did Jesus teach about the power of prayer in faith?
3. How would the rejection of the Jews actually accomplish God's plan of salvation?

Day 215: The Last Supper

Matthew 26:14–29; 1 Corinthians 11:17–34

Notes

Matthew 26, Verse 17. Passover. Passover was celebrated on Nisan 14, and the Feast of Unleavened Bread began the next day. Sometimes the entire time was called either "Passover" (Luke 22:1) or the Feast of Unleavened Bread. Further, Galileans and Judeans reckoned a day differently, Galileans from sunrise to sunrise and Judeans from sunset to sunset. Thus, for Galileans, Nisan 14 fell on Thursday, while for Judeans it fell on Friday. This is how Jesus and his disciples (Galileans) could celebrate Passover on Thursday night, while Jesus was crucified on Friday during Passover by Judean reckoning.

Verse 26. This is my body. Jesus clearly meant that the bread represented his body, not that it was literally his body.

1 Corinthians 11:23. I received from the Lord. This is the official proclamation in the New Testament that a recreation of the Last Supper should be regularly observed by churches in remembrance of Christ's sacrifice on the cross for our sins. Most scholars believe that 1 Corinthians was written before the gospels, so this was the first biblical account given of the Lord's Supper.

Summary

The Last Supper instituted an important ordinance of the church in remembrance of the broken body and shed blood of Christ on behalf of his people. In the ancient world, to sit at a table with someone signified free and open communion. Consequently, the Lord's Supper is a picturesque way to signify that we have full communion with God through Christ's death for us, and that we also share communion with others of Christ's followers.

Questions for Reflection

1. Why did Paul give careful instructions about the Lord's Supper?
2. What do the bread and cup represent in the Supper?
3. What does the whole meal represent?

Week 44: Jesus's Death and Resurrection

Weekly memory verse:

Isaiah 53:5 - "But he was pierced for our transgressions; he was crushed for our iniquities; upon him was the chastisement that brought us peace, and with his wounds we are healed."

Weekly hymn:

"Stricken, Smitten, and Afflicted"

Weekly catechism:

What is the Lord's Supper?

The Lord's Supper is an ordinance of the New Testament, instituted by Jesus Christ, to be a sign of the believer's communion with Christ and his church through his broken body and shed blood.

Stricken, Smitten, and Afflicted

O MEIN JESU, ICH MUSS STERBEN

WORDS: Thomas Kelly, 1804 8.7.8.7.D

MUSIC: *Geistliche Volkslieder*, Paderborn, 1850

Day 216: Judas Betrays Jesus

Matthew 26:30–56; Psalms 46–48

Notes

Matthew 26, Verse 30. Hymn. This was likely Psalm 118, the last of the Egyptian Hallel (praise) psalms, which were traditionally sung as part of the Passover celebration.

Verse 39. This cup. A cup is often a symbol of God's wrath against sin. *Will.* This is not a conflict between the persons of God; rather it is an example of Christ in his humanity voluntarily submitting to the will of the Father, certainly a mystery related to the Trinity.

Verse 51. One of those. John identifies this as Peter and the servant as Malchus (John 18:10). Luke indicates that Jesus healed Malchus's ear (Luke 22:51).

Verse 53. Twelve legions. A legion was 6,000 soldiers, so this would be more than 72,000 angels.

Summary

Jesus willingly gave himself to suffer for the sins of his people, and yet he knew that the experience of God's divine justice upon him would be terrible. Yet he submitted himself to this in order to bring his Father glory and for the sake of sinners. All of this had been foretold in Old Testament prophecy, and so even the traitorous actions of Judas were intended by God to accomplish the redemption of many.

Questions for Reflection

1. Why did Jesus ask that the cup pass from him?
2. How did Jesus demonstrate submission to his Father?
3. Why was Peter's action wrong?

Day 217: Jesus Tried by the Religious Leaders

John 18:12–27; Mark 14:53–65; Matthew 27:1–10

Notes

John 18, Verse 12. Bound him. The houses of Annas and Caiaphas may have shared a common courtyard since this is where Peter appears to be while Jesus is taken back and forth between the two houses. Annas had been high priest from AD 6–15, and his son-in-law Caiaphas held the office from AD 18–36. This trial, which occurred sometime between midnight and 3:00 am, was illegal based on Jewish law.

Mark 14, Verse 62. I Am. This was an unambiguous claim that Jesus was God himself.

Matthew 27, Verse 9. Jeremiah. This is actually a quote from Zechariah 11:12–13; however, since in the Hebrew Old Testament, Jeremiah came first in the section of Prophets, the whole section was sometimes referred to by his name.

Summary

The religious leaders carefully plotted the arrest and trial of Jesus in the dead of night, since they knew he was popular among the people. This trial was illegal by Jewish standards, but God used the sinister actions of his enemies to accomplish his good purposes. Jesus, innocent of all the false charges, remained silent, although when asked if he was Messiah, Jesus answered with an unambiguous claim to be God himself.

Questions for Reflection

1. Why did the religious leaders put Jesus to trial at night?
2. What is the difference between Peter's denial and Judas's betrayal?
3. Why did Caiaphas tear his garments?

Day 218: Jesus Tried by the Political Leaders

Luke 23:1–25; Isaiah 53

Notes

Luke 23, Verse 2. Tribute to Caesar. This was a deliberate lie; Jesus had explicitly defended the necessity to pay taxes to Caesar (Luke 20:20–25).

Verse 7. Herod's jurisdiction. This was Herod Antipas, who ruled Galilee and Perea and who had killed John the Baptist.

Verse 18. Barabbas. John indicates that the Jews had a custom to free a criminal during Passover (John 18:39); Pilate wished to free Jesus, who he believed to be innocent, but the crowd chose Barabbas, a thief (John 18:40) and murderer (Luke 23:18–19), instead.

Verse 21. Crucify him. Crucifixion was a disgraceful form of Roman torture and execution.

Summary

Unlike the religious leaders, Pilate genuinely desired to determine whether Jesus was innocent or guilty. Having determined him to be innocent, Pilate attempted to both pass the matter off to Herod and free Jesus in a way that would appease the people. However, under the public pressure, he gave in and delivered Jesus to be crucified.

Questions for Reflection

1. Why was Jesus silent during much of his trial?
2. Why did the people demand Jesus's crucifixion?
3. In what ways did the events of Jesus's trial and crucifixion fulfill Isaiah's prophecy?

Day 219: The Death of Jesus

Matthew 27:27–61; Psalm 22

Notes

Chapter 27, Verse 27. Battalion. Usually around 600 men.

Verse 32. Cyrene. A city in North Africa.

Verse 33. Golgotha. Luke uses the name "Calvary," from the Latin word for "skull." This may have been a skull-shaped hill or simply known as a place of death.

Verse 45. Sixth hour. This was noon. The crucifixion had begun at 9:00 am (Mark 15:25), and verse 46 indicates that Jesus's death occurred at the ninth hour, 3:00 pm.

Verse 46. Forsaken me. In quoting Psalm 22, Jesus was not claiming that God had actually forsaken him; rather, he was using the psalm to express deep lament.

Verse 52. Bodies of the saints. Matthew is the only gospel that records this, and nothing more is said of them. They apparently appeared to many (v. 53) and then likely ascended to heaven.

Summary

Jesus willingly gave himself to be crucified, knowing that in this action he would accomplish the redemption of his people. That fact that he did indeed accomplish this was displayed no more perfectly than when the veil of the temple was torn in two from top to bottom, indicating that the barrier between God's presence and his people was now eliminated.

Questions for Reflection

1. In what ways did Psalm 22 foretell aspects of Christ's crucifixion?
2. How do we know that Jesus died voluntarily?
3. What did the tearing of the veil indicate about Christ's death?

Day 220: The Resurrection of Jesus

Matthew 27:62–28:15

Notes

Matthew 27, Verse 4. Like dead men. This probably indicates that they were struck unconscious because of what they had seen.

Verse 7, Galilee. Jesus's disciples saw him several times before they saw him in Galilee, but it would be there that he would appear to "over five hundred brethren at once" (1 Cor 15:6).

Summary

Jesus rose from the dead, just as he promised he would. His resurrection is a key element of the gospel, as it proved his victory over sin and death and the fact that his sacrifice had been accepted by God. The fact that he was seen by many is also an important component of the gospel message.

Questions for Reflection

1. Why did the religious leaders want to seal and guard the tomb?

2. Why was it important that Jesus be seen after his resurrection?
3. Why was Jesus's resurrection important?

Week 45: Jesus Ascends and Sends the Holy Spirit

Weekly memory verse:

1 Corinthians 15:21-22 - "For as by a man came death, by a man has come also the resurrection of the dead. For as in Adam all die, so also in Christ shall all be made alive."

Weekly hymn:

"Jesus Lives, and So Shall I"

Weekly catechism:

What benefits do believers receive from Christ at their death?
Believers are at their death made perfect in holiness and immediately pass into the presence of God forever.

Jesus Lives, and So Shall I

ZUVERSICHT

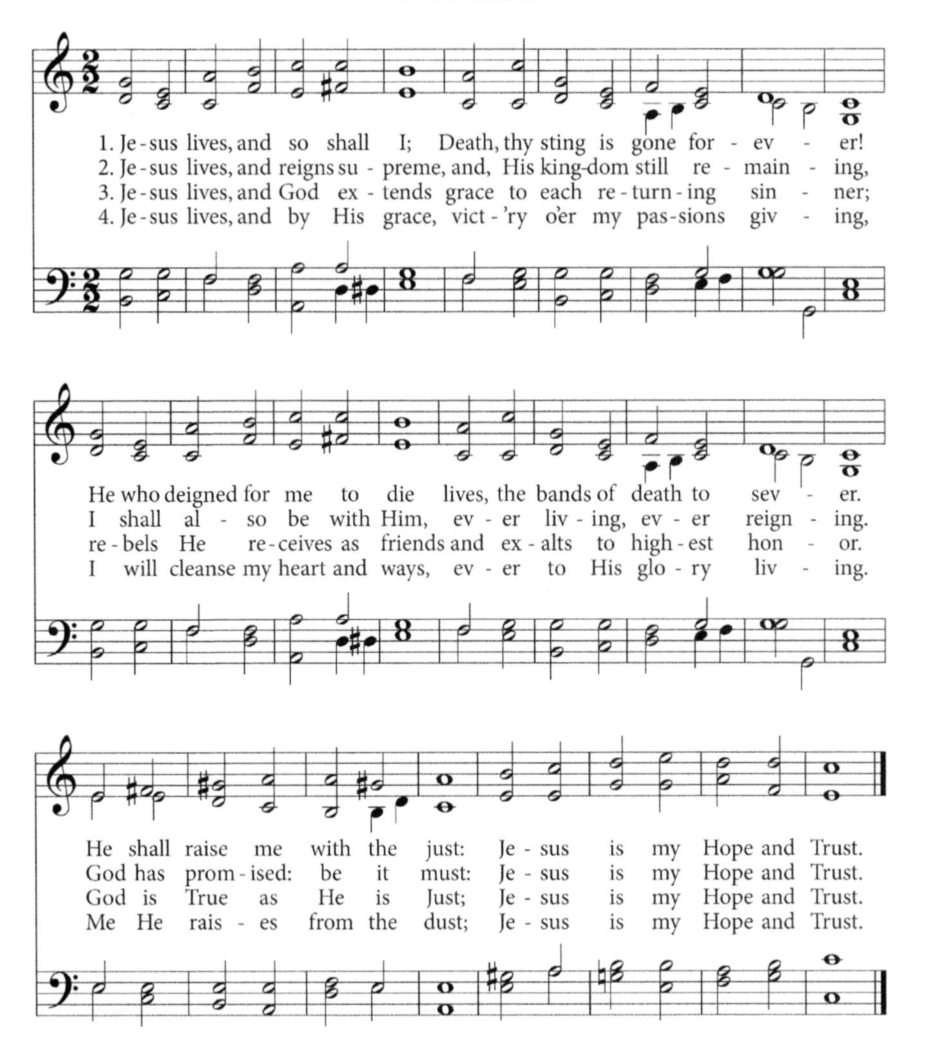

5. Jesus lives! I know full well
nought from Him my heart can sever,
life nor death nor pow'rs of hell,
joy nor grief, henceforth forever.
None of all His saints is lost;
Jesus is my Hope and Trust.

6. Jesus lives, and death is now
but my entrance into glory.
Courage, then, my soul, for thou
hast a crown of life before thee;
thou shalt find thy hopes were just;
Jesus is the Christian's Trust.

WORDS: Christian F. Gellert, 1757; tr. John Dunmore Lang, 1826 — 7.8.7.8.7.7
MUSIC: Johann Crüger, 1653

Day 221: Jesus Appears to His Disciples

Luke 24:13-45; Psalms 138-139

Notes

Luke 24, Verse 13. Two of them. These apparently were not any of the 11 disciples. Verse 18 indicates one of them was named Cleopas. *Emmaus.* The exact location of this city is unknown.

Verse 31. Vanished. Jesus had a true body, indicated by the fact that he could eat, but it was now a glorified body.

Verse 34. Appeared. Scripture indicates that Jesus appears on at least ten separate occasions between his resurrection and ascension (see 1 Cor 15:5-8).

Summary

As proof that he did indeed rise from the dead, Jesus appeared on at least ten different occasions to hundreds of people. He had a glorified body that nevertheless still retained the scars of his crucifixion, as additional evidence that he was who he claimed. All of what happened, both his death and resurrection, had been prophesied in the Old Testament.

Questions for Reflection

1. Why did Jesus need to appear to people between his resurrection and ascension?
2. How were Jesus's death and resurrection prophesied in the Old Testament?
3. What are evidences that the risen Christ had a physical body?

Day 222: Jesus Appears to Thomas and Other Followers

John 20:24-21:25; Psalm 140

Notes

John 21, Verse 1. Sea of Tiberias. Another name for the Sea of Galilee (see John 6:1).

Verse 3. Fishing. This was in obedience to Christ's command that they wait for him in Galilee (Matt 28:16).

Verse 7. Disciple whom Jesus loved. A common self-description of John.

Verse 19. Death. Peter would later die at the hands of Nero, being crucified upside down since he did not want to be crucified exactly as Christ had been.

Summary

Jesus further confirms his resurrection by appearing to his disciples, giving them undeniable evidence that he was who he claimed to be and he was truly alive. Christ lovingly challenged Peter in what would be necessary to serve him going forward, and Peter did indeed faithfully follow Jesus's instructions for the rest of his life.

Questions for Reflection

1. How did Jesus's response to Thomas's doubts reveal his compassion?
2. How did Jesus's challenge to Peter reveal his compassion?
3. According to John, why did he write his Gospel?

Day 223: Christ Ascends to Heaven

Matthew 28:16–20; Luke 24:44–53; Acts 1:1–11

Notes

Matthew 28, Verse 16. Eleven disciples. Other followers of Jesus were also with them, as is clear by the fact that "some doubted" (v. 17).

Verse 19. Make disciples. The primary command of Jesus's "Great Commission" to his disciples is to make disciples. This includes going, proclaiming the gospel (Mark 16:15), baptizing new converts, and "teaching them to observe all that I have commanded you."

Acts 1, Verse 1. First book. Luke wrote Acts as volume 2 of his explanation and defense of Christianity. *Theophilus.* The secular ruler to which Luke wrote both volumes.

Verse 5. Baptized. First Corinthians 12:13 indicates that all believers are baptized with the Holy Spirit into the body of Christ, although the disciples had to wait ten days for the inauguration of this act.

Verse 6. Restore the kingdom to Israel. The disciples still believed that Christ would establish an earthly kingdom. Jesus did not correct their thinking; rather, he indicated that what was prophesied in the Old Testament was still yet to come.

Verse 11. In the same way. This is a clear prophecy of the bodily Second Coming of Christ.

Summary

Between his resurrection and ascension, Jesus taught his disciples what they would need to know in order to establish his church after he left. He commissioned them, and by extension all Christians, with making disciples of all nations, and he gave them the ability to do so.

Questions for Reflection

1. How could some of Jesus's followers doubt even though they saw him risen?
2. What elements are included in Jesus's Great Commission to his followers?
3. According to Jesus and the angels, what will happen when he comes again?

Day 224: The Coming of the Holy Spirit

Acts 1:12–2:47

Notes

Chapter 2, Verse 2. Suddenly. The coming of the Holy Spirit was not something the disciples were seeking or praying for. Christ sent the Holy Spirit just as he promised he would.

Verse 4. Filled with the Holy Spirit. This was a unique filling with the Holy Spirit that empowered the apostles for special tasks in the book of Acts. This is different both from Spirit baptism, which is a one-time act for all Christians at the moment of their salvation (1 Cor 12:13) and being filled *by* the Spirit with the Word of God. Only the last of these (being filled by the Spirit) is commanded of Christians (Eph 5:18). This special Spirit-filling on the day of Pentecost was evidenced by rushing wind, tongues of fire, and the God-given ability to speak in languages that the disciples had not previously known.

Verse 6. Language. While the term "tongues" in verse 4 may initially be ambiguous, the term "language" here clearly indicates the definition of speaking in tongues—speaking in a known language that the speaker has never before learned.

Verse 16. Joel. Joel's prophecy was clearly not completely fulfilled that day, as many of the visible signs he prophesied did not occur. Yet Peter indicates that this day was a pre-fulfillment that was initiated by the coming Holy Spirit.

Verse 38. Be baptized. Just as Jesus had commanded in his Great Commission, Peter challenged his audience to repent of their sins, followed by immersion in water as a sign of their union with Christ by the Spirit. Baptism does not produce remission of sins, but it is so closely connected with true repentance as to be considered a complementary act.

Verse 42. The breaking of bread. This refers to the observance of the Lord's Supper, along with dedication to apostolic teaching, fellowship, and "the prayers," likely indicating formal worship prayers known to them from the Synagogue.

Summary

Just as Jesus had promised, he sent the Holy Spirit upon his followers on the day of Pentecost, fifty days after his resurrection. At that moment, Christ's followers were baptized with the Holy Spirit into the body of Christ, which formed the foundation of the church. They also received special signs and abilities in order to confirm their authority and ministry. In response to Peter's powerful sermon, 3,000 people were saved, baptized, and added to the church, devoting themselves to the apostles' teaching, to fellowship, to observing the Lord's Supper, and to the prayers.

Questions for Reflection

1. Why did Jesus send the Holy Spirit?
2. What did it mean that the disciples spoke in tongues?
3. What were the core commitments of the early church?

Day 225: The Apostles Preach the Gospel and Are Persecuted

Acts 3:1-4:31; Psalm 2

Notes

Acts 3, Verse 11. Portico called Solomon's. A portico that surrounded the temple court.

Chapter 4, Verse 3. Already evening. Jewish law forbids trials from taking place at night.

Verse 8. Filled with the Holy Spirit. This is the same unique, special filling the apostles experienced in Acts 2.

Verse 25. By the Holy Spirit. This introduction to the quote from Psalm 2 is a clear description of the fact that Scripture was written by human authors by the Holy Spirit.

Verse 12. Signs and wonders. These were miraculous works of the Holy Spirit through apostles in order to authenticate them as legitimate messengers of God (2 Cor 12:12, Heb 2:3).

Summary

Just as Jesus predicted, and on the basis of the power he himself provided by sending the Holy Spirit, Jesus's disciples began to boldly preach the gospel. The same Jewish leaders who conspired to kill Jesus opposed this preaching as well. Yet Peter answered the charged with respect and boldness, confident that what was happening was consistent with what God has predicted.

Questions for Reflection

1. What was the content of the apostles' sermons?
2. Why did the religious leaders arrest them?
3. What was the apostles' response to the persecution?

Week 46: The Persecution of the Early Church and Spread of the Gospel

Weekly memory verse:
Acts 1:8 - “But you will receive power when the Holy Spirit has come upon you, and you will be my witnesses in Jerusalem and in all Judea and Samaria, and to the end of the earth.”

Weekly hymn:
“The Church’s One Foundation”

Weekly catechism:
What will be done to the wicked at death?
The wicked will at their death be cast into the torments of hell.

The Church's One Foundation

AURELIA

WORDS: Samuel J. Stone, 1866
MUSIC: Samuel S. Wesley, 1864

7.6.7.6.D

Day 226: The Fellowship of the Early Church

Acts 4:32-5:16

Notes

Chapter 4, Verse 32. Everything in common. This was not a forced socialism, but rather a voluntary sharing of goods.

Verse 35. Distributed. The early church recognized the wisdom of having the leadership determine the best way to help those who had material needs within the congregation.

Chapter 5, Verse 4. Lied. This statement, along with the parallel statement in verse 3, both demonstrates the personality and deity of the Holy Spirit.

Verse 11. Church. This is the first occurrence of the Greek word *ekklesia* in Acts, a word that means "called out assembly" and becomes the most common word to describe assemblies of Christians. The English word "church" comes from the Greek word *kuriakos*, which means "belonging to the Lord" (1 Cor 11:20, Rev 1:10).

Summary

The early Christians shared a deep fellowship with one another, rooted in their common belief in Jesus Christ. This caused them to care for each other's needs. Yet this was not required, and the hypocritical deceit of Ananias and Sapphira revealed that joining this new called-out body of believers in Jesus Christ was not something to take lightly.

Questions for Reflection

1. What led the early Christians to care for each other's needs?
2. Why were Ananias and Sapphira punished?
3. What was the purpose of signs and wonders?

Day 227: The Church Chooses Deacons

Acts 5:17-6:7

Notes

Chapter 5, Verse 34. Gamaliel. The most prominent Jewish rabbi of the time. His most well-known student was Paul (22:3).

Chapter 6, Verse 1. Hellenists . . . Hebrews. "Hebrews" were native Jews that lived in Palestine, while "Hellenists" were Jews living outside Israel. Hellenists commonly absorbed Greek culture, which made the Palestinian Jews suspicious of them.

Verse 2. Serve. The word translated "serve" here is *diakonein,* which is why the men chosen in this passage are called "deacons." Deacons are chosen by the congregation (v. 3) and confirmed by the elders (v. 6), helping to take care of the church's material matters so that the elders can give themselves to prayer and the ministry of the Word (v. 4).

Summary
When the commands of men and God conflicted, the apostles chose to obey God, refusing to stop spreading the gospel message. Even though they were unjustly imprisoned and beaten, they rejoiced that they could suffer for the honor of Jesus's name. This only led to the church's increased growth, to the degree that the large numbers of Christians necessitated setting apart deacons to help meet the material needs of the congregation.

Questions for Reflection
1. What was the response of the apostles to their imprisonment?
2. What was Gamaliel's advice to the council?
3. What is the purpose and role of deacons within the church?

Day 228: Stephen, the First Christian Martyr
Acts 6:8–8:3

Notes
Chapter 6, Verse 8. Stephen. One of the men chosen to be a deacon (v. 5).

Verse 9. Synagogue. This verse appears to describe people from three synagogues: (1) the Freedmen, descendants of freed Jewish slaves living in Rome, (2) Cyrenians and Alexandrians, those from two cities in North Africa, and (3) Cilicians and Asians, those from Romans provinces in Asian Minor. Paul likely attended the synagogue in Cilicia.

Summary

Persecution against the new Christians reached a climax with the martyrdom of Stephen, one of the first deacons of the church. Stephen proclaimed a clear message to his Jewish audience, arguing through an extended rehearsal of God's work in the Old Testament that God cannot be contained. This was an indictment against the unbelieving Jews and laid an important theological basis for the evangelization of the whole world.

Questions for Reflection

1. Why were the Jews upset with Stephen?
2. What was Stephen's primary message to the people?
3. What was the response of the people?

Day 229: The Conversion of Samaritans and the Ethiopian Eunuch

Acts 8:4–40

Notes

Verse 4. Philip. One of the men chosen to be a deacon (6:5) and the first to be given the title "evangelist" (21:8).

Verse 15. Receive the Holy Spirit. In a manner that was not to become typical, God chose to delay baptizing the new Samaritan converts with the Spirit in order to authenticate that this truly was of God since these were the first non-Jewish converts. They likely spoke in tongues when they received the Spirit (v. 17), just like the Day of Pentecost (2:4) as authentication. Normally, every Christian is baptized with the Spirit into the body of Christ at the moment of salvation (1 Cor 12:13).

Verse 27. Eunuch. Although this Gentile governmental official from Ethiopia was apparently a convert to Judaism, his physical emasculation prevented him from entering the Jewish assembly (Deut 23:1).

Verse 28. Isaiah. He was reading in Isaiah 53.

Summary

After Stephen's martyrdom forced Christians to flee Jerusalem, the gospel began to spread to more than just Jews. Samarians, a mixture of Jewish and Gentile ancestry, believed Philip's message and were baptized with the Spirit into the same church. Likewise, a cursed Jewish proselyte from Ethiopia was likewise joined to the church when he believed in Christ. All who call upon the name of the Lord, regardless of ethnicity, become part of the church.

Questions for Reflection

1. Why would it have been surprising for a Samaritan to join Jews in becoming Christians?
2. Why did God delay baptizing the Samaritan converts with the Holy Spirit?
3. Why would it have been surprising for an Ethiopian eunuch to become a Christian?

Day 230: The Conversion of Saul

Acts 9:1-31

Notes

Verse 2. Damascus. The ancient capital of Syria, northeast of Jerusalem.

Verse 10. Ananias. The leader of the church in Damascus.

Verse 11. Tarsus. A city in the Roman province of Cilicia in Asian Minor.

Verse 17. Filled with the Holy Spirit. This is the same unique empowering for ministry given to the apostles in Acts 2.

Verse 23. Many days. Saul spent three years in the Arabian desert, where God uniquely prepared him for the ministry to which he was called (Gal 1:17-18).

Verse 30. Caesarea. A city on the north coast of the Mediterranean Sea.

Summary

God supernaturally converted Saul, a man committed to the destruction of Christians, on the road to Damascus. Yet all conversions are supernatural, though they may not happen in as dramatic a fashion.

God uniquely called Saul to be his minister to the Gentiles, spreading the gospel and seeing many churches formed.

Questions for Reflection

1. Why did Saul want to persecute Christians?
2. What are some evidences that Saul was completely transformed?
3. To what ministry did God uniquely call Saul?

Week 47: The Gospel Spreads to the Gentiles

Weekly memory verse:

Romans 10:12 - "For there is no distinction between Jew and Greek; for the same Lord is Lord of all, bestowing his riches on all who call on him."

Weekly hymn:

"How Sweet and Awful Is the Place"

Weekly catechism:

Where is Christ now?
Christ ascended into heaven and sits at the Father's right hand.

How Sweet and Awful Is the Place

ST. COLUMBA

WORDS: Isaac Watts, 1707, alt.
MUSIC: Irish melody; harm. *The English Hymnal*, 1906

CM

Day 231: Peter's Early Ministry

Acts 9:32-43; Psalm 141

Notes

Acts 9, Verse 32. Lydda. A central city situated at the meeting of roads from Egypt to Syria and from Joppa to Jerusalem.

Verse 36. Joppa. A coastal town.

Verse 43. Tanner. Tanners were shunned by Jews since they handled the skins of dead animals.

Summary

While Jesus called Paul to be the primary apostle to the Gentiles, Peter, too, had a successful ministry among them as well. Despite future tensions between these two men, both Paul and Peter served the same Lord and committed their life to the same mission of the spreading the good news of forgiveness from sin for those who trust in Christ.

Questions for Reflection

1. How were Peter's miracles similar to miracles Jesus performed?
2. Why was it remarkable that Peter stayed in Joppa with Simon, a tanner?
3. What should be our prayer when we find ourselves in trouble?

Day 232: Gentiles Are Added to the Church

Acts 10:1-11:18

Notes

Chapter 10, Verse 2. Feared God. This indicates that Cornelius had forsaken his pagan religion and converted to worshiping the God of the Jews.

Verse 12. All kinds of animals. These included both clean and unclean animals in terms of Jewish dietary restrictions (cf. Lev 11:25-26).

Verse 44. Holy Spirit fell. Because this was the first public occurrence of significant Gentiles coming to faith and uniting with Christ's body, the Holy Spirit chose to visibly demonstrate the unity of the church—Jews *and* Gentiles—by giving them the gift of tongues.

Chapter 11, Verse 2. Circumcision party. Jewish Christians.

Summary

The conversion of Cornelius marks the first significant occurrence of Gentiles coming to faith in Christ and being added to the church. God uniquely informed Peter that division between Jews and Gentiles was abolished in the church. The Holy Spirit visibly demonstrates that God accepts Gentiles, too, by granting them the gift of tongues, just as he had for the apostles and the Samaritans.

Questions for Reflection

1. Why did God give Peter the vision of the animals?
2. Why was it so significant that the Holy Spirit came upon the Gentile converts?
3. Why were the Jewish Christians upset with Peter?

Day 233: The Church in Antioch

Acts 11:19-30; Psalm 142

Notes

Acts 11, Verse 19. Antioch. The third largest city in the Roman empire, located on the northern coast of the Mediterranean Sea. The church here becomes the most important Christian church after the church in Jerusalem and is a major missionary hub.

Verse 20. Hellenists. Greek-speaking non-Jews.

Verse 26. Christians. A derisive term meaning "little Christs."

Verse 28. Agabus. One of the Jerusalem prophets who would later have a significant role in Paul's ministry (21:10-11).

Verse 30. Elders. This is the first mention of the pastor-overseers of the church.

Summary

The influence of the gospel begins to spread outside Jerusalem and

Judea to the doorway of the rest of the world. As more Gentiles come to faith in Christ, the church in Antioch forms as a central hub for missionary activity. Followers of Christ there begin to be noticed as having a distinct identity, and they soon come to claim the name, "Christians."

Questions for Reflection

1. Why was the church in Antioch important?
2. Why did the followers of Christ welcome the term "Christians"?
3. What does the growth and significance of this church reveal about the apostles' obedience to Christ's commission to them?

Day 234: James Killed and Peter Imprisoned

Acts 12; Psalm 143

Notes

Acts 12, Verse 1. Herod. This is Herod Agrippa I, grandson of Herod the Great.

Verse 12. Mark. A cousin of Barnabas (Col 4:10) and an acquaintance of Peter in his youth (1 Pet 5:13). This is the same Mark who would later write the Gospel, likely with Peter's help.

Verse 15. His Angel. Jewish superstition taught that each person had his own guardian angel.

Verse 17. James. The brother of Jesus and the head of the Jerusalem church.

Summary

Persecution of the church continued to rise, now coming from the government. James becomes the first apostle to be martyred, and Peter is once again imprisoned. Yet God miraculously saves Peter, enabling him to continue in ministry as the primary focus of God's missionary activity shifts to Paul.

Questions for Reflection

1. Why did Herod kill James and imprison Peter?

2. Why did God allow James to be killed but freed Peter?
3. What did Herod's death reveal about God's control of it all?

Day 235: Paul Begins His First Missionary Journey

Acts 13

Notes

Verse 4. Cyprus. This was Barnabas's home and only a two-day journey from Antioch.

Verse 5. Salamis. A large commercial port of Cyprus. *John.* Also known as Mark (cf. 12:12).

Verse 6. Paphos. The capital city of Cyprus.

Verse 51. Shook the dust from their feet. A symbolic act of condemnation.

Summary

Paul set out on his first missionary journey, accompanied by Barnabas and his cousin Mark, the latter of which would choose to leave them after a short time. He established the practice of first visiting the Jewish synagogue in any town he visited, but it was quickly apparent that the Jews would continue to reject Jesus as their Messiah, and so Paul shifted his ministry attention to the Gentiles.

Questions for Reflection

1. Why did Paul visit Jewish synagogues in each town first?
2. Why did most Jews continue to reject Jesus as their Messiah?
3. Why did Paul shift his ministry attention to the Gentiles?

Week 48: The Gospel Moves into Europe

Weekly memory verse:

Romans 8:38–39 – "For I am sure that neither death nor life, nor angels nor rulers, nor things present nor things to come, nor powers, nor height nor depth, nor anything else in all creation, will be able to separate us from the love of God in Christ Jesus our Lord."

Weekly hymn:

"And Can It Be"

Weekly catechism:

How does Christ's resurrection benefit you?
Christ's resurrection is a certain promise of my glorious resurrection.

And Can It Be

SAGINA

WORDS: Charles Wesley, 1738, alt.
MUSIC: Thomas Campbell, 1825

LMD

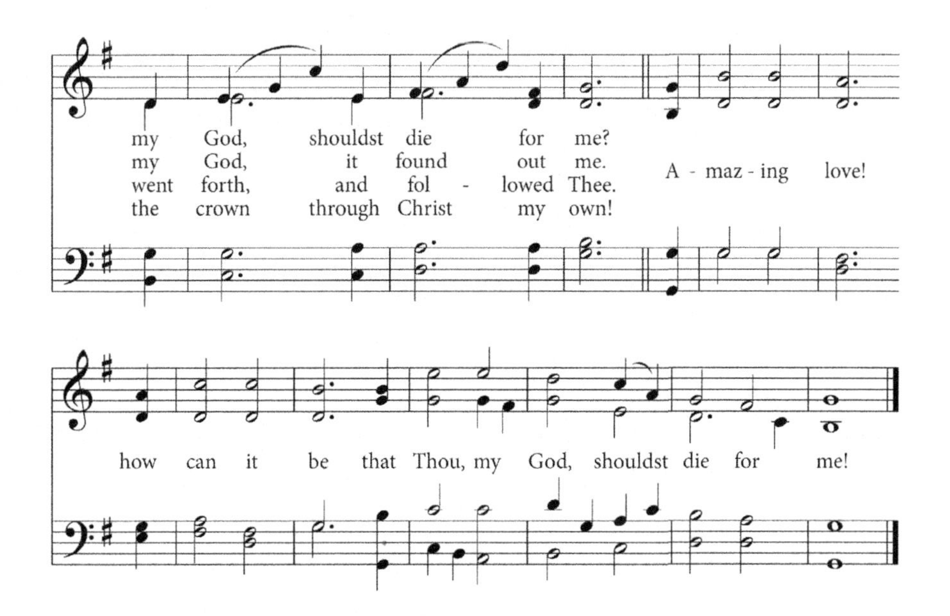

Day 236: Paul Completes His First Missionary Journey

Acts 14; Psalm 144

Notes

Acts 14, Verse 1. Iconium. A melting pot of several cultures, including Phrygians, Greeks, Jews, and Romans.

Verse 11. Gods. Lystran folklore taught that Zeus and Hermes had visited the city in the past, and so they interpreted current events in that light.

Verse 26. Antioch. This ended Paul's first missionary journey.

Summary

Paul and Barnabas set a standard for what a gospel missionary should be. They were evangelists, proclaiming the good news of Jesus Christ to all who would listen. They were preachers, faithfully expounding the Word of God. And they were church planters, organizing new converts into establishes congregations who would continue the work of making disciples, even when the missionaries left.

Questions for Reflection

1. Why did Paul and Barnabas perform signs and wonders?
2. Why did the people of Lystra think Paul and Barnabas were Zeus and Hermes?
3. Why did the people stone Paul?

Day 237: The Jerusalem Council

Acts 15; Psalm 145

Notes

Acts 15, Verse 1. Some men. These were Judaizers, false teachers who insisted that obedience to the Mosaic Law was necessary for salvation.

Verse 8. The Holy Spirit. This is why God delayed giving the outward sign of the Holy Spirit to the Samaritans and later to Gentiles (4:8, 31; 6:5; 7:55); it confirmed clearly that these non-Jews were accepted, even though they were not obedient to the Mosaic Law.

Verse 13. James. The lead elder of the Jerusalem church.

Verse 39. Sharp disagreement. Paul and Barnabas eventually reconciled (1 Cor 9:6), and Paul eventually forgave Mark and considered him a useful son (2 Tim 4:11, 1 Pet 5:13).

Summary

The Jerusalem Council established important principles regarding the nature of the gospel by grace alone in Jesus Christ alone by faith alone balanced with the importance of holiness once a person comes to faith apart from works. It condemned the legalistic Judaizers as heretics, but nevertheless urged new Gentile believers to live holy lives and be sensitive to the consciences of their Jewish-Christian brothers and sisters.

Questions for Reflection

1. Why was the Jerusalem Council necessary?
2. What did the council decide about the relationship between saving faith and good works?
3. Do you think either Paul or Barnabas were wrong in their opinions about Mark?

Day 238: Wise Words

Proverbs 23-24

Notes

Proverbs 23, Verse 10. Ancient landmark. These were boundary stones that marked the borders of ancestral lands. To secretly move one was to steal land not one's own.

Verse 11. Redeemer. This refers to a kinsman redeemer, a more prosperous near family member who would rescue one in need (see Lev 25:25).

Verse 31. Wine when it is red. This verse is one of the most direct prohibitions of drinking intoxicating beverages.

Summary

The book of Proverbs is filled with wise words. Some of the instructions given here have direct application to ancient Near Eastern customs, and yet their principles remain valid to this day. Other instructions have direct, if not even more powerful, application for issues in today's society.

Questions for Reflection

1. Why must we be careful when sitting with a powerful person?
2. What are the negative effects mentioned that come with drinking "wine when it is red"?
3. What should be our attitude toward our enemies?

Day 239: Paul Begins His Second Missionary Journey

Acts 16

Notes

Verse 3. Circumcised him. Clearly, as evident in the previous chapter, Paul did not believe circumcision was necessary for salvation. Yet for the sake of gospel ministry, Paul taught that we should be willing to give up our freedoms.

Verse 9. Macedonia. The region on the mainland of Greece, the first entrance of the missionaries into Europe.

Verse 10. We. This indicates the Luke joined Paul, Silas, and Timothy at this point.

Summary

Paul continued to spread the gospel and plant churches, this time clearly led by the Holy Spirit to leave Asia and begin working in Europe, on the mainland of Greece. God providentially prepared the way for the mission team, working in the hearts of key individuals who would be important founders of churches in the cities.

Questions for Reflection

1. Why did Paul circumcise Timothy?
2. Why did God send the vision of man from Macedonia to Paul?
3. What did Paul tell the Philippian jailer when he was about to take his own life?

Day 240: Paul in Thessalonica and Athens

Acts 17; Proverbs 25

Notes

Acts 17, Verse 18. Epicurean and Stoic philosophers. Epicureans were materialists and Stoics were pantheists.

Verses 22. Religious. This carried the idea of "superstitious" and would not have been considered a compliment.

Verse 28. Your own poets. The first quote is from the Cretan poet Epimenides (c. 600 BC), and the second is from the Stoic poet Aratus (c. 315-240 BC). He quotes them to demonstrate the lack of internal coherence of their own religious beliefs.

Summary

Paul carefully considered his audience when proclaiming the gospel. With the Jews in Thessalonica and Berea, he could assume their knowledge of the Old Testament Scriptures and build upon that to convince them that Jesus was the promised Messiah. For the philosophical and superstitious Athenians, Paul had to begin with proclaiming that God was the true Creator and Ruler of all. Either way, Paul relied on the sufficiency of God's truth in proclaiming the gospel to all people.

Questions for Reflection

1. How did the Bereans prove to be more noble than the Thessalonicans?
2. Why was Paul provoked when he entered Athens?
3. What was the varied response to Paul's message?

Week 49: Paul Begins His Final Missionary Journey

Weekly memory verse:

Philippians 2:9-11 - "Therefore God has highly exalted him and bestowed on him the name that is above every name, so that at the name of Jesus every knee should bow, in heaven and on earth and under the earth, and every tongue confess that Jesus Christ is Lord, to the glory of God the Father."

Weekly hymn:

"Look, Ye Saints, the Sight Is Glorious"

Weekly catechism:

How does Christ's ascension into heaven benefit you?
Christ is my advocate in heaven before his Father and my certain promise that he will take me up to himself.

Look, Ye Saints, the Sight Is Glorious

CORONAE

WORDS: Thomas Kelly, 1809

MUSIC: William Henry Monk, 1871

8.7.8.7.4.7

Day 241: The Fool's Folly
Proverbs 26–27

Notes
Proverb 26, Verse 4. According to his folly. When addressing a fool (an unbeliever), he should not be given the impression that his presuppositions are correct, lest he think he is right.

Verse 11. Vomit. Peter quotes this Proverb in 2 Peter 2:22.

Verse 17. Dog. Dogs were not domesticated in ancient times.

Proverbs 27, Verse 14. Loud voice. In other words, mere flattery.

Verse 22. Mortar . . . pestle. Utensils used to crush grain into powder.

Summary
The progressive deterioration of a fool like is incongruent aspects of the natural order and will move from bad to worse. A wise person, on the other hand, thinks before he speaks, benefits from the sharpening of others, and will be blessed.

Questions for Reflection
1. What kinds of pictures does the Proverb use to describe the fool?
2. What are characteristics of a wise person?
3. What are some blessings a wise person can expect to enjoy?

Day 242: The Wicked Condemned
Proverbs 28–29

Notes
Proverb 28, Verse 8. Interest. The law prohibited Jews from charging interest to other Jews (Deut 23:19–20).

Verse 21. Piece of bread. A small bribe.

Proverbs 20, Verse 13. Give light to the eyes. This literally means to give life.

Summary

Wicked people's lives are characterized by injustice and immorality. But they will ultimately receive the fruit of their own wicked actions—eternal condemnation.

Questions for Reflection

1. What are specific acts of injustice described in these proverbs?
2. How do wicked acts result in condemnation for the wicked?
3. How are the actions of righteous people contrasted with those of the wicked in these proverbs?

Day 243: Paul Completes His Second Missionary Journey

Acts 18; Proverbs 30

Notes

Acts 18, Verse 1. Corinth. This was the most important commercial and political city in Greece.

Verse 2. Aquilla . . . Priscilla. This couple was probably part of the church in Rome.

Verse 11. A year and six months. This was Paul's longest stay in one city except for Ephesus (20:31) and Rome (28:30).

Verse 19. Ephesus. This was the most important city in Asia Minor.

Verse 22. Went up. Because Jerusalem was elevated, this indicates that Paul visited in the church at Jerusalem before heading to Antioch. This ended his second missionary journey.

Proverb 30. This is a collection of proverbs likely written by a student of Solomon.

Summary

Paul strategically chose important cities for his missionary endeavors, seeking to establish churches in these cities that would then continue evangelizing the area. Yet ultimately, it was God who had chosen many people in those cities, and he worked sovereignly to lead Paul and save key individuals for the foundation of these churches.

Questions for Reflection

1. Why did Paul choose Corinth and Ephesus to minister in?
2. How were Aquilla and Priscilla helpful in Paul's missionary work?
3. How do the events in this chapter illustrate human responsibility and God's sovereignty in evangelism?

Day 244: Paul's Third Missionary Journey

Acts 19

Notes

Verse 1. Paul passed through. Paul's third missionary journey began after he left Antioch in Acts 8:22.

Verse 6. Holy Spirit. Tongues and prophecy once again served to confirm that these converts were part of the church.

Verse 14. Sceva. There is no record of such a Jewish high priest, so he may have assumed this title falsely.

Verse 21. Spirit. Probably Paul's spirit, not the Holy Spirit (the Greek word for "spirit" is the same as "Spirit").

Summary

The power of the gospel to save is clearly evident during Paul's ministry in Ephesus. The gospel has power to convert sinners and join them to Christ's body; it has power to sanctify new converts, causing them to reject their former sinful life; and it has power such that the unbelieving community will notice the life-transforming change that occurs for someone who trusts Christ.

Questions for Reflection

1. Why was it important for God to confirm that the Ephesian converts were truly part of the church?
2. What are some evidences that the new Ephesian converts were truly saved?

3. Why were the unbelieving people of Ephesus upset?

Day 245: Paul's Letter to the Corinthian Church

1 Corinthians 1–2, 13

Notes

Chapter 1, Verse 1. Sosthenes. Probably a former leader of the Corinthians synagogue who was converted and became Paul's personal secretary (Acts 18:12–17). This letter was probably written while Paul was in Ephesus, during his third missionary journey.

Verse 11. Chloe. Probably a prominent member of the Corinthian church who had visited Paul in Ephesus and told him of divisions in the Corinthian church.

Summary

In Paul's recounting of the power of the gospel among the Corinthians, he reveals that he did not come to them seeking to appeal to their preferences or in any way that changed the message of the gospel. Rather, he preached to them the clear gospel, which was actually a stumbling block to natural people, both Jews and Greeks. And yet that same gospel penetrated the hearts of some, bringing them to faith in Christ and into the unity of the body.

Questions for Reflection

1. Why was Paul thankful for the Corinthian believers?
2. Why does God choose to use weak things to bring unbelievers to faith in Christ?
3. What is the nature of true, biblical love?

Week 50: Life by the Spirit and Word

Weekly memory verse:

Titus 2:11-13 - "For the grace of God has appeared, bringing salvation for all people, training us to renounce ungodliness and worldly passions, and to live self-controlled, upright, and godly lives in the present age, waiting for our blessed hope, the appearing of the glory of our great God and Savior Jesus Christ."

Weekly hymn:

"Savior of the Nations, Come"

Weekly catechism:

Will Jesus Christ come again?

Jesus Christ will come a second time in power and glory, which is the joy and hope of all believers.

Savior of the Nations, Come

NUN KOMM, DER HEIDEN HEILAND

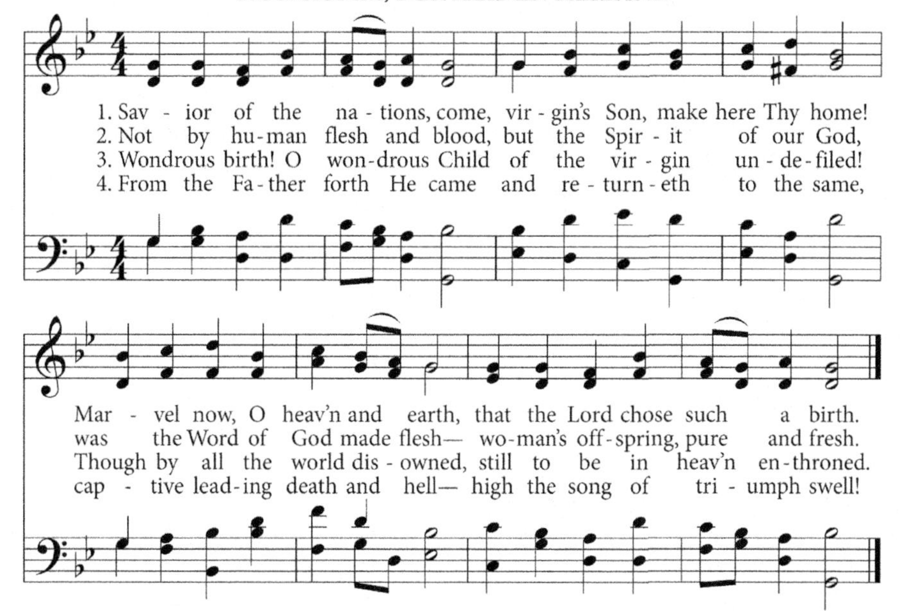

5. Thou the Father's only Son,
hast o'er sin the victory won.
Boundless shall Thy kingdom be;
when shall we its glories see?

6. Brightly doth Thy manger shine,
glorious is its light divine.
Let not sin o'ercloud this light;
ever be our faith thus bright.

7. Praise to God the Father sing,
praise to God the Son, our King,
praise to God the Spirit be
ever and eternally.

WORDS: Attr. Ambrose of Milan, 4th cent.; German version, Martin Luther, 1523; tr. William M. Reynolds, 1880, alt.

7.7.7.7

MUSIC: *Enchiridia*, Erfurt, 1524; harm. Seth Calvisius, 1594

Day 246: The Word of the Lord

Psalm 119

Notes

Verse 1. Law. This is the longest chapter in the Bible. It is an acrostic psalm, composed of 22 stanzas, each with 8 lines; each of the 8 lines in subsequent stanzas begins with consecutive letters of the Hebrew alphabet. Its theme is God's Word.

Verse 75. Afflicted me. The psalmist is confident that God's sovereign goodness reigns even over his afflictions.

Verse 164. Seven. Seven is a figure of speech representing perfection or completeness.

Summary

The Word of God is eternally settled in heaven; it is good and trustworthy, something in which believers can place their confidence, trust, and delight. It is a Word in which believers come to truly know God, its instructions are worthy of obedience, and its truths worthy of belief and defense.

Questions for Reflection

1. What kinds of images does the psalmist use to describe the Word of God?
2. Why is the Word of God worthy of delight?
3. What benefits does the Word of God deliver to those who love it?

Day 247: Living Filled by the Spirit

Ephesians 5:18–6:20

Notes

Chapter 5, Verse 18. Be filled. This is a command given to believers that describes their submission to the Holy Spirit's work in their lives, specifically filling them with the Word of Christ (Col 3:16).

Verse 19. Psalms, hymns, and spiritual songs. These terms are not meant to designate carefully defined kinds of songs but rather signify a variety of songs.

Verse 21. Submitting. This literally means to "arrange under" and describes a voluntary willingness to follow the lead of others. This kind of attitude characterizes all of the relationships described in the following verses.

Summary

A Christian who is filled by the Spirit with the Word of Christ will gather with his people for worship and edification, will live faithfully in the various vocations to which he or she is called, and will actively fight against the attacks of Satan. A Spirit-filled believer is controlled by the Word, glorifying God with every thought and action.

Questions for Reflection

1. What does it mean to be Spirit-filled?
2. How does being Spirit-filled manifest itself in the church assembly?
3. How does being Spirit-filled manifest itself in the Christian's life?

Day 248: Christian Living

Philippians 3-4

Notes

Chapter 3, Verse 2. Evildoers. In context, this specifically refers to the Judaizers, who required obedience to the Law as necessary for salvation.

Verse 18. Belly. This refers to the physical appetites, which, although God-given and good, must be controlled. An enemy of Christ is driven by appetites.

Chapter 4, Verse 8. Whatever. Qualities in this list characterize the three transcendent categories of truth, goodness, and beauty, by which all things must be measured.

Summary

Although salvation does not come through works, a Christian who has a changed heart will desire to pursue holiness, ruled by love for God, and dedicated to do whatever pleases the Lord.

Questions for Reflection

1. How is the Christian life like a race?
2. What kinds of actions and attitudes should characterize a Christian's life?
3. How can the list in Philippians 4:8 apply to what a Christian enjoys in life?

Day 249: The Gospel of Christ

Romans 1, 3

Notes

Chapter 1, Verse 7. Rome. Paul wrote this letter to the church in Rome while he was in Corinth, evidenced by his reference to individuals in Corinth such as Phoebe (16:1), Gaius (16:23), and Erastus (16:23).

Verse 16. Power. The word "dynamite" comes from this Greek word.

Verse 18. Revealed. This passage describes general revelation, what God communicates to all people through his creation. Although this general revelation plainly reveals that there is a God, only his Word and Spirit effectually reveal him to people for their salvation.

Chapter 3, Verse 25. Propitiation. This Word refers to the appeasement of God's wrath that was secured in the sacrifice of his Son.

Verse 30. Justify. This is a legal term which means to "declare righteous."

Summary

The gospel of Jesus Christ is the power of God unto salvation for anyone who believes. The sacrifice of Christ on the cross appeased God's just wrath and allowed him to justly justify (declare righteous) unjust people who trust in him.

Questions for Reflection

1. Why is Paul not ashamed of the gospel of Christ?
2. What does God's general revelation accomplish?
3. How can God justly justify the unjust?

Day 250: Life in the Spirit

Romans 8, 12

Notes

Chapter 8, Verse 6. Mind. Those whose minds are set on the flesh describes all unbelievers, and all Christians are spiritually minded.

Verse 9. Dwells. All believers have the Spirit of God dwelling within them, evidenced by his active work of sanctification in their lives.

Verse 26. Groanings. The Spirit intercedes on behalf of Christians in ways they cannot even express.

Chapter 12, Verse 2. Conformed. This refers to an outward expression that does not reflect an inward reality.

Summary

Those who are in Christ will not be condemned; rather, they are spiritually minded and indwelt by the Spirit, living as sacrifices of worship to God whose lives are being transformed by the Word of God rather than being conformed to this present evil age.

Questions for Reflection

1. What does it mean that Christians are spiritually minded?
2. What are the benefits of the Spirit dwelling within believers?
3. In what ways should Christians present their bodies as living sacrifices to God?

Week 51: Paul on Trial

Weekly memory verse:

Revelation 20:12 – "And I saw the dead, great and small, standing before the throne, and books were opened. Then another book was opened, which is the book of life. And the dead were judged by what was written in the books, according to what they had done."

Weekly hymn:

"Joy to the World"

Weekly catechism:

What will happen to believers after Christ comes again?
Believers will live with Christ forever in a new heaven and a new earth.

WORDS: **Psalm 98**; Isaac Watts, 1719 CM

MUSIC: George Frederic Handel, 1742; arr. Lowell Mason, 1848

Day 251: Paul Heads Toward Jerusalem

Acts 20:1-21:16

Notes

Chapter 20, Verse 3. Three months. Paul likely spent most of this time in Corinth.

Verse 5. Us. The first-person plural indicates that Luke joined Paul in Philippi.

Verse 7. First day of the week. This is evidence that Christians had begun to meet regularly on Sunday, rather than Saturday, since this was the day on which Christ rose from the dead. They had to meet early in the morning and late at night since it was a work day.

Verse 28. Flock . . . overseers. This passage is one of the clearest evidences that the one church office of elder (v. 17) were also called "pastors" and "overseers."

Summary

Compelled by the Holy Spirit, Paul heads toward Jerusalem to deliver the offering collected from churches, which would be his last visit there. On the way, Paul is able to visit many of the churches he helped to plant, further encouraging them and instructing them in the faith.

Questions for Reflection

1. Why did Paul want to go to Jerusalem?
2. Why did the Jews hate Paul?
3. On what basis did Paul tell the Ephesian elders that he was innocent of the blood of all (v. 26)?

Day 252: Paul Is Arrested in Jerusalem

Acts 21:17-22:29

Notes

Chapter 21, Verse 18. James. This is the half-brother of Jesus and head of the Jerusalem church.

Verse 38. Egyptian. Several years earlier, an Egyptian false prophet had led a revolt against Rome. His army was defeated, but he escaped.

Lysias assumed Paul was this same man who had returned to finish his revolt.

Chapter 22, Verse 25. Roman citizen. Roman citizens were exempt from torture.

Summary

During Paul's final visit to Jerusalem, he was able to report to James and the other Jerusalem elders how God had worked to bring Gentiles to a saving knowledge of Jesus Christ. This same good news for Christians, however, made the Jews angry, leading to Paul's eventual arrest. This arrest gave Paul key opportunities to clearly proclaim what God had done.

Questions for Reflection

1. Why was it important for Paul to report to James and the Jerusalem elders about what God did among the Gentiles?
2. Why did the Jews arrest Paul?
3. How did Paul respond to the charges against him?

Day 253: Paul Before the Jewish Council

Acts 22:30–23:35; Proverbs 31

Notes

Acts 23, Verse 2. Ananias. This is not the Annas of the gospel accounts; rather, Ananias was one of the most corrupt high priests who sided with Rome over the Jews and was later assassinated during the revolt of AD 66.

Verse 26. Felix. The governor of Judea from AD 52 to 59.

Verse 31. Antipatris. A Roman military post about 30 miles from Jerusalem.

Summary

Paul spoke strongly against the false claims and corrupt leadership of the Jewish Council, yet he remained respectful to the authorities God had put in place. He emphasized that what he had been doing for Christ was a fulfillment of the Jewish Scriptures, not contrary to them.

Questions for Reflection

1. Why did Paul back down his rhetoric once he realized he was speaking to the high priest?
2. In what ways did Paul insist that his missionary activity was a fulfillment of the Jewish Scriptures?
3. How would the Lord's visit to Paul have encouraged him?

Day 254: Paul on Trial

Acts 24-26

Notes

Chapter, Verse 24. Drusilla. Felix's third wife was the youngest daughter of Agrippa I, not yet 20 years old at this time.

Chapter 25, Verse 13. King Agrippa. Herod Agrippa II was son of the Herod who put Peter in prison and killed James, brother of John (12:1). His great uncle was the Herod of the gospels, and his great-grandfather was king when Jesus was born.

Summary

Paul continued to stand firm in his conviction that his conscience was clean, even in his trial before the political leaders of Judah. Paul was not surprised, however, that the Jews rejected him and his message since God had told him it would be so.

Questions for Reflection

1. What defense did Paul give in response to the charges against him?
2. Why did Paul preach about the resurrection of Christ, even though he knew his audience would not believe?
3. Did any of the political leaders find Paul guilty of the charges against him?

Day 255: Paul Sails for Rome

Acts 27; Psalm 146

Notes

Acts 27, Verse 9. The Feast. This was the Day of Atonement.

Verse 17. Syrtis. Sandbars just off the coast of Africa, where many ships were run aground.

Verse 27. Adriatic Sea. This is not the present Adriatic but rather the central Mediterranean Sea.

Summary

God further confirmed Paul and his mission, even during his journey toward Rome. God providentially protected Paul, and Paul's personal character and leadership engendered respect even among the unbelieving people.

Questions for Reflection

1. In what ways did God protect Paul on his journey to Rome?
2. How did Paul take leadership, even as a prisoner among unbelievers?
3. How did the events of this journey further confirm Paul and his mission?

Week 52: Jesus Comes Again

Weekly memory verse:

Revelation 22:17 – "The Spirit and the Bride say, 'Come.' And let the one who hears say, 'Come.' And let the one who is thirsty come; let the one who desires take the water of life without price."

Weekly hymn:

"Lo! He Comes with Clouds Descending"

Weekly catechism:

What is your only hope in life and death?
My only hope in life and death is that I am not my own but belong to God and to my Savior Jesus Christ.

Lo! He Comes with Clouds Descending

HELMSLEY

WORDS: Charles Wesley, 1758, alt.

8.7.8.7.4.4.4.7

MUSIC: Thomas Olivers, 1763; harm. Ralph Vaughan Williams, 1906

Day 256: The Coming of Christ

Galatians 4:4–7; Titus 3:3–7; 1 Timothy 1:15–17

Notes

Galatians 4, Verse 4. Son. This emphasizes Jesus's full deity. *Woman.* This emphasizes Jesus's full humanity.

Verse 5. Adoption. Those who are redeemed become children of God.

Titus 3, Verse 7. Justified. A legal declaration of righteousness based on Christ's righteousness imputed to those who believe.

1 Timothy 1, Verse 15. Trustworthy. Paul uses this phrase to denote a statement that summarizes key doctrine.

Summary

Jesus Christ came into the world to save sinners. Jesus, who is fully God and fully man, lived a life in perfect obedience to the law of God, thus earning the righteousness that no person could earn, and died to take the punishment for sin. Those who trust in him are given his righteousness and the forgiveness he secured. He now sits at the Father's right hand, waiting to come again to free his people from the very presence of sin.

Questions for Reflection

1. Why did Jesus come into the world?
2. Why will Jesus come again?
3. How do both comings of Christ give hope to the Christian?

Day 257: Paul Arrives in Rome

Acts 28; Psalms 147-148

Notes

Acts 28, Verse 1. Malta. An island south of Sicily.

Verse 11. Twin gods. The Greek gods Castor and Pollux, Zeus's sons, who were believed to protect sailors.

Verse 12. Syracuse. Tradition holds that Paul established a church in this important city in Sicily during his short stay there.

Verse 31. Without hindrance. Luke finished writing Acts before Paul's first release from Roman prison (ca. AD 60-62).

Summary

God providentially brought Paul to Rome, which was a deep desire of his, through quite unusual means. Yet Paul's imprisonment allowed him to faithfully preach the gospel there, defending the Christian faith, and helping to establish a strong Christian presence in that powerful city.

Questions for Reflection

1. How did Paul faithfully fulfill his mission even during his imprisonment?
2. What was the central message of Paul's defense of Christianity to the Jewish leaders?
3. How can God's providential work in Paul's ministry give us confidence today?

Day 258: The Second Coming of Christ

Revelation 1, 4-5

Notes

Chapter 1, Verse 1. Revelation. This is the Greek word from which we get the English word "apocalypse," which means to uncover or reveal.

Verse 4. Seven spirits. This is likely a reference to the seven-fold ministry of the Holy Spirit prophesied by Isaiah (Isa 11:2).

Verse 8. Alpha and Omega. These are the first and last letters of the Greek alphabet, signifying that Jesus is the beginning and end of all things.

Verse 9. Patmos. A Roman penal colony where John was imprisoned.

Verse 10. Lord's Day. In Christian writings following the completion of the New Testament, including by authors close to John, this refers to the first day of the week, the day on which Jesus rose from the dead, which became the central day of worship for the Christian church.

Verse 20. Angels. This term means "messengers" and here likely refers to the pastors of the seven churches to which John is writing.

Chapter 4, Verse 4. Twenty-four elders. These elders represent the church.

Chapter 5, Verse 1. Scroll. This represents the title deed to the Kingdom of God.

Summary

John's vision foretells the time when Jesus will come again in power and might to establish his Kingdom on earth. Anticipation of such a coming is meant to cause Christians to take account of their lives now, making sure that they are fervently following Christ and looking for that blessed hope.

Questions for Reflection

1. What should anticipation of the coming of Christ cause us to do?

2. What does John's vision of the worship of heaven teach us about our worship?
3. Why is Jesus the only one worthy of opening the title deed to the Kingdom of God?

Day 259: The New Heaven and the New Earth

Revelation 21; Psalm 149

Notes

Revelation 21, Verse 2. Bride. This is a key metaphor in the New Testament for the church (Eph 5:25–27). The New Jerusalem becomes the dwelling place for the church.

Verse 8. Lake. This is the place of final, eternal punishment for those who do not trust in Christ.

Verse 27. Lamb's Book of Life. This journal in which God has written the names of all whom he has chosen to save.

Psalm 149. These final psalms command us to praise the Lord in all circumstances of life, whether it be in corporate worship, in social settings, in the home, or even in the midst of battle.

Summary

One day, God will create a new heaven and a new earth where he will forever dwell with his people in perfect harmony, just has he has promised. There, Christ will be the source of all satisfaction, and there will be no tears or sin. All unbelieving people will be sent to the eternal lake of fire.

Questions for Reflection

1. In what ways does the new heaven and earth bring to remembrance God's plan for Adam and Eve in the Garden of Eden?
2. Why will there be no tears in the new earth?
3. What does the description of the New Jerusalem teach us about the eternal dwelling of God's people?

Day 260: Jesus Is Coming

Revelation 22; Psalm 150

Notes

Revelation 22, Verse 7. Quickly. Jesus's coming again is imminent; it could happen at any time.

Verse 10. Seal up. Prophecies were typically sealed, but this prophecy is to be proclaimed, both as a warning to those who do not believe, and as an encouragement and admonition to believers.

Verse 15. Dogs. In New Testament times, these were undomesticated animals, and thus represent those filthy with sin.

Verse 17. Come. The fitting response of the church to this letter is anticipation of such a coming again.

Summary

Jesus will soon come again. His coming, which could happen at any time, will bring with it judgment to sinners, but eternal life and blessing to those who repent of their sins and trust in him alone for their salvation. Anticipating his coming should cause us to live holy lives, faithfully proclaim the good news to unbelievers, and live with hope and confidence in the good plan and promises of God.

Questions for Reflection

1. When could Jesus come again?
2. What should this letter cause Christians to do?
3. What is our only hope in life and death?

Printed in Great Britain
by Amazon